Better Than Rubies

A History of Women's Education

Phyllis Stock

Capricorn Books

G. P. Putnam's Sons • New York

Second Impression

SBN: 399-12081-5 (hardcover)
SBN: 399-50381-1 (softcover)

Library of Congress Cataloging in Publication Data

Stock, Phyllis H
  Better than rubies.

  Bibliography
  Includes index
  1. Education of women—Europe. 2. Education of women—United States. I. Title.
LC2031.S76 1978   376'.94   77-21318

PRINTED IN THE UNITED STATES OF AMERICA

TO BOB
Who provided for this woman's education

For wisdom is better than rubies;
and all the things that may be desired
are not to be compared to it.

PROVERBS 8:11

CONTENTS

PREFACE

Man has no nature, said the Spanish philosopher Ortega y Gasset, only a history. And what of woman? There has been a good deal of speculation about her nature, though not nearly as much as about man's. But only in recent years has there been a notable effort to recover women's past. Not only is it now apparent that we know very little of the way one-half of the human race has lived, but also it appears that such knowledge might illuminate the situation of women in the present. At the same time there has been an upsurge of interest in the history of education, as a key to how people saw their world in the past and how society attempted to prepare them to live in it. Considering the pertinence of the topic to our understanding of women, it is surprising how little work has been done in the field of women's education.

The world that women have lived in has always been circumscribed by what they have been taught. In turn, they have passed this view on to daughters, who usually retained it for their lifetime, and to sons, who usually managed to transcend it through further education and experience in the world outside the home. However, all people, male and female, begin their lives in the world of women.

The importance of this female world is now recognized in the fields of family history and psychohistory, as well as in women's studies.

In modern society education serves as one of the most important keys to status. But even in older societies, where birth, wealth, or sheer brute force brought power and position to their owners, access to education, or the lack of it, indicated the status of particular groups. Thus when we wish to discover the position of women, or of a particular class of women, in another age, we must include in our questions, first, whether these women were formally educated in comparison with their men, and second, how they were educated, what they learned. The answers provide clues to many other aspects of life in the society under examination.

In discussing the education of women, one must first consider the questions raised by education in general, questions that apply to both sexes. As used in English, the term *education* either embraces two distinct words in French, or replaces one of them. *Education* means development of the character of the student; *instruction,* development of the intellect. It is particularly important to distinguish between the two when speaking of the education of women, since in many societies only character-training has been considered important for the female sex. Sometimes even the education of the intellect has been considered solely in its relation to moral development, following Plato's concept of knowledge as leading to the good. Only in rare cases has the intellectual development of girls been considered a benefit in itself, or a means of fulfillment of the individual personality.

Almost all education, however, has a social, rather than individual function. The aim of the educator is to produce an adult who will play a certain desired role in society. With reference to women, it is necessary to discover the type of woman postulated as ideal in a particular period, in order to understand the education provided for her. What role would the type of education offered have enabled her to play? How was it related to the role implied for the male by his education? For certain periods one can discover the social or political need that a certain training was intended to fulfill. Naturally, in any time when men and women were viewed as totally different beings, the education provided them also differed. It is often significant that certain studies, standard in the male curriculum, were omitted from the female curriculum. Thus the education of the two sexes reflect actual social and power relationships between men and women in the society.

Another distinction—that between formal and informal education—concerns women's education even more than men's. Formal education is usually offered in the interests of preserving the society that provides it. It is therefore conservative; it affords women little opportunity to break out of the mold in which society has cast them. Informal education, on the other hand, often escapes the boundaries of the accepted and opens new opportunities to the individual. Unfortunately for women, there is one large exception to this rule: training girls in the home for the role of housewife, which they are expected to fulfill in exactly the way their mothers did. In societies where girls' education in the home for housewifery only has been the norm, the establishment of any formal education for them by society has represented progress. Nevertheless, there have been historical periods in which informal education of women in a setting dominated by female values has been more liberating than formal education at the hands of male teachers. It is a matter of who controls the concept of the ideal woman, which in turn determines the education of women.

Throughout most of history the view of woman as housewife and mother was unavoidably predominant. However, there were some loopholes. Examples of women who, by denying their traditional role, had the opportunity to develop intellectually include the learned prostitute of the ancient world and the nun of medieval times. But there were also times when the patriarchal system weakened, when women became socially, economically, or politically independent; then women freed themselves from the male concept of them and to some extent controlled their own intellectual life and values. It is easier to find this freedom among the upper classes, where records are more complete; however, it also existed in the lower classes, when men lost control of whole areas of life and women filled the gap. In many societies the widow of all classes was freed by her husband's death to take over his role, and often was wholly competent to do so as a result of informal education by her mother, her husband, or other women.

One can divide women's education into six general types: (1) informal moral education, usually combined with housewifery, provided by female members of the family or others *in loco parentis;* (2) formal moral education, usually based on some knowledge of reading and provided by nuns or other women in schools and convents; (3) vocational education in a trade, provided by parents, others *in loco parentis,* or husbands; (4) intellectual education aimed at character formation, usually provided at home by parents or male tutors; (5) intellectual education for the fulfillment of a particular role in society (court lady, mistress of the estate, first educator of the children) and supplemented with training in the social graces, provided by tutors, convents, schools; and (6) intellectual training for individual fulfillment, a career, or both, usually provided in formal educational settings.

These types of education vary according to social class. In general, three classes are referred to in this book, though they frequently overlap. The noblewoman, or lady, belonged to the hereditary aristocracy which traced its rank and privileges to land tenure. Allied to this class were those families who acquired noble status by other means—through conquest, as the *condottieri* princes of the Italian Renaissance, or through service to the king, as the nobles of the robe in seventeeth-century France—as well as that top level of the moneyed middle class whose fortunes enabled them to mingle socially with the aristocracy.

The requirements of aristocratic social life dictated a certain type of education for women of this group. Moreover, the training they received was often reproduced in families of the middle class who aspired to higher social rank. The attitudes of the broad middle class, often known as the bourgeoisie, varied considerably, but its view of women was almost exclusively as a good housewife and mother.

The lowest and most numerous class, consisting of day laborers in town and country, is unfortunately the one we know least about. Although its most prosperous representatives adopted bourgeois standards, for the most part necessity, not choice, dictated the opportunities for learning open to a working-class girl. Even the most elementary education—moral training combined with housewifery—was often unavailable to her. But she was usually no more disadvantaged than her brothers, whose education was similarly ignored.

In discussing education, basic training in morality and religion, the three Rs, and manual vocations are generally subsumed under the heading of primary education. This is the education (when education is provided for them at all) considered sufficient for the lower classes and for women throughout most of history. Further learning based on reading and writing—history, literature, languages, science, and philosophy—is considered either secondary or higher education. The distinction between these two is sometimes difficult to draw; women were often given a "higher" education that was really only secondary. Because they were denied entrance to the universities until about a century ago, very little of what is today considered higher education was available to them.

It is axiomatic in the history of education that a change in the social and economic structure of society usually results in a change in educational content and practice. This is also true of women's education, but not to as great a degree as it is of men's. Some changes that fostered intellectual expansion in the world of men did not do so in the woman's world. Conversely, there were periods when women in certain classes of society were intellectually superior to their husbands; this was usually the case when intellectual pursuits were valued less highly than such male activities as war and commerce. One thing is certain: in a society dominated by men, women's education is determined by men, at least to the extent that it does not run counter to the interests of society at large. In describing the course of female education, it is therefore necessary to account for changes by relating them to the interests of the male-controlled society, and, as much as possible, to all the varied factors that affect social life.

The outlines of the history of women's education are becoming visible, despite lack of attention in the past. So many histories of education, so many pedagogical treatises, so many accounts of various types of schooling make no reference at all to the female sex. The occasional official decree, "the children shall be taught . . . " usually turns out to mean male children. Occasional references to girls in schools often give no indication of whether schooling for girls was the norm, or of how many girls were included in the educational process of the time. It is as if, for the historians of education, the female sex did not exist.

The main reason for these lacunae applies to many areas of women's history: women have just not been considered important up to now. The occasional exception to the rule is added for color: *even girls* were educated in this school; a certain beautiful young woman displayed her erudition on a ceremonial occasion; a particular queen was learned in languages and history. As La Bruyère said, in the seventeenth century, a learned woman was like a gun that was a collector's item, "which one shows to the curious, but which has no use at all, any more than a carousel horse."[1]

Now that scholars have taken an interest in women's education, they are beginning to ask questions about what is presently known: What different types of education have been available to women in the past? Under what conditions are women likely to be offered education, and why? How is women's education related to the social structure and to their relations with men?

The sources at hand are, first, men's writings on the nature and capabilities of women, particularly their mental capabilities. These indicate the roles men have seen women as fulfilling in their society and the attitudes men have held about the wisdom of educating women. To these are added occasional assessments by women in modern times of their own roles and abilities. Another group of sources are accounts of women who were learned, which must be handled carefully. In most cases these women represented, not the broad mass of their sex in their class, but only themselves; they cannot be taken as the norm for their time. Another type of source is the rare treatise devoted to female education, along with the occasional reference to women in works on male education. These are more useful, since they may express the attitudes of a whole class in a particular time and place; but they also must be used gingerly. The ideal of women's education laid out in them often pertained to only a very few women. The most difficult information to acquire is the extent of education of ordinary poor girls. Broad programs intended to educate the masses may turn out to have had only minimal results in terms of the number of girls involved. It is not until the nineteenth century, when European governments began to take a serious view of universal education, that material is abundant on women's education. From that point it is necessary to select what seems significant out of a plethora of information.

From these disparate sources I have essayed a survey of women's experience with learning. In preparing this volume I have made use of work now in progress, and generously shared, by a number of individuals. Among those who have discussed it with me, advised me, enlightened me, I would like to thank, first the members of the women's history section of the Institute for Research in History in New York, who are seriously attempting to define the problems and methods of women's history. They, in addition to women in the field all over the country, are sharing, not only their insights, but their materials and research, the use of which I gratefully acknowledge.

I would particularly like to thank those whose unpublished papers are listed in the bibliography, and those who allowed me to read their recent articles before publication. Also my colleague at Seton Hall University, W. Scott Morton, read the manuscript and offered invaluable advice. Diane Vivinetto, my student, who gathered statistics for me, and my typist, Peggy Willig, have been indispensable. To all of them, and to my editor at Putnams, Sandra Soames, I owe a debt of gratitude.

INTRODUCTION

"There is no special faculty of administration in a state which a woman has because she is a woman, or which a man has by virtue of his sex, but the gifts of nature are alike diffused in both; all the pursuits of men are the pursuits of women also, but in all of them a woman is inferior to a man."[1]

The failure, until recent times, to provide women with an education equal to that of men had always stemmed from the presumption that women were the intellectually inferior sex. This belief was based, in turn, upon a general presumption of female inferiority, which is manifested in the laws and customs of all civilized societies. There is evidence that this was not necessarily so in primitive conditions, where women's childbearing and agricultural abilities were highly valued. There is even room for speculation that the legal oppression of women after the rise of the state might have been some kind of compensation on the part of males for the procreative abilities they envied in females. We only know that, from the dawn of civilized society, women were considered the weaker, less intelligent, subordinate sex.

Plato, who made the statement quoted above in his *Republic*, is often considered to have been an early defender of women. His important theory of Platonic love was attributed to a woman, "wise in this and many other kinds of knowledge." He argued that women should be included in the guardian, or ruling, class of the Republic; they should receive the same extended education as male guardians and share in all the duties of guardianship, even in the defense of their country. However, in the distribution of labors, the lighter were to be assigned to the women, because of their "weaker natures." Thus one of the earliest proponents of women's education modified his argument by his presumption of the natural inferiority of the sex. This distinction is made quite clear in Plato's speculation in the *Symposium* on the origin of the sexes. Originally three sexes—male, female, and androgyny, human beings were all split in two by the gods because of their insolence. Since then each half continuously seeks his other half, in order to become whole again. But it is those males who seek their other half in males who are valiant and become statesmen.

Of course, this fable reflects the customs of Greek society, where homosexual love was valued more highly than heterosexual. But it also reflects the tendency on the part of most writers about women to try to prove that female inferiority originated far back, in the very nature of things. Hippocrates, writing of the act of procreation, stated that male seed was stronger than female seed; if the stronger seed was more abundant the child would be male. Aristotle saw the generative act purely as a labor of creation on the part of the male. The man was the active partner, who provided the form of the new life, while the woman, passive, provided only the material. He even compared the male to the carpenter and the female to the wood. As for the resulting foetus, the male was more active, being hotter; the female nature was colder and weaker. And Aristotle concluded, "We should look upon the female state as being as it were a deformity, though one which occurs in the ordinary course of nature."[2]

This concept of the male as hot and active, the female as cool and passive, was generally accepted in the ancient world. Galen stated that the female was more imperfect than the male because she was colder, by analogy with inferior species. "Just as man is the most perfect of all animals, so also, within the human species, man is more perfect than woman. The cause of this superiority is the male's superabundance of warmth, heat being the primary instrument of nature."[3] Galen considered the male sperm to be the formative principle of the animal, as did Aristotle. (Galen labeled women's ovaries internal testicles for production of the female seed. When this was noted in the sixteenth century it caused some alarm. It was concluded by the Italian anatomist Borgarucci and the Spanish anatomist Valverde that nature had properly hidden woman's testicles from her to restrain her natural arrogance and desire to dominate.)

Aristotle's biological views on the inferiority of the female sex persisted and were influential until the sixteenth century. In his political writings he placed the male in control of the primary unit—the family—on the basis of his rational superiority: "The slave has no deliberative faculty at all; the woman has, but it is without authority, and the child has, but it is immature." It was the same with moral judgment; women had it, but to a different degree. "The temperance of a man and of a woman, or the courage and justice of a man and a woman are not, as Socrates maintains, the same; the courage of a man is shown in commanding, of a woman in obeying."[4]

It is not surprising to learn, then, that Greek girls, confined as they were to the *gynaeceum,* or women's quarters, never received more than an elementary training in reading and writing, if that. Their brothers were exposed to higher wisdom at the *gymnasium,* where the men gathered. Women's judgment was considered weak; therefore they must always be subject to the guardianship of males. The education of a wife was entirely domestic—first under her mother's supervision, where she learned to sew and spin and was "meant to see, hear and ask as little as possible"; then under the tutelage of her husband, who taught her how to manage his household. As Xenophon described it: "It seems to me that God adapted woman's nature to indoor and man's to outdoor work. . . . It is more proper for a woman to stay in the house."[5] Therefore the average Greek woman's knowledge was entirely confined to hearth and home. Those famous learned women of Athens, such as Pericles' Aspasia, usually were not Athenian citizens, or else lived during the Hellenistic age, when Roman and Egyptian customs weakened the sexual barriers. The famous school of Sappho on Lesbos might be considered an exception. However, the emphasis in the curriculum, centered on music, poetry, and dancing, was upon feminine charm that would please men, and not on learning for its own sake.

Along with Greek philosophy in general, the Romans adopted the Greek belief in female inferiority. But the stronger emphasis among the Romans on family life elevated the position of women, particularly the Roman matron. Unlike Greek women, Roman women of the upper class were educated—not so much for their own sake as to make them better mothers for boys who would grow up to take part in civic life. The most famous example is Cornelia, mother of the Gracchi brothers, who was credited by Quintilian and Cicero with contributing, through her own learning, to her sons' eloquence in the tribune. Daughters of the wealthy shared their brothers' tutors. There were also schools available to the poorer classes, which provided an education in the literary classics. The Roman tradition of education for both sexes was to be reborn later in the courts of Renaissance Italy.

In the intervening period, there rose a new attitude toward women, which affected their opportunities for learning. The Christian view of woman was ambiguous at best. She was Eve, the temptress and source of evil in the world; she was also Mary, the virginal mother of Christ who atoned for sin. Augustine's description of original sin is pertinent to our topic, because it speaks to the question of woman's relationship to irrationality. In *The City of God* Augustine insisted that lust (which would have had no part in procreation had the sin of Adam, brought on by Eve, not been committed) was an evil for human beings because it was not controlled by their will and reason. He insisted that in a state of innocence the necessary generation of offspring would have taken place "at the discretion of the will." The emphasis on Eve was thus a continuation of the classical myth of Pandora, who released into the world vice and passion, among other ills.

The vision of Mary, however, was an advance for women, provided they remained chaste. The new religion taught also that man and woman were both possessed of immortal souls. "There is neither Jew nor Greek, there is neither bond nor free, there is neither male nor female: for ye are all one in Christ Jesus,"[6] wrote Saint Paul. In the very early Church women were allowed to preach and prophesy. They were not set apart from the men, as they had been in the Jewish synagogue, where only males were educated to read the sacred books. However, the writings of Paul, so important in the early Church, reveal the paradox in the Christian view of women. Though he stated the equality of women in the quotation above, he later commanded women to keep silent in the churches. If a woman wished to learn anything, she should ask her husband at home, and not draw attention to herself in public. The reason given for subordination of women was drawn from the Old Testament. Adam was formed first, in the image and glory of God; then Eve was formed in the image of Adam. A less perfect being, woman was deceived by the devil; therefore she should maintain silence and not teach or hold a position of authority. Childbearing and obedience were her role. Woman should submit herself to her husband as to the Lord. The early Church Fathers, including Augustine, followed this line. Later theologians, including Aquinas, combined it with Aristotle's views. Women were the occasion of sin, "the devil's gateway," as Tertullian put it. Having brought evil into the world, they must be viewed as dangerous and irrational, never to be placed in a position to make decisions. The only real escape for a woman lay in the total abnegation of her sex—that is, virginity. And indeed, it was only the cloistered female of the convent who received any education throughout the period of the Church's ascendancy.

By the sixth century the schools left by Roman civilization, and also those educated enough to teach in them, were rare. From then until the eleventh century there is no record of any formal education for girls outside the Church. Daughters of good families were placed in convents to acquire the minimum learning necessary for a religious vocation. They were taught by the abbess, who often was herself only educated enough to read the prayers and some of the Church Fathers. The educational renaissance that took place under Charlemagne did not include the nunneries, although women of the emperor's own family were educated along with the men at the famous palace school run by Alcuin. At this time some other noble women acquired the same education as men—the classical curriculum, somewhat degenerate and capped by theology. But in general women were more closed off from learning by the end of the ninth century than before; girls were no longer allowed to attend the monastic and episcopal schools with boys.

The curriculum of the nunnery, the only source of female education, included reading, writing, and singing, all for religious purposes; some grammar and arithmetic; occasionally, drawing and painting for use in copying and illuminating manuscripts; and often, some medical knowledge, to avoid the use of male physicians. Until the twelfth century, convent education had the great advantage of preserving Latin as a living language, long after civil society had abandoned it. This made reading ancient poetry possible, and even, in the case of Saint Radegonde and others, writing Latin verse. But secular literature soon gave way to exclusively religious writings. Education in a nunnery was considered a way of keeping young women from dangerous idleness; and no distinction was made in early medieval times between the instruction of novices and boarding students.

In the twelfth century, Latin was abandoned in the nunneries altogether, and ecclesiastical authors were translated into the vernacular. The rise of the universities completed the decline of women's education in the late Middle Ages. All the intellectual vigor left the monastic and episcopal schools for the faculties of higher learning, taking with it Latin and the whole intellectual tradition of Christianity. Convent education suffered concordantly. Many men disapproved of teaching women to read and write unless they were destined to become nuns, since they would only write love letters and fall into sin. However, in the same period the idealization of virtuous women, along with the cult of Mary, raised certain individual women to higher status. A number of double monasteries (male and female, separate but on the same site) were governed by abbesses.

There is some reason to believe that women were not entirely absent from the universities, at least in Italy. These early universities rose in response to secular needs. When the Crusades opened up the Near East, where the learning of the classical age had been preserved by Byzantines and Arabs, the universities dealt with the resulting wave of scholarship. And as trade quickened and began to undermine the feudal system, kings sought the authority of ancient texts to establish domination over their nobles. Thus the first universities were formed around secular disciplines such as law and medicine.

Italy, never completely feudalized in the Middle Ages, was the first area where town life was restored, through her participation in the Mediterranean trade. The first university at Bologna, and indeed all Italian universities, included lay teachers and students. (Later universities in northern Europe, founded around schools of theology, were confined to clergy.) There are many references to women teaching law, philosophy, rhetoric, and medicine at Bologna and other Italian universities in the thirteenth century. However they seem to be exceptions, rather than the rule. Some women may have been well educated enough, through their fathers' efforts, to teach under special conditions and write the books attributed to them. In the intellectually active and free atmosphere of urban Italy, professors may have wished to show off a star pupil who happened to be a daughter. But it is fairly certain that even in Italy, universities provided women with neither a formal education nor a license to teach.

As cities spread to all parts of Europe, women found a place in the guild system. The hand work that had always been done by women at home—weaving, baking, cooking, beer brewing—now afforded them paying positions. This meant that they were now more welcome to stay at home as an alternative to going into a convent. Sometimes whole guilds were made up of women; where they were mixed, women received equal pay and treatment. (This was a condition never again to be attained.) A girl's apprenticeship was usually at home. Some trades, connected with serving the public, were considered dangerous for a woman's morals. Normally a woman learned the trade at home or with a neighboring artisan, married an artisan in that trade, and helped him in his livelihood. But in England women had almost a monopoly in the guilds of spinning, weaving, bread baking, and beer brewing, which were carried on in the home. At this time many European convents were converted into veritable workshops for unmarried women, where they produced religious objects, made lace, illuminated manuscripts. Some of these women's communities lost their religious character altogether.

Clearly women's education was now moving out of the Church's hands. Noble families began to provide tutors for their boys, sometimes for their girls. But the boys received a more intensive religious training, the girls a more social and literary one. Music and dancing were important, also games like checkers and chess. Girls also learned astrology and some medicine and surgery. But the basis of their education, by the end of the thirteenth century, was literary. It was now the exception for women to learn Latin. In France the girls learned and recited the *fabliaux* and *chansons de geste*. These in turn were the basis of manuals on *civilité*, as French women started on the road to becoming arbiters of taste, both in speech and manners.

However, for the most part it was considered enough for a woman to be properly religious. The main goal of education was to preserve sexual purity and produce proper behavior in society. Bourgeois women sometimes had tutors, and of course the convents were open to them. But the level of education they attained was mediocre. The main emphasis was on housewifely duties; Xenophon's *Economist* was eventually to be translated for them. There was little interest among the poor in education, even less in women's education. Surviving famine, plague, and war was their main objective.

Women often gain in status and power in society, not with the advent of a new social structure, but with the breakdown of an old one. This was true in the period of Rome's decline; it also occurred as the feudal period began to break down in the late Middle Ages. During the Crusades, as throughout the medieval period in general, fighting ability was the most highly prized male quality. Indeed the most powerful feudal nobles were often absent from their estates, engaged in warfare. This left the secondary virtues, such as economic and intellectual interests, to the lady of the manor. Left behind to manage feudal estates, great ladies acquired property rights and even political power. In France feudal lands not requiring military service on the part of their holders passed to female heirs when there were no males. This was more often the case in the late Middle Ages, when warfare resulted in a dearth of men. Female control of property was reflected in the retention of the mother's name, particularly during the crusading period. Since all power during the Middle Ages originated in land tenure, this unusual situation created a small number of powerful feudal ladies. They, in turn, were able to dominate a portion of the intellectual life of their time, that part reflected in the courtly literature.

For the most part, the medieval lady was herself as unschooled as her husband. However, through her patronage of the troubadours who sang their stories at the courts, she was able to a great extent to determine the vernacular literature of the day. In the twelfth and thirteenth centuries, this literature came increasingly to revolve around the concept of courtly love. In some cases (Countess Beatrice of Die, Marie of France), women contributed their own works to the growing repertoire. But the more usual situation was a great lady—Eleanor of Aquitaine, for example—presiding over a court where troubadours sang songs celebrating the love of pure and noble women.

The drama of courtly love usually involved a woman already married, often the lady of the manor whose husband was away fighting. Ideally it was a pure love, with a minimum of physical contact. The woman imposed tests of love upon her courtier, who must be washed and perfumed and address her in poetic language. In return, the lover could dream that some day his lady-love would take his hand, or perhaps bestow a kiss. Codes of love described the ways in which he might address his lady, according to her place in society and his. They also prescribed the graduated levels of favors she might bestow upon him. "Courts of love" whiled away hours deciding such questions as whether it was within the code for the lady to allow her petitioner a glimpse of her nude body, and under what conditions. Whether or not the purity of such love actually conformed to the ideal, the lady in the game was clearly idealized.

In cultural terms, courtly love was more than a game. It placed the lover in a relationship of vassalage to his lady which was not simply romantic; it paralleled the true relationship of a lesser knight to his noble lady. It gave the woman control over the love relationship—which would not have been possible had the woman not actually held a superior position. It has been pointed out that as a reflection of real power, courtly love also enabled women to escape the prison of marital fidelity. But for our purposes women's powerful position in twelfth-century courts has other implications. From this position, the courtly lady—in her relationships, in her role as literary patron, and in her "courts of love"—performed an educative function. She taught men, who in their medieval state were cruel, crude, and unwashed, how to behave in the genteel society of women. Control over manners, usually exercised by men over women, was, in the limited area of society where women predominated, now exercised by women over men.

This civilizing function created the idea of the gentle man, who would be acceptable to women. Eleanor herself, first Queen of France and then of England, brought with her the manners of courtly love. From her court at Poitiers later in life she and her daughter, Marie of Champagne, influenced young noblemen who became the ruling class in France, Italy, Sicily, and Spain, and carried with them the literature and arts of courtesy.

Thus, while some men ruled through prowess in war, albeit often far away from home, and others ruled through a monopoly of Latin letters, in Church and university, the noble lady became the queen of a vernacular literature that reflected real feudal relations. Although in the centuries that followed, women acquired more education, they lost control of the educational process, and could no longer shape the intellectual life of their time to their own needs. This was a reflection of loss of real power in society.

CHAPTER I

The Learned Lady of the Renaissance

The Renaissance is one of the great ages in the history of the
Western world, a time in which the spectrum of mankind's knowledge became immeasurably widened. The "opening to the East" resulting from the Crusades brought a revival of trade and a renewed
interest in the thought of the ancient world, a legacy that had been
largely lost to the West during the Middle Ages. For a time the universities absorbed the new learning; but eventually it spilled over
into the secular world, where it was eagerly received in courts and
in the cities that were burgeoning throughout Eruope.

For those who could afford to take part in it, the Renaissance was
a true rebirth of the intellect. Both in Italy and in the north, Renaissance learning touched women in the early stages of humanism. But
for the Renaissance lady education was by no means as liberating as
it was for men. The social and political changes of the fourteenth
and fifteenth centuries tended to return the noble woman to her traditional role in the home. Within the limits of her household, she
could participate to some extent in culture. But it was a culture elaborated by and for men.

HUMANIST ITALY

The Renaissance society of Italy was an urban society; the opening of East-West commerce after the Crusades had strengthened and renewed the trading cities in the north of the peninsula. In this new urban setting, a different type of nobility was pushing to the fore, a nobility based upon military prowess and native cunning rather than upon birth. *Condottieri*, soldiers of fortune at the head of mercenary armies, fought their way to control of city-states. Then they attempted to make their rule hereditary, while taking on the trappings of nobility and ornamenting their courts with patronage of the new learning. In their origins these self-made men were hardly different from the new class that had arisen with the revival of town life and trade—the bourgeoisie. The two groups subscribed to the common value of making their way in the world through their own efforts. And both were attracted to Renaissance humanism.

Humanism was based upon the works of the classical world; its wisdom seemed more relevant to a flourishing urban society based on trade than the prescriptions for the good life prevalent in medieval Europe. A man could gain fame for his ability to decipher the Latin authors, and more if he could also read Greek. This was bound to affect the life of women in society. The example of ancient Rome, often referred to by the first Renaissance men of Florence, made the family the microcosm of the state, as Aristotle had described it. The father, as ruler, was the active principle that determined the lives of his wife, children, and servants, as in ancient Rome.

This emphasis on the family was strengthened throughout the Renaissance by demographic factors. From a high point in the mid-fourteenth century, population in Italy fell drastically, by as much as two-thirds in Tuscany, and stabilized at this level throughout most of the fifteenth century. The Black Death accounted for at least part of this crisis, which was more acute in urban areas than in rural. Thus in the centers of Renaissance thought the very survival of the family was threatened; writers began to examine the problem and idealize traditional family roles. Leon Battista Alberti's essay *On the Family,* discussed below, was written with the idea of providing his own relatives and his readers with a prescription for the survival of the bourgeois family.

Another factor in the position of women in Italian Renaissance society was marriage age. Girls were never much older than twenty at first marriage, often much younger in the cities. Men, however, never married before twenty-five, and sometimes waited until forty. The average male age at marriage dropped to thirty in the fifteenth century, perhaps because of the need to renew families hit by plague, and then rose again as the death rate fell in the sixteenth century. The female average did not change throughout the period. In any case, there was always a great difference in age between husband and wife (13.6 years in Florence during 1427–28), which made of the wife a child-bride.

In Alberti's discourse on the family, he described his young wife as longing for her family after marriage. It was he who took charge of her education, for her mother had taught her only how to spin and sew, and how to be virtuous and obedient. As head of the household, he considered it proper that he conduct the external affairs of the family, while his wife, once instructed, supervised the domestic arrangements, for "it would hardly win us respect if our wife busied herself among men in the marketplace, out in the public eye." He felt it would be demeaning for him to remain shut up in the house with the women, "when I have manly things to do among the men, fellow citizens, and worthy and distinguished foreigners." Alberti explained that women were by nature "timid, soft, slow, and therefore more useful when they sit still and watch over things," while men had more elevated minds and were suited to action. Perhaps for this reason, he did not confide important affairs to his wife, and scorned men who did. In what, then, did her education consist? In practical lessons on how to manage the household and the servants; but mainly on how to conduct herself in a chaste, modest, and sober manner. His description of the foolish behavior of some wives, which she was to avoid, indicated that she was a typical teenage girl married to a middle-aged man. For exercise she was to inspect the house from top to bottom a few times a day, checking on the servants' activities. And when she seemed melancholy, he admonished her that it was her duty to greet him happily when he came home from a hard day at men's work.[1]

Typically, the inspiration for this discourse was antiquity—the *Economist* of Xenophon. As a picture of the lot of the bourgeois Renaissance wife, it recalls the Greek lady, shut up in the *gynaeceum*, more than the Roman, and indicates a woefully low level of education compared to that of her husband. It falls into the category of informal moral education enriched only with housewifery. But what of the noble lady, who presided so brilliantly over the courts of the newly established princes of Italy? The history of the period is sprinkled with names of women illustrious for their learning, and there is no question that many were highly educated.

The study of the humanities by noble women was not regarded unfavorably by the public, unless they made too great a show of their abilities. However, women were expected to put not only chastity, but also propriety, before learning. (Isotta Nogarola, celebrated for her Latin prose and verse, was socially ostracized in Verona because she carried on a humanist correspondence with her former tutor Guarino.)

The first in a long line of studious women whom we know of was Baptista di Montrefelto, who was drawn to poetry and ancient literature in the late fourteenth century. She was best known for the Latin oration with which she greeted the Emperor Sigismund when he passed through her native Urbino in 1433, and which was printed as late as fifty years afterward.

Lionardo Bruni, later Apostolic Secretary, dedicated a treatise to Baptista, *De Studiis et Literis*, in the form of a letter hailing her distinction in the field of learning. It is the first Italian humanist work, and one of the few, devoted entirely to the education of women. Like all writings of the time on this subject, it conforms to the category of intellectual education for the formation of character. It is typical also in that it assumes only the aristocratic lady will seek education. The basis of all studies, Bruni wrote, for women as for men, was a thorough knowledge of Latin and Latin style in writing. Armed with this knowledge, one should read the Church Fathers, Cicero, Vergil, and Livy. But for women a certain discrimination in learning was necessary. He did not recommend "subtleties of Arithmetic and Geometry," or even "the great and complex art of Rhetoric." All forms of rhetoric—public discussion, forensic argument, logical fence—lay, he maintained, "absolutely outside the province of woman." This omission must be considered important in a society where participation in public life was an ideal. From that very

Cicero whom Bruni urged Baptista to read, the Florentines in particular had derived the concept of the active civic life, modeled on that of republican Rome. Clearly Bruni did not conceive of women, however learned, as actively participating in the new civic life.

The subject for woman, which was particularly her own according to Bruni, was "the whole field of religion and morals." Hence the importance of the Church Fathers, particularly Augustine. (He did not recommend current moral writings, because of their deficiencies of style.) In addition, the moral philosophy of Greece and Rome raised questions he thought worthy of discussion by men and women alike. These two sources were therefore most important for the Christian lady. However, as a broad education was the goal, she should extend her studies to include history, which deepened the understanding of contemporary affairs and provided moral lessons. He recommended concentration on ancient historians, and on the great orations of antiquity, which provided moral concepts emotionally expressed.[2]

Unlike many preceptors of women in the Renaissance, Bruni thought women should read poetry. Poets were referred to by ancient writers; they conveyed philosophical ideas. Alone of the writers of his time, Bruni seemed to trust women's ability to remain virtuous when exposed to poetic tales of dubious morality; yet the treatise ends with an admonition to concentrate on authors and subjects related to religion and ethics. Renaissance works on the education of men also stress the subordination of learning to character training.

This is certainly true of the most renowned of Italian educators, Vittorino da Feltre. A fifteenth-century humanist scholar of high repute, he took students into his home and guided not only their intellectual, but also their moral development. When Gianfrancesco Gonzaga, *condottiere* prince of Mantua, desired to adorn his court with humanist studies, he asked Vittorino to tutor his children. Attracted by the idea of training future leaders and assured of a free hand in doing so, Vittorino agreed to establish at Mantua the first great school of the Renaissance. Given a house on the Gonzaga estate formerly known as the House of Pleasure, he stripped it of its luxuries and lived there with the Gonzaga boys and girls, plus sons of other nobles and deserving boys of poor families. Barbara von

Hohenzollern, later married to the Marquis of Mantua, also attended the school for a time. The range in age was six to twenty years, the older ones helping to teach the younger.

The curriculum included critical scholarship in Latin and Greek, taught as a key to understanding the ancient world through its literature, philosophy, and history. Declamation and reading aloud served to train the students in eloquence. Arithmetic was taught as an exercise of the mind; geometry was joined with its practical adjuncts of drawing, measuring, and surveying; astronomy, not astrology, was included. The study of logic served as a guide to exact thinking; of Greek ethics, to proper living. Vittorino alternated study with physical exercise to develop the ancient ideal of a sound mind in a sound body. But the emphasis was on Christian humanism—the combination of the best in ancient thought with the ethics of Christianity.

Cecilia and Lucrezia Gonzaga learned the same things as their brothers at the Mantua school, and Cecilia's scholarship equalled that of her brothers. The school is an example of how some noble girls could escape the restrictions placed upon female education by being schooled along with male relatives. The Gonzaga girls received the training in mathematics and eloquence that Bruni would have denied to Baptista. This situation must have existed in other noble families. However, humanist culture was sought and attained by wives and daughters of only a few families, predominantly in the cultural centers of northern Italy. And the treatises on education, when they made some mention of women, always prescribed a more limited curriculum than that for men.

The restrictions on women's education reflect a limited view of women, well expressed by the influential Baldassar Castiglione in the *Book of the Courtier*. This is a series of conversations, which supposedly took place at the court of Urbino, on the subject of the ideal courtier. It was agreed that he should have skill at arms, physical prowess, and courtly grace. He should be adept at speaking and writing in classical style, and should be acquainted with music, painting, drawing, and languages. Castiglione here illustrated the milieu in which the educated lady was supposed to move. And yet the actual participation by women was limited, serving usually to move the conversation along. All substantive matters were dealt with by the men; two of the four women did not speak at all, but provided, at one point, a little dance.

The ideal court lady was a subordinate topic, discussed mainly in terms of her relationship to men. It was agreed that she should have the same virtues of mind as men—prudence, magnanimity, continence, kindness, discretion—plus the ability to manage her children and her husband's property. She should also be schooled in letters, music, and painting. In fact, she was considered to be intellectually capable of understanding everything a man could. But other qualities were emphasized as more important than intellect in a woman: beauty and modest behavior. Above all, she should display "a certain pleasing affability . . . whereby she will be able to entertain graciously every kind of man with agreeable and comely conversation suited to the time and place and to the station of the person with whom she speaks."[3] She must be "agreeable, witty, and discreet." In other words, the court lady was to be educated in order to complement the courtier and provide him with a knowledgeable partner for polite conversation. It was the role of the courtly medieval lady in reverse.

There were also things a woman should not learn, according to Castiglione—those "robust and strenuous exercises" intended to fit the courtier for war. Like the strictures of Bruni against rhetoric for women, the absence of physical training here signified the elimination of any political role for women. In place of arms and athletics, the lady might take up dancing; but even here, she should not "make movements that are too energetic and violent." In music also, she should play gently, and only on appropriate instruments for women, certainly not on fifes, drums, or trumpets. However, she should have knowledge of the physical skills that she was not herself allowed to develop, in order that "she may know how to value and praise cavaliers more or less according to their merits."[4]

Castiglione also emphasized in these conversations the overwhelming importance of chastity, without which a woman was nothing. One by one he introduced the classical views of women's inferiority (that she was an imperfection in nature; that she provided only matter, to which the male gave form; that she was cold and passive, while man was warm and active; that in the form of Eve she brought death and sorrow to mankind). He then allowed the proponents of women to defend them in endless tales of ladies who retained their virtue under hazardous conditions.

It is clear that the ideal court lady was to be educated as part of the conspicuous consumption of her newly rich or newly powerful family. Her husband's virtues were to be demonstrated in the public arena; hers, in the private life of her home, which she decorated with taste and adorned with clever conversation. As the bourgeois Renaissance lady exemplified the Ancient Greek wife, she was to exemplify the Roman. For both, the success of the family required that she be chaste and confined.

Other detailed descriptions of the education of court ladies were written in the sixteenth century. They all emphasized education of women for the moral life. Some writers, like Ludovico Dolce in mid-century, accepted the ancient belief that the good is fostered and developed by knowledge, and outlined fairly comprehensive readings in Latin. (Greek was not usually considered necessary for women.) To the writings of Plato, Seneca, the philosophers, Vergil, the moral portions of Horace, Cicero, and the ancient historians, Dolce added the modern works of Petrarch, Dante, Bembo, and Castiglione. The aim of women's education, he wrote, was not so much knowledge or abstract thought as the ability to feel and judge. In history, facts were not important; instead, a girl should be made to feel the moral conflicts involved. In philosophy the aim should be comprehension, not of great metaphysical principles, but of the existence of evil and unhappiness in life. This model prefigures later ones for female education calculated to develop the specifically "feminine" characteristics.

Other writers felt that reading, although necessary for the noble lady, must be monitored carefully. Silvio Antoniano stated that since women were vain by nature, learning would make them want to rule the household. All agreed that women's education should be limited by her future role and station in society; most considered education of the intellect completely unsuitable to women who were not noble.

Bruni provided a picture of what the Renaissance lady should properly learn; Vittorino, of what she might learn if she was lucky enough to be educated with her brothers. All writers on the subject agreed that the purpose of learning for women was character training. Castiglione provided another purpose for women's education: the adornment of the social life of the Renaissance courts. But even here, maidenly modesty was emphasized. Women were not to shine, but to provide a background against which men could display their brilliance. And even this role was limited to the very few aristocratic women.

Giovanni Michele Bruto produced a more typical prescription for a lady's education. He dedicated it to Marieta Catanea and addressed it to her father. This work was translated into French and English and widely circulated. Bruto recommended that the father choose a virtuous and wise gentlewoman who would guide his daughter to detesting vice and loving chastity. The girl must be kept from the acquaintance of servants, who would tell her vulgar tales. Her reading must be severely restricted. Bruto did not agree that learning would keep women from succumbing to vice; the dangers of learning outweighed the advantages. Reading opened the door to ancient authors' tales of adultery and fornication. A girl should never be given amorous works to read or songs to learn; rather, she should concentrate on the lives of virtuous and renowned women of the past.

Even then, in going over the learned women of the past, Bruto concluded that any man of good judgment would rather have an unlearned and modest daughter than one schooled in philosophy but suspect in her morals because she engaged in public disputation. Women, he wrote, were given to men as companions, to govern their households: "It becometh not them like Draco, Lycurgus, Solon, Numa Pompilius, to prescribe laws, whereby men must govern themselves: they must live well and moderately, and not like professors of sciences and faculties, in schools to teach the wisdom of lawes and of Philosophie." If a girl desired learning, she should be shown how much more suitable needlework and spinning were in gaining an honest reputation "than the book and pen with an uncertain report." It was sufficient that a woman be taught how to run a household well.

However, Bruto would not forbid the lady reading, which could be an ornament to her, provided she not read love lyrics or fables such as those of Boccaccio. (If men read them it was for the sake of their style, and not the subject matter, he noted.) The Scriptures, the lives of famous women, and the lives of female saints were suitable reading. The important thing was that education lead to true religion and piety, which in turn would lead to humility and obedience.

Bruto also decided that music opened the gate to vices—mainly, it seems, because it was practiced by common people and accompanied banquets and other occasions of merriment. Since Ulysses himself could not resist the siren's song, how could a "weake and delicate young gentlewoman, not only hearing, but learning so pleasant an art," not become licentious and morally weak? He would even keep young women from the kind of gathering described in Castiglione's *Courtier*. The more acquaintances she had, the more danger of moral pollution. Ideally she should have only one companion, and should be silent in the presence of those wiser than she. She must deport herself modestly, "with a little blushing," show a cheerful countenance tempered with seemly gravity, and keep her eyes down whenever she spoke.[5]

Thus the education recommended for the sixteenth-century noble lady was remarkably similar to that recommended for the fifteenth-century bourgeoise. The sole difference was that the noble woman was allowed to read, though in a severely limited area. Concern about chastity was the salient feature of Bruto's treatise, as it was of all Renaissance writings on women. Development of the moral qualities considered necessary to female innocence—humility, simplicity, modesty, piety, patience, obedience—were always emphasized. The Italian Renaissance lady, unlike the Renaissance man, was to be passive and sheltered within the home, which she adorned with her modest beauty.

The Gonzaga court at Mantua, the Sforza court at Milan, and the d'Este court at Ferrara produced a considerable number of educated Renaissance ladies. Baptista Malatesta, to whom Bruni dedicated his treatise, was a Gonzaga. Later, Vittorino's school educated Cecilia Gonzaga, who read the Church Fathers in Latin at age eight and wrote Greek well at twelve. Elizabeth Gonzaga, the lady who presided over the conversations of Castiglione's *Courtier*, was educated in Latin, dancing, and singing. Baptista's great-granddaughter and namesake, born a Sforza at Milan, learned her letters at three and was mistress of Latin rhetoric at an early age. Like her great-grandmother, she welcomed illustrious visitors to Milan with prepared and extempore Latin speeches. Married at fourteen to the Duke of Urbino, she was also capable of serving as regent in his frequent long absences. She took part in diplomatic exchanges in Rome in 1462, which prompted the Pope to remark that her eloquence was equalled only by her discretion.

The girls of the Sforza family were frequently assigned to welcome visiting worthies with Latin orations. Maria was chosen over her elder brothers to welcome Pius II when he visited Milan; Ippolyta, married to a Bentivoglio, performed the same role when that Pope visited Calabria. The dukes displayed the learning of their daughters and wives as they displayed their palaces, their works of art, their precious manuscript libraries—as adornment of their power. Noble girls were often sent at a young age to the courts of their future husbands to be schooled, as Barbara von Hohenzollern was in Vittorino's school at Mantua.

But for the women, education was by no means an avenue to power. True, noble ladies often ruled their lords' estates in their absence—provided that the estates were secured by military might commanded by their husband or other male relatives. In northern Italy there was no title to power, only power itself. That is why, in a Renaissance chronicle of Ferrara, one reads: "A daughter was born this day to the Duke. . . . And there were no rejoicings, because everyone looked for a boy." One Sforza woman of the late fifteenth century, Caterina, was married to the Count of Forli, nephew of Pope Sixtus IV; three times she rode at the head of her troops to quell uprisings after the assassination of her husband. But when her uncle fell from power at Milan and his support was lost to her, she was forced to give in to the might of the Borgias.

Typical of educated Italian women were the sisters Beatrice and Isabella d'Este, of Ferrara. Educated by the scholar Guarino, they learned the Latin authors, Greek and Roman history, French, music, dancing, riding, and hunting. Isabella was an outstanding Latin scholar, who spoke the language with ease in the classical style. She read all the modern languages, played the clavichord and the lute, designed and executed embroidered masterpieces. As a married woman she ruled Mantua while her husband Francesco fought against the French. At the same time she built up an outstanding collection of art and rare editions. Like all of these women, she was a prolific correspondent. Almost two thousand of her letters have been preserved. Her sister Beatrice, Duchess of Milan, patronized poets and musicians.

At the d'Este estate in Ferrara, Renée of France, married to the Duke, presided over a circle of poets in the early sixteenth century. She was frequently visited by Vittoria Colonna, Marchioness of Pescara. Born in 1490 in Naples, betrothed four years later, married at nineteen, and widowed at thirty-five, Vittoria is best known for her extraordinary friendship with Michelangelo. An intellectual and Platonic relationship, it began when she was forty-eight and he was sixty-three. To Ferrara came also the brilliant Olympia Morata, then only twelve, to oversee the education of Renée's ten-year-old daughter, Anna. Olympia, daughter of a professor of the classics, was well versed in Greek and Latin literature and rhetoric. At age fourteen she was writing Latin letters, as well as dialogues in the style of both Cicero and Plato. At sixteen she was asked to lecture at the University of Ferrara on the philosophical problems in Cicero's *Paradoxes.*

Olympia's career may provide a clue to the origin of stories about female professors at Italian universities. A member of the bourgeoisie, taught by her scholarly father, she acquired entrée into both noble and university circles, like male scholars. But her lectures at the university did not constitute a permanent post. What is unusual is her role of tutor to noble girls; most girls were tutored by males, who controlled the intellectual life of the time.

RENAISSANCE FRANCE

As feudalism began to give way to centralized monarchy in France, the nobility lost status in general, noble women particularly. There had been a conflict all along between the rarefied view of women set forth by the troubadours and the misogyny of the clergy and *fabliaux.* The clergy tended to see woman as Eve, source of all evil. The *fabliaux* were tales told to groups of common people as entertainment. In them women were pictured as vicious, perfidious, dangerous animals who must be controlled and forced to be dutiful to their husbands. Husbands beat wives and locked them up; wives fought back, biting and scratching. What the woman got, she got by trickery. And of course, the ultimate trickery was adultery. The bourgeois wife of Orléans was able to cuckold her husband and trick him into being beaten as well, thus showing the scheming and deceitful nature of women.

The troubadours had celebrated the nobility of women. They had also proclaimed that true love could be found only outside marriage, a logical viewpoint in an age when noble marriages were based upon political and economic alliances between estates. The *fabliaux* concentrated on the married state, and maintained that a wife could only be a sore trial to man. The two views of women—romantic and vicious—were marvelously exemplified in the most celebrated work of the thirteenth century, the *Roman de la Rose*. Written by two different authors, with a separation of forty years between them, the two parts of the work reflect the entire range of attitudes on love in the century. The first half, by Guillaume de Lorris, is an allegory of courtly love; the second, by Jean de Meung, an attack on women in the manner of the *fabliaux*. The second author, unlike the first, was a bourgeois, not an aristocrat, and his portion reflected the more popular view of women. This did not prevent its acceptance by the aristocracy. It may be pertinent that the second part was written as the power of the French monarchy reached its medieval height during the reign of Philip the Fair (1285-1314). The French nobility was beginning to lose its political predominance; perhaps the individual noble, insecure in his public position, was determined to be sure of power in his domestic domain. The ideal wife would be, not the courtly lady of the past century, but Chaucer's Patient Griselda of the next, who endured, in wifely obedience, all manner of cruel tests imposed upon her by her husband.

The *Roman de la Rose* ushered in the first stage of French dialogue about the nature and value of women, which lasted into the seventeenth century. At times serious, at times only literary, it was known as the *querelle des femmes*. Up to this point, attitudes toward women had been expressed by men. The quarrel over the *Roman* was spearheaded by a woman who was the first proponent of women's education.

Christine de Pisan was raised at the court of Charles V of France, where her father was court philosopher and astrologer. Although her father wished to give her a good education, her mother felt that only a domestic training in preparation for marriage was advisable. Her studies when young were limited, though she heard scholarly discussions in her father's house. Later in life she lamented that she had not taken more advantage of them. She was married at the age of fifteen, the average for her time, and she suffered within ten years the death of the three men upon whom her livelihood depended— her father's patron the king, her father, and her husband. At twenty-five she was a poor widow with three children trying to salvage a living from an estate that was being milked by rapacious lawyers.

Christine then made two decisions that were unusually brave for a woman of her time: not to marry again, and to present her own case to the new royal court in an attempt to salvage her rights. Her visits to court were attended by whistles and ribald shouts in the streets, palace corridors, and anterooms. She was only partly successful in retaining some income for herself and her children. This may be the first recorded instance of a woman's feminist consciousness being raised by her life experience. Christine managed to place her children in good positions in noble retinues (or, in the case of her daughter, in a convent). Then she decided to educate herself, learning Latin, reading history and literature. She began to write poetry, which gradually became popular in court circles. Her poems and other writings show an extensive, if not always firsthand, knowledge of the main authors of the ancient world and her own time.

Reading the *Roman de la Rose* aroused Christine's latent feminism. It was not only that she opposed the misogyny of the second part of the work; she resented the general attitude of men toward women, reflected in the weakening of chivalry and the antifeminist preaching of the clergy. In her poem "Epistle to the God of Love" written in 1399, Cupid presents to the other gods a women's petition asking for an end to the outrages they are forced to bear. The poem was a *cause célèbre*. A royal secretary replied, attacking the audacity of a woman who criticized a great work of literature, the clergy, and men in general. Christine was defended, however, in a limited way by the famous theologian Jean Gerson, who stated that the *Roman* was an immoral work. Others entered the quarrel on both sides. Christine presented her case to the queen of France, humbly avowing that she was no match for these learned men, but asking that the case be judged on its merits.

The quarrel came to no clear conclusion, of course. But it was the first literary quarrel in French history—that is, the first literary debate that took place outside the university faculties. It concerned morality and attitudes toward women, and one of its chief protagonists was a woman.

Some of Christine's later works were aimed at a female audience. In the *City of Women* she created, with the aid of three female goddesses (Reason, Uprightness, Justice), a city to justify her sex. Reason provided her with the foundation, a long list of women rulers. When asked if women were capable of learning, Reason supplied samples of female scientists and inventors. Uprightness peopled the city with virtuous women, and protested against those who thought it was morally dangerous to educate women. Justice crowned the city with women who aroused respect; the Virgin and the female saints defended it from harm. (Christine seems to have used Boccaccio's *De Claris Mulieribus* as a source for her famous women.)

Christine's resentment of her own limited education, as compared with that of men, emerged in this book. She wrote: "If the custom were to put little girls in school and if one commonly made them learn the sciences as one does boys, they would learn as perfectly and would understand the subtleties of all the arts and sciences as [the boys] do."[6] She admitted that although women had the understanding to make laws, they lacked the strength to enforce them. But she also claimed that many women had, as widows, run estates as well as their husbands did. Not that men were not superior intellectually, as well as physically; but women, she felt, had more subtlety of mind.

In the same year (1405) Christine wrote her *Book of the Three Virtues,* addressed to noble ladies, ladies-in-waiting, and bourgeois or common women. Here she was mainly concerned with the development of female virtues appropriate to women of different social strata. As for intellectual development, women's education should be narrower than men's, she said, because their tasks in life were different. Noble women should learn to read so as to study devotional books and those encouraging good morals: the Bible, Boethius,

Seneca, Titus, Valerius Maximus. They should acquire a good vocabulary in order to converse well; they should be musical. Noble women living on estates should know common law and the laws of warfare. Bourgeois women should know how to manage the home. In general, Christine justified knowledge for women with both moral and pragmatic reasons.

There has been some discussion about why she did not maintain that girls should study Latin, *lingua franca* of the educated of her time. Nor did she recommend that women follow her example and devote themselves to the literary life; she placed her own daughter in a convent. Of course, she may have refrained from suggestions that would have made her plea for female education unacceptable. Or it may have been that her own experience of defending herself, acquiring an education, and making her own living had been so difficult that she could not recommend it to others. She did recommend that women should be educated enough to manage their persons and their business affairs in a man's world, in case they should be unlucky enough to be without a man; and she maintained that women were perfectly capable of intellectual development.

At this point she was supporting herself by writing—the first women in history known to do so. Her poems were mostly the lyrical love ballads popular in the courts of her time. She worked with famous illuminators to produce them in costly manuscript editions for wealthy collectors, such as the Duc de Berry. Her long poems tell stories in which women resist the temptation to succumb to a dishonorable love, pointing out pitfalls that lie in the path of a woman who is naive, uneducated, and helpless in a man's world. It was a world she knew from her own experience.

Christine's praise of intellectual women, if not her personal example, may have inspired later Renaissance ladies, Her works were widely published; over two hundred manuscripts and printed copies in French, English, and Dutch still exist, published in the century after her death in 1430. The *City of Women*, besides being the most widespread, was commemorated in a tapestry made in 1513 for Marguerite of the Netherlands. Copies of this tapestry were owned by Queen Elizabeth of England and by the mother of Mary, Queen of Scots; Elizabeth's hung in her wardrobe room. In 1530 Anne of Beaujeu, Queen of France, wrote her *Teachings* for the use of her daughter Suzanne, outlining a moral and philosophical education that included study of the ancients and the Church Fathers, and emphasizing the development of reason and practical abilities. It seems to be modeled on the ideas of Christine. (However, she did not imitate Christine's feminism. In a letter to her daughter she characterized herself as "the least foolish of women in the world, for there are no wise women.")

Mention of these women, all queens, points to a development in women's intellectual life during the Renaissance. In France, where noble women lost real power during the period, they also lost their position in the intellectual world. Christine was an anomaly. By the sixteenth century, when the Renaissance reached its height, few women outside the royal court presided over intellectual and literary circles, and even royal women's ideas were censored in a country such as France, where only men could actually rule.

The French invasions of Italy in the late fifteenth century caused a cultural interaction between Italian humanism and the classical learning introduced into France in the twelfth century. Anne de Beaujeu read Plato and arranged for her daughter's education in the tradition of Christine de Pisan while serving as regent for her son, Charles VIII. It was this king whose officers brought Italian humanism back to France after numerous campaigns. Charles's wife, Anne de Bretagne, who brought Brittany to the French crown, was the first French queen to fill her court with educated ladies and demand respect for women from men. She encouraged writers to exalt women and Platonic love, and she had Boccaccio's *On Famous Women* translated into French.

With the decline of feudalism and the centralization of the monarchy in France, the royal court became the center of secular intellectual life. There the King's sister-in-law Louise of Savory educated the future king, Francis I, and his sister Marguerite by the principles of Italian humanism. Louise was well read and au courant with the latest literary developments; but she knew her own worth depended on whether her son, in the absence of a direct heir, attained the throne. Probably because Louise valued her two children differently, Marguerite, who surpassed her brother in scholarship and was the most educated woman of her time in France, always depicted herself a satellite of her royal brother.

Marguerite's education, although not as broad as that of some Italian women, included Latin, religious history, philosophy, Italian, and Spanish. But she has been described as a woman who spent her entire life enlarging her intellectual horizons, both through scholarship and through personal contact with great philosophical and literary minds of her day. She studied law, mathematics, cosmography, medicine, geography, the Bible, and the lives of the saints. She is perhaps best known for the *Heptameron*, modeled on Boccaccio's *Decameron* and often as crude in its sexual allusions, but written with a different purpose.

Like Christine de Pisan, but with more subtlety, Marguerite wrote about the difficulties borne by women living in a man's world. Her stories illustrate the brutality and insincerity of men who wish only to satisfy their immediate physical impulses. But they also suggest that if women knew how to handle men, they could civilize the dangerous beasts. Thus her work links the earlier tradition of courtly love and the later tradition of the salon, both French women's attempts to "handle" men. In neither Marguerite's time nor the salon period, however, did women have any real power, even if they were, like Marguerite, of royal blood. Under the Salic Law, no French woman could rule. Marguerite was protected by her brother, the king, although she was often accused of heresy for dabbling in reformist religious ideas. Among the circle around her after her marriage in Navarre were many reformers, such as Lefèvre d' Etaples and even Calvin, to whom she gave refuge. But many times she had to withdraw in deference to political considerations. She was unable to save her friend Etienne Dolet from burning at the stake for translating one of Plato's dialogues.

Women's dependence on male power, common to all European societies, produced a response characteristic of French noble women, though adopted to some extent by others. Perhaps attempting to revive the chivalry accorded them in the period when they had power, French women tried to charm men in order to have their own way. A French lady's education was therefore calculated to emphasize her feminine qualities, rather than her reason. It was basically a literary education, useful in clever conversation. Most French women did not parade their knowledge. However, in line with their medieval heritage, they patronized literature, as Italian women patronized the arts.

Marguerite seems to have been somewhat more of a feminist than was typical. In a work now lost, she defended her sex as more intelligent than men and more capable of ruling justly. She implied that women had ruled the first civilized societies until men usurped power. (Perhaps there was acutally more ambivalence than her biographers have detected in her attitude toward her royal brother.) Her lifetime saw publication of many works dedicated to the praise of women and supporting their education. Jean Bouchet's *Poetic Judgment of Female Honor,* published in 1538, celebrated the superiority of women; it repeated many of the arguments used in Henry Cornelius Agrippa's treatise *Excellence of Women.* This work, written in Latin in 1509 and dedicated to the learned Marguerite of the Netherlands, was translated into French in 1530. Agrippa's reward was a university chair, and later the position of imperial historiographer to Charles V.

On the death of Marguerite of Navarre, Charles de Sainte-Marthe wrote *Funeral Oration on the Death of the Incomparable Marguerite,* a panegyric on the learned woman. He recalled that Marguerite believed women should be educated, and read and study the Bible and its commentators. It was indefensible, he wrote, to deny women the study of philosophy. Although such things as war and government might be proper only to men, the virtues taught by philosophy and Bible study were proper to both sexes. Sainte-Marthe was defending Marguerite from the disapproval she had brought on herself by her studies of religion and her support of religious reformers. Marguerite was an example of widespread female interest in reformed religion. It would be interesting to know to what extent this interest represented women's rebellion against their position in the traditional society.

Later in the century the French court was to hear another defense of female education. At the age of thirteen Mary Stuart, betrothed to the Dauphin, declaimed a Latin oration she had written, maintaining, "against common opinion," according to a contemporary, that it was proper for women to know letters and the liberal arts. Raised at the French court from the age of five to be Queen of France,

Mary read Greek, Latin, Italian, and Spanish; her personal library included Horace and Livy, Herodotus, Sophocles, Euripides, and Plato, besides Italian Renaissance works and a great deal of history. Ronsard and du Bellay introduced her to the greatest of French poetry, which she loved and read all her life, as well as writing some herself. Mary later became Queen of Scotland and pretender to the throne of England.

In France as in Italy, a few bourgeois girls received an education during the Renaissance. The most famous of these was the poet Louise Labé of Lyon, *"la belle cordière."* Lyon was a center of progressive thought close enough to the Italian border to be a Renaissance city. The town set up schools for orphans, where girls were taught sewing, spinning, and reading in French, while the boys studied Latin classics. Louise's father was a well-to-do ropemaker who indulged his daughter's fancy for education, although he could not even write his name. She was instructed in Latin, Greek, Italian, Spanish, music, needlework, dancing, and horseback riding. At sixteen she was a prodigy of learning, a poet, a horsewoman, and a good shot. Although she did not, as legend has it, take part in the French siege of Perpignan in 1542, she did participate, bearing heavy arms, in the tournaments that attended the Dauphin's passage through Lyon.

Louise married another ropemaker, who allowed her to continue her intellectual interests, including collecting books and manuscripts. She held a salon, certainly the first bourgeois salon in France, featuring music, conversation, and the reading of Latin, Italian, and Spanish works from her collection. Her own literary output consisted mainly of poetry, some of which has been recovered. The only work published during her lifetime (in 1555) was a typical Renaissance prose dialogue, *The Debate of Folly and Love,* which ran into three editions. It was dedicated to a friend, Clémence de Bruges, herself a learned poet and talented musician.

The dedication, in the form of a letter, is an appeal to women to educate themselves: "I can do no more than implore virtuous ladies to raise their minds a little above their distaffs and their spindles. It is for them to rouse themselves and show the world that, even if we were not born to command, we should not be despised as companions . . . of those who are born to rule."[7] The language of this uncommon commoner reaches across the intervening centuries with more urgency than that of noble ladies.

HUMANIST ENGLAND

The Renaissance came late to England, not until the sixteenth century. Yet in the short period before it blended with the Reformation, English humanism provided precedents for the education of women, both aristocratic and bourgeois. The primary movement rose from the happy circumstance that a leading English humanist, Sir Thomas More, was the father of three girls, whom he provided with the same broad education as his son, hiring the best of tutors and taking part in their education himself. In More's *Utopia,* which he presented to Henry VIII in 1516 as a memoir on government and society, he included a system of education for boys and girls together; he also provided for adult education for "men and women of all ranks who possess studious tastes," through lectures at dawn each day. When absent from his home on official business, More expected to receive from each of his children a carefully constructed daily letter in Latin, telling him what they were learning. He also corresponded with their tutors.

In a letter to one of these tutors in 1521 More wrote, concerning the "fruits of learning":

> Neither is there any difference in harvest time, whether he was man or woman, that sewed the first corn; for both of them bear name of a reasonable creature equally, whose nature reason only doth distinguish from brute beasts, and there I do not see why learning in like manner may not equally agree with both sexes; for by it reason is cultivated, and (as a field) sewed with the wholesome seed of good precepts, it bringeth forth excellent fruit.[8]

Commenting on the current belief that women were morally weaker than men, he argued that if it was so, there was all the more reason to redress the defect by good instruction.

More's daughter Margaret was the outstanding scholar among his children; she mastered Greek and Latin, and studied philosophy, as-

49

tronomy, physics, arithmetic, logic, rhetoric, and music. More's pride in her leaves no doubt that he considered women intellectually equal to men; he showered her with affection for her abilities, and showed her letters to other scholars. Yet he expected her to show womanly modesty about her attainments. After informing her that Cardinal Pole could not believe her masterly letter was written by a woman, he went on to praise her for being content only to have her husband and father as audience.

Although Margaret may have worked mainly for her father's praise, she was not without ambition. As a married woman she translated Erasmus' treatise on the Paternoster into English and allowed it to be published in 1524. The introduction by Richard Hyrde was the first Renaissance defense of the education of women in English. Hyrde directed the arguments for learning in women to a woman interested in her own education, Frances of Suffolk. He first disposed of the argument that, since women were frail and disposed to vice, learning would be morally bad for them. He accused men of being envious, lazy, and unashamed of their own faults. If learning was the cause of immorality, he noted, men should not acquire it either, since they had more occasion to sin than women. Learning was safer than ignorance, since it kept one from idleness and fantasy. Urging Frances to educate herself, he pointed to Margaret as a good example.

It was not by chance that Margaret's work was a translation of Eramus. The famous scholar had been a guest in the More household in 1509, where he had written *In Praise of Folly*. His personal experience with the Mores' family school had won him over to the view that women should be educated as well as men. In his colloquy "The Learned Young Woman," Erasmus portrayed an educated woman defending her learning as an aid to the moral life, in answer to the mindless anti-intellectualism of an abbot. As a humanist, Eramus believed that character was based on thought and judgment, and that the lives led by typical upper-class women were conducive to neither. Nor did he approve of forcing girls into convents. His view of women's education was directed toward making young women into good wives and mothers in the traditional sense. On the subject of women as teachers, he wrote: "It is unnatural for women to have control over men."[9]

Thus the example of More's daughters, influential in England, gained wider currency through the impression it made on the greatest of northern humanists. But at the same time it was fortified in England through the Spanish connection. Catherine of Aragon, unlucky first wife of Henry VIII, brought with her from Spain a tradition of humanism in which women could take part. In the late fifteenth century her mother, Isabella of Castile, had gathered a Renaissance court around her. She was herself a student of several modern languages, as well as Latin, which she learned from one Doña Beatriz Galindo, who may have been connected with the University at Salamanca. Numerous scholars refer to women teaching at the universities of Salamanca and Alcalá. In any case, Catherine, born in 1485, learned to read and write Latin in her childhood, and was also admired by Erasmus. (It was at her request that he wrote his treatise *On Christian Matrimony*, where he strongly supported women's education.)

When Catherine arrived in England, she was welcomed by More in Latin verse. All efforts on behalf of women's education in the early sixteenth century are in some way associated with these two. Catherine's greatest contribution was to appoint her countryman Juan Luis Vives director of the education of her daughter Mary Tudor. Educated at the University of Valencia, Vives had attended Erasmus' lectures at Louvain; he arrived in London in 1523 to lecture at Oxford, and became attached to the English court. Henry VIII, himself a humanist and patron of learning, agreed that his daughter should be provided with the finest education. Thus it came about that the most comprehensive treatise on women's education of the sixteenth century was written by Vives in 1523 and dedicated to Catherine. At the same time he produced a textbook, the *Satellitum*, dedicated to Mary and used also by Edward VI and Elizabeth I in their schooling.

The *Instruction of a Christian Woman* was written in Latin and translated into English in 1540. It appeared in forty editions, in Spanish, English, Dutch, French, German, and Italian, to become the leading sixteenth-century work on women's education in any language. It was most influential in England where a veritable campaign for aristocratic education was taking place. The English nobility, like that of other European nations, was beginning to decline.

Aristocratic claims to power and privilege, based on military exper-
tise, were weakening as the demand for fighting ability gave way to
the demand for commercial talents. The latter was the province of
the middle class, with its intellectual and organizational abilities. In
the mid-sixteenth century nobles who could not read and write began to seek education; this new interest in learning extended to aristocratic women. For this purpose, Vives' treatise combined the Italian Renaissance tradition and the example of earlier educated wom-
en, such as More's daughters.

Vives set the tone for his treatise by noting that innumerable
things must be taught to men, who are active at home and abroad,
while women could be taught easily, since their only concerns were
honesty and chastity. In childhood, a girl must never be exposed to
evil; she should play only with girls of her own age, supervised by
her mother or a nurse. She should learn cooking and spinning, as
well as her letters. In discussing the question of educated women,
Vives found no defects in their ability to learn. Although educated
women were often morally suspect, and learning might be an aid to
deceit rather than to virtue, good women, if they were "fenced in
with holy counsels," would not be harmed by knowledge. The important thing was to separate wisdom from lust. He recalled that
Pallas Athena, goddess of knowledge, was a virgin.

Vives was later to agree with Erasmus that women should not be
teachers. But a virtuous and learned woman could be a girl's first
teacher. If her first teacher was a man, he must be one "either well
aged, or else very good and virtuous, which hath a wife, and that
right fair enough, whom he loveth well, and so shall he not desire
another." The girl should learn to read from books that teach good
manners; to write, with "some sad sentences, prudent and chaste,
taken out of Holy Scriptures, or the sayings of philosophers. . . ."
However, discretion in the choice of philosophical works for girls
was important; only those that trained her character for life in the
"womanly sphere" should be chosen. "For it neither becometh a
woman to rule a school, nor to live amongst men, or to speak
abroad, and shake off her demureness and honesty. . . ."[10] Wom-
en were weak, as Saint Paul said, and should not teach, lest they
spread "false opinions."

Women's weakness necessitated forbidding them certain books

and songs, which Vives named; romantic works would lead them astray—better not to allow a girl to read at all if such books are what she likes. He recommended the Bible, the Church Fathers, Plato, Cicero, and Seneca. Many chapters of the treatise deal with the problem of preserving virginity; Vives preferred girls to have no contact with males at all. To preserve themselves from the "heat of youth" they should also fast a good deal up to marriage, drinking only water and eating small quantities of plain food. For, "how can a young woman that hath a body hot with meat be sure of herself?"[11] (Meat here means all solid foods.) Vives thought that spiced and delicately prepared foods also inflamed the terrible lust of youth. To guard against this lust, a girl should, like the Apostles, weary her body and subdue it to her mind by not sleeping too long or having too soft a bed. "For the Devil's subtlety never cometh more sooner than in idleness."[12]

During her waking hours also, body and mind must both be busy—at prayer, at the loom, at her books. Vives agreed with Erasmus that study for a woman was a remedy against dangerous idleness and vain interests in clothing and personal adornment. (Erasmus felt study was preferable to needlework, which left the mind unoccupied.) Both men saw danger in a girl's participation in trivial gossip; even allowing the mind to wander was a problem. "A woman's mind is unstable and abideth not long in one place. It falleth from the good to bad without any labour."[13] Venturing out of the house was also to imperil her beauty, honesty, demureness, wit, shamefastness, and virtue. If she must do so, a girl should prepare herself as if she were going forth to defend her principles and her chastity. Of course, she would be chaperoned; she should walk at a moderate pace, her countenance and gestures sober. Vives disapproved of weddings and banquets as potentially harmful to the youth of both sexes. For a woman, church should be the sole destination; and even there she should be well covered up so as not to attract attention.

It is clear that Vives was concerned primarily with confining women to their limited roles of wives and mothers; hence the emphasis on everything that had even remotely to do with chastity. His view of women as inferior creatures, in a work dedicated to a queen, was expressed in such a way as to indicate its wide acceptance. Behind his admonitions lurked the idea that, if women were allowed to break out of their traditional roles in any way, chaos would result. He admonished: "A woman shall use no man's raiment, else let her think she hath the man's stomach [courage]."[14] He seemed frightened at this prospect.

The plan of studies Vives outlined for young Princess Mary was somewhat broader than his general strictures might indicate. Literature, mainly in Latin, was to be used to form character. Besides the Latin philosophers previously mentioned, he named Plutarch, some historians, Lucan, and Horace, as well as the Christian poets. If one compares his reading list for girls with that for boys, one finds more pious works and fewer "heathen poets" on the girls' list. Even Vergil, considered essential for boys, was omitted. But he would allow Erasmus and More's *Utopia*.

This was a course of study for a princess. Most women were destined only to be wives. In 1527 Vives published *On the Duty of Husbands*, translated into English in 1550, in which he discussed the wife's education. Defending learning for women, he argued that if they were educated to virtue, learned women might be more moral than the unlearned. It was important for women who had been admitted to the mysteries of religion to understand it, he maintained, not by superstitious belief, but by true knowledge. Therefore they should read moral philosophy, and, if they liked poetry, the Christian poets. "And as for the knowledge of grammar, logic, histories, the rule and governance of the commonwealth and the art mathematical, they shall leave it unto men." Nor was eloquence "convenient nor fit for women."[15] A well-instructed woman would be able to govern the household and to instruct the children in virtue. However, in an aside reminiscent of Alberti, he warned husbands not to tell their wives their secrets.

Here also Erasmus was in agreement. He felt it was a real pleasure for a man to have an intelligent and instructed wife who could appreciate his true excellence. An instructed wife was also easier for a husband to guide by reason. Both Vives and Erasmus disapproved of the fashionable court-lady of the Italian mode. Vives made some exceptions in terms of worldly knowledge—history, Latin poetry, some modern works—for a princess who might become Queen of England. Otherwise he saw women's education as a limited endeavor, aimed at cultivating the wifely and motherly virtues.

There is one other document connecting the subject of women's education to Catherine. In the 1530s Sir Thomas Elyot, part of the humanist group around More, wrote an imitation of a Platonic dialogue called *The Defense of Good Women*. In the dialogue Candidus maintained against Caninus that woman, like man, was differentiated from beasts by reason. A queen, Zenobia, was brought in to settle the argument. She told how she married late, having spent the years between sixteen and twenty studying moral philosophy. She described how she put her knowledge to good use as wife, mother, and queen. Caninus was won over to the view that women could be brought up to be equal to men, not only in reason, but in fidelity and constancy.

Although More and Catherine, the main proponents of women's education in sixteenth-century England, figure among the losers of history, their efforts were not lost. Throughout the century English women of the upper classes displayed a veritable thirst for learning, best exemplified by Elizabeth I, one of the great learned ladies of the Renaissance.

Like her cousin Mary of Scotland, Elizabeth was precocious. At the age of eleven she presented to Queen Katherine Parr her own handwritten translation of Marguerite's mystical poem "The Mirror of the Sinful Soul," one hundred twenty-eight pages, which she had bound in canvas and artfully needlepointed in silk thread. A combination of typical woman's work and impressive woman's learning, this gift symbolized the talents Elizabeth would later bring to the throne. As a princess she consciously prepared herself to rule, spending three hours a day reading history. Her studies also included astronomy, mathematics, logic, philosophy, architecture, and poetry. She was fluent in Latin and good in Greek, which she continued to study after attaining the throne. As Queen of England, she was to converse on at least one occasion with ambassadors of three different countries at the same time, each in his own language.

One of her tutors was Roger Ascham, who wrote in 1550 that there were many ladies who now surpassed More's daughters in learning of all kinds, but none could touch Elizabeth: "Her study of true religion and learning is most energetic. Her mind has no womanly weakness, her perseverance is equal to that of a man, and her memory long retains that which it readily grasps."[16] He noted her skill in languages, classical and modern, and in music. She read all of Cicero with him and much of Livy, as well as Greek tragedy and religious works. Her morning was devoted to reading the New Testament in Greek.

Elizabeth was the only Renaissance lady who truly ruled. In England the succession was established in the Tudor family, and did not depend upon military prowess, as in Italy; women were not denied the right to rule, as in France. Of course, her male advisors expected to direct her reign. At least, they expected that she would make a diplomatic marriage and, diplomatically, allow her husband to manage the affairs of the realm with their help. Neither expectation came to pass. Elizabeth's education had provided her with a thorough knowledge of the rights of the crown, and she refused to give them up.

At the same time, she soothed the ruffled vanity of the men she dealt with by occasionally adopting the demeanor of the weaker sex. When the French ambassador, de Maisse, remarked late in her reign that her knowledge of languages was a great virtue in a princess, she replied that there was no marvel in a woman learning to speak, but that there would be in teaching her to hold her tongue. She fended off demands that she choose a husband with a demureness that was almost coquettish.

The combination of playing the weak woman and asserting her own judgment appears in her response in 1563 to one of many petitions from the House of Commons that she marry:

> The weight and greatness of this matter might cause in me being a woman wanting both wit and memory some fear to speak, and bashfulness besides, a thing appropriate to my sex: But yet the princely seat and kingly throne, wherein God (though unworthy) hath constituted me, maketh these two causes seem little in mine eyes, though grievous perhaps to your ears, and boldeneth me to say somewhat in this matter, which I mean only to touch, but not presently to answer.[17]

Elizabeth's education had prepared her to succeed by being modest as a woman and absolute as a ruler.

The English Renaissance was at its height when Castiglione's *Courtier* was translated in 1561. It reinforced the trend toward education for aristocratic women. However, the English Reformation was consolidating itself at the same time. Already by the death of Elizabeth one could distinguish two types of learned women—Cavalier and Puritan. The theory behind the education of the first was that of the predominantly Catholic Renaissance; the reform ideas behind the second were to lead to a typically Protestant view of women's education.

CHAPTER II

Protestant Versus Catholic In Primary Education

During the Renaissance it was agreed that the elite of society should be educated; the period was unusual in that some women were included in the small circle of those who became learned. For the formal education of women is usually closely tied to that of the masses who are to be led, rather than to that of the elite who are to lead. Like the lower classes, women usually are without power. The aim of education given to both groups is socialization—to train them to fit into society as envisaged by the powerful. This is the role of primary education, which is deemed necessary to the extent that a complex social order renders socialization by the family inadequate. Males, who operate in the public arena, are the main consideration of primary education. But the process usually includes females to some extent also, since they are acknowledged to play an important role in the primary socialization of children.

During the Middle Ages the Church was the repository, not only of all knowledge, but of the social ideology that supported a hierarchical feudal system. It provided whatever formal education existed, as well as the informal education offered by religious ritual and prescription. From the religious point of view, ordinary people only needed education enough to follow the religious liturgy and have an elementary understanding of Church dogma. A minimal education was also essential for a religious vocation. Thus it was in convents, monasteries, and episcopal schools that children of both sexes received elementary schooling. The education available to girls under this system had already declined in quality and quantity by the twelfth century. Convent education was transmitted by nuns who were themselves almost illiterate.

At about this time the Church's monopoly over education—even of the lower classes—began to break down. The quarrel between Church and State in the Holy Roman Empire and the Netherlands prompted some territories to set up their own schools, which were not generally open to girls. The rising burgher class in the towns of the Hanseatic League began to turn its back on the Latin schools run by the Scholastics of the Church—schools that had been open to girls on the primary level. Finding scholastic, theologically oriented education unsuited to new conditions in their burgeoning commercial centers, they prepared to send their children to "German" schools, usually private, where they had some control over the curriculum. Here the difficulty of finding female teachers tended to eliminate girls.

However, two movements originating in the Netherlands pioneered secular education for girls. The Brothers of the Common Life, known for their pietist and humanist education of boys, set up sister-houses throughout the Netherlands and northwest Germany, which provided girls' schools. In the same territories elementary education for girls was also provided by the *beguines*, communities of women who lived together but did not bind themselves by religious vows. Thus in these areas, even before the Reformation, there was a tradition of elementary education, outside the purview of the Church, which included girls.

The Reformation itself provided a tremendous impetus to education throughout Europe. Most important, it was a first step toward universal education. In the areas touched by reform, convents and monasteries were closed, eliminating the education they had provided; it seemed necessary to replace them with other institutions. But the battle between the new and old religions made mere replacement clearly insufficient. Suddenly, in the sixteenth century, it became important to leaders all over Europe that everyone be trained in the tenets of the one true faith—Catholic in France, beleaguered by Calvinists; Protestant in northern Germany and the Netherlands, threatened by a Catholic emperor. The impulse set loose at this time was not to find its full expression until the nineteenth century, when all Western nations adopted universal education. Along the way, it was to benefit boys more than girls. But in the long run women, like men, were to benefit from the Reformation belief that every person should be able to read the Bible.

The two great Protestant areas of Europe by the end of the sixteenth century were England and the northern German states of the Holy Roman Empire. The different course taken by the Reformation in these areas determined the difference in their development of popular education. The Holy Roman Emperor, failing to save Germany as a whole for the Catholic Church, was forced by the middle of the century to allow each German prince to decide which religion might be practiced in his territory (*cuius regio, eius religio*). The princes of the north had backed Luther in his reforms; under Lutheranism Church and State worked hand in hand. Thus in each area where Lutheranism had taken hold, schools were founded for the faithful by the churches under the orders of the State. In England, on the other hand, the religious movement took a wavering course between reform and counterreform, ending up in a national Church late in the century. Although broadly based on Protestant dogma, the Anglican Church excluded a large portion of Protestants, who became dissenters. The religious split in England prevented the development of any kind of national education system until as late as the nineteenth century. As a result, primary education in England, although religious in its inspiration, remained private longer than that in any other Protestant country.

READING AND REFORM IN GERMANY

In 1520 Luther called upon the German nobility to reform Christianity in their territories. He particularly opposed the interpretations of religion handed down by Church and University, and maintained that the Bible was the single source for all Christians.

"Above all," he declared, "in schools of all kinds the chief and most common lesson should be the Scriptures. . . . And would to God each town also had a girls' school, in which girls might be taught the Gospel for an hour daily, either in German or in Latin."[1] In 1524 he published a letter to mayors and aldermen of Germany, asking that they take over the work of education, since he disapproved of convent and university teaching. He argued that even if there were no soul, and no religious need for education, schools would be necessary for both the maintenance of civil order and the proper regulation of households by men and women. "Even a girl has enough time that she can go to school for an hour a day and still perform her household tasks," he insisted.[2] This was as much time as he asked for boys, who, he felt, should spend the rest of the day learning a trade. Only the brightest should have more than an elementary education, so that they could go on to become teachers and preachers. Luther's ideal elementary curriculum was not, however, confined to reading the Scriptures. He said he would want his own children to know languages and history, singing and instrumental music, and "the whole course of mathematics."[3]

In 1533 Elsa von Kaunitz offered Luther her house and services for teaching girls in Wittenberg. The Wittenberg school was unusual in that the girls learned some arithmetic. The more usual program was reading, and sometimes writing, in German; religion, including catechisms, psalms, hymns, maxims, Bible history; and often, needlework. Actual reading of the Bible was rare in both boys' and girls' schools; Luther soon lost faith in the ordinary man's ability to interpret the Scriptures properly. By the late sixteenth century catechisms written by him were standard reading fare in schools and Sunday schools.

There is only one reference to girls in John Calvin's works. He decreed that girls have separate schools, indicating that he expected girls to benefit from some kind of primary education. But his main emphasis was on secondary schools, open only to boys. There is no mention of female education in the educational plan of John Knox, Calvin's Scottish disciple.

Other Protestant leaders also concerned themselves with education. Philip Melanchthon, second only to Luther in the German Reformation, surveyed the churches and schools of Saxony in 1527-28.

He was responsible for setting up Latin schools, probably only for boys, which were imitated in many other states. However, he ordered that schools be set up for girls, not too far from their homes, taught by schoolmistresses of good Christian character. The curriculum was to be reading, a rather complete exposition of religion, and hymn singing. One or two hours a day for a year or two would suffice for this program; girls should spend the rest of the time at home, helping their parents and learning to keep house. "From such girls who have laid hold of God's word there will come useful, skillful, happy, friendly, obedient, God-fearing, not superstitious and self-willed housewives, who can control their servants and train their children in obedience and to respect them and to reverence God."[4]

The pedagogue Johannes Agricola wrote a text in 1527 for girls' schools in Eisleben, *One Hundred Thirty Common Questions for Young Children in German Girls' Schools*. Another reformer, Johann Buzenhagen, expanded the old burgher schools in the Hanseatic cities, establishing Latin and Protestant German schools in northern Germany and Denmark. This area was a generation ahead of the rest of Germany in founding popular schools. The method by which this was done was the *Schulordnung*—a decree by a prince or a city council that the Church should establish schools in the area (also called *Kirchenordnungen*). After the decree was adopted, Buzenhagen actively participated in the establishment of schools.

One of the first *Kirchenordnungen* reforming the Church and setting up schools for girls as well as boys was that of Hesse, in 1526. Brunswick's decree in 1528 provided for four girls' schools; Hamburg's in 1529, Lübeck's in 1531, Bremen's in 1534, Pomerania's in 1535, and Schleswig-Holstein's in 1542 were similar. The curriculum for girls was to be reading, religion, the New Testament, and hymn singing. The course ran one or two hours a day for two years at most. In 1533 Luther's own Wittenberg required every town in the territory to have a girls' school, where they would read each morning, write and sing psalms and hymns in the afternoon, and learn arithmetic. On Wednesday and Saturday, school was to meet only mornings, for religious training. Most other girls' schools did not do as well. Indeed, many of them existed on paper only. Outside the big cities only about one-fourth of the religious decrees provided for a girls' school; when they did, the qualifying clause "when possible" was often added.

The first decree to provide for an entire system of schools under state control was issued by Duke Christopher of Württemberg in 1559. It noted that "in as much as in some German schools not only the boys, but also the little girls are sent to school, we determine that in such schools the children be separated . . . the little girls also be separately placed and taught. . . . "[5] The German school (or people's school) spread to every part of the territory in the next hundred years, and by 1649 included obligatory attendance for all children until fourteen years of age. The children learned reading, writing, memorizing, and singing, the latter two connected to religious training. (Perhaps because women were not allowed to sing in church choirs, they did not learn singing in Württemberg.) Because of its long and almost unbroken involvement in education for girls, Württemberg was to come into the nineteenth century with an unusually high literacy rate for women.

Pomerania's decree of 1563 provided for a girls' school in every large town, which would teach reading and writing four hours a day. It was stressed that religious texts were important for girls as well as boys, so that they too could be brought to a knowledge of God and virtue. While it was assumed that the girls would become homemakers, ethical training was emphasized, so that "those also who may fail of an opportunity to marry may end their life in blessed chastity."[6] The decree posed the problem of caring for such women in the absence of convents.

One of the reasons that the decrees often remained a dead letter with respect to girls was that teachers were not always available, even though the requirements stressed moral qualities more than intellectual ones. In a typical decree, the ideal for a teacher of girls was "a respectable, mature and unblamable woman," or "a pious and honorable man with a respectable and pious wife." It was difficult enough to acquire a teacher for a boys' school who had a basic education; in teachers of girls, formal education was not considered to be absolutely necessary. They should be able to read and write, although even this was not required in all cases. It was more important that they be capable of providing religious and moral training. One early decree (1526) reads:

> It would be well to appoint a suitable woman as schoolmistress to in-
> struct the girls in the matter of discipline, writing and reading for two
> hours a day. . . . The Scriptures do not belong to men alone, but to
> women also, who expect heaven and eternal life just as do men.[7]

It refers to Saint Paul's admonition in *Titus* that the old women should teach the young girls to be sober.

In most cases it was considered preferable for women to teach the girls. But even the male teachers were often wanderers who happened to be partly educated, stopped in a place for a time, and performed work for which they were little suited, moving on as they tired of it. They received less income than day laborers, and were not highly regarded in the community. For women, who could not live a wandering life and whose pay was even less than that of male teachers, a career as an educator held little attraction. Those women who were available for the task were often the wives of male teachers, less educated than their husbands, or wealthy women engaging in the work for idealistic reasons, such as Frau Magdalen von Staupitz, who taught in the girls' school at Grimma from 1529 to 1548.

The lack of teachers for girls was one problem; another was parents' lack of interest in educating them. Luther's "Sermon on the Duty of Sending Children to School," written to be delivered by all Nuremberg pastors, indicated that parents were failing to send even boys to school, now that education did not lead to a career in the Church. In it he referred to the different secular careers for educated boys. These, of course, were not available to girls. And education was not free, except for the poorest. Teachers' salaries were almost always paid mainly out of tuition received. This accounts for the low income of female teachers, who often received little in addition, except a free dwelling. It also partially accounts for the unwillingness of families to send their girls to school as well as their boys.

In addition to the financial burden, unwillingly assumed by parents of girls, there was the strong and lasting feeling that education, except in religion and homemaking, was not only superfluous but even harmful to girls. Superfluous, because marriage was her destination, for which intellectual interests might be a disadvantage; harmful, because literacy rendered the preservation of a girl's innocence of wordly things less sure. School decrees into the eighteenth century include passages like the following: "The parents must not forbid girls the right to learn to write; they can as well learn to write holy things as evil things."[8]

German pedagogues, however, continued to insist on the value of education for girls. Early in the seventeenth century Wolfgang Ratke, who prescribed the same basic education for girls and boys, established a normal school in Frankfurt to train male and female teachers. Initially composed of 181 boys and 131 girls, the school later trained both sexes in almost equal numbers. He also set up schools for girls in Cöthen and Weimar which extended into three classes, and taught the three Rs. Johann Amos Comenius, the pedagogue of the century, wrote his *Great Didactic* in 1627-32, in which he supported education for both sexes. Not only the children of the rich and powerful, not only the males, but "boys and girls, both noble and ignoble, rich and poor, in all cities and towns, villages and hamlets" should be sent to school. They are all rational creatures, he wrote, and we do not know what God has in mind for any particular person; anyone can be an instrument for His glory. Therefore there was no reason to exlude girls from education, either in the vernacular (German) or in Latin. They too were formed in the image of God, were endowed with equal, and sometimes even superior, sharpness of mind and capacity for knowledge. Although he pointed out that women had often ruled and advised men, and had studied medicine, he stated that the main purpose of education was to make a girl a better wife and mother. And, perhaps to convince his readers further, he quoted the New Testament (Timothy I, 2:12) to the effect that women should not be forbidden to read.

Others also used the Bible as justification. Veit Ludwig von Seckendorff, in his *Christian State* of 1693, pointed out that the Turks kept women in gross ignorance because they wanted them only for sensual pleasure. Christians know, as Saint Paul pointed out, that women have a soul. Therefore they must have a basic education. The idea that wisdom would lead women to prudence and morality was in constant conflict with the fear that too much knowledge would cause weak women to surrender to the evils of the world. Comenius advised that women should read only virtuous books. Other pedagogues, like Hanss-Michael Moscherosch, felt that religious books were the only ones appropriate for girls. Light reading, he said, led away from God and toward the devil.

The Thirty Years' War (1618-48), which wreaked devastation on the German states, brought dislocation to the still tentative establishment of primary education. Sweden seems to have been an exception, since King Gustavus Adolphus systematically enforced universal education. In 1637 it was boasted that not one peasant child could be found in the country who could not read and write. However, the war was not fought in Sweden. After midcentury, some German princes set up common elementary schools for both sexes, with a curriculum usually consisting of reading and the catechism. But the number of public schools for girls had decreased, as had the number of female teachers. Many men, incapable of manual labor because of wartime injuries, turned to teaching in the state schools as a career. Female teachers were almost totally confined to private schools, including those attached to churches. However, the tendency was now to limit private schools in favor of public schools, as the middle classes came into the state civil service. By the early eighteenth century state standards were established in many territories for teachers of private schools. The people's schools, run by churches, declined in relation to the state schools, catering to the middle classes. Since the latter served mainly males, girls' education suffered accordingly.

The regeneration of the German, or people's, school in the eighteenth century is only partly attributable to Enlightenment ideas. Also important was the growth of pietism, which renewed the educational ideals of the Reformation. But the reform was to a great extent indirect and slow. The pietist August Hermann Francke's first interest was in aristocratic education; his belief in education for women equal to that of men really only extended to elementary schooling. Most people still thought of teachers as people who had no other skills; they feared the effect of education on the lower classes, and on women.

Real advances came mainly from enlightened leadership in the state. As we have seen, as long as it was left to parents to decide on their children's education, girls would receive less schooling than boys. In the eighteenth century all the major Protestant princes issued decrees requiring a school in every village; most of them included compulsory attendance of both sexes and tuition-release for poor children. Prussia was a leader in this movement, which engaged the personal interest of Frederick William I and his son Frederick the Great. Both saw education as a social duty of the state, and attendance at school as the duty of the citizen. The social status of teachers rose as state examinations were set for them and normal schools were founded to train them. But there were no normal schools for female teachers; thus the girls' schools usually acquired the male teachers rejected by the state system. This tended all the more to push female teachers into the private schools. The qualified schoolmaster in the state schools for both sexes would usually teach the boys, leaving the training of the girls to his wife, who might or might not be well educated.

Public primary education for girls did not catch up with that for boys in the eighteenth century. In the cities, most girls were sent to private or church schools. Nevertheless, by the end of the eighteenth century, the German lands had acquired the highest literacy rates in Europe—over 95 percent for males. Since girls were legally as obligated to attend school as boys, one must assume a high literacy rate for them also, even assuming the relative inferiority of their education. The original Reformation impulse toward universal education for religious reasons, gradually supplemented by the concept of training for citizenship, was beginning to yield fruit.

EDUCATION AS CHARITY IN ENGLAND

In England the dissolution of the monasteries by Henry VIII closed down the nunnery schools, which had been almost the only source of education for lower-class girls. Although there was some recognition of the necessity to found new schools for boys, there was no outstanding figure like Luther to call for the education of girls. The strongest voice was the reformer Thomas Becon's, whose *New Catechism* of the mid-sixteenth century was inspired by Lutheranism.

If it be thought convenient . . . that schools be set up for the right education and bringing up of the youth of the male kind, why should it

not be thought convenient that schools be built for the godly instruction and virtuous bringing up of the youth of the female kind? Is not
the woman the creature of God as well as the man, and as dear to God
as the man?

He urged that public authorities establish schools for girls in "every
Christian commonweal, and honest, sage, wise, discreet, sober,
grave and learned matrons made rulers and mistresses of the same."
They should be paid to teach young women "to be sober-minded, to
love their husbands, to love their children, to be discreet, chaste,
housewifely, good, obedient to their husbands. . . . " Women, he
pointed out, were necessary to the state, for good mothers produced
good children.[9]

But the grammar schools for boys, founded in the reigns of Henry
VIII, Edward VI, and Elizabeth I, did not usually include girls.
Some, like Bunbury Grammar School in Cheshire (founded in 1594)
admitted girls only until the age of nine, or until they learned to read
English. Others, like Harrow, expressly forbade them. As on the
continent, the commercial bourgeoisie was interested in education.
In 1561 the Merchant Taylor's School was founded in London, with
Richard Mulcaster as headmaster. This was one early English elementary school that taught girls. In his *Positions*, written in 1581,
Mulcaster defended the education of women, although it was not as
necessary as that of boys, on secular, rather than religious
grounds—soundness of mind and body, development of natural capacity—arguments that partake more of the Renaissance than the
Reformation. And he did not approve of schooling for the lowest
classes.

The first schools for ordinary girls were established by reformers
exiled from Holland and France, who taught reading, religion, and
industrial arts such as spinning and weaving. At first intended for the
refugees' own children, these schools, conducted in the home, were
extended to include other children and thus provide a living for the
exiles. Older women also began to instruct the young in whatever
they knew for a fee. These "dame schools" in the villages were
available to all but the very poorest, and were probably attended by
some girls. But as in Germany, parents were suspicious of the value
of education for girls. A manuscript in the British Museum by Eliza-

beth Jocelyn, who died in childbirth, asks that if the child be a girl, she may be brought up learning the Bible, writing, good housewifery, and good works. But she maintains that a girl needs no more education than this, lest she have "greater portions of learning than wisdom."[10] This reflected a general seventeenth-century belief held by English women, that too much learning might be a danger, not only to a girl's social, but even to her moral, life.

Children on poor relief were also given some education. In 1535 the ordinances on this subject of the town of Ypres in the Spanish Netherlands were translated for Thomas Cromwell, minister to Henry VIII. Derived from a treatise by Vives, they decreed that abandoned children, both boys and girls, should be institutionalized and educated. Household duties and handwork were the subjects for girls; but "if any girl show herself inclined for and capable of learning, she should be allowed to go further with it."[11] Most of these schools led destitute girls into domestic service, but sometimes these girls also learned to read and write.

The "charity school" was to be the basic form of popular education in England. Poor Law legislation continued to be enacted in the reigns of Elizabeth and the first Stuarts, providing for vocational education for both sexes, leading to apprenticeship for boys and for some girls. Girls' schools sometimes became small workshops, in which the schoolmistress was paid by the income derived from pupils' work; this formula would later be abused. Public responsibility for charity schools was indicated by a grant, made by Parliament in 1649, of £20,000. Although charity schools derived from a religious impulse, they were not in the early stages connected with religion as such; there was even some concern manifested by the authorities that the informal nature of English schooling might foster heresy.

The move to set up good Protestant establishments resulted in upper-class boarding schools rather than popular education. The best schooling by a religious sect in the seventeenth century was provided by the Quakers, whose leader, George Fox, believed in female education. By 1671 there were fifteen Quaker boarding schools, offering languages, literature, science, and vocational preparation. Two of these schools were for girls and two were coeducational. Promising students of both sexes were trained as teachers.

The humanitarian impulse responsible for the charity schools reached its height in the late seventeenth century under Queen Anne. It was further prompted by reaction to the moral frivolity of the Restoration earlier in the century. However, after the escape of the nation from a Catholic monarchy, it was not only morality, but orthodoxy, that seemed important. In 1698 the Society for Promoting Christian Knowledge was founded, with the aim of teaching poor children reading, writing, and the catechism. English Protestants had come to the view—stated over 170 years before by Luther—that education was a necessary handmaiden of reformed religion.

The new charity schools, many of them started in areas of Jesuit activity, were viewed as security against the return of Catholicism. "How will they stoop to Beads and Latin charms who have learnt so many plain forms of sound Words in their Catechisms, Psalms, and Prayer-Books," asked Dr. White Kennett rhetorically before 3,000 charity school children and their supporters at St. Sepulchre's Church in 1706. "All our present Charity-Schools, though not opened directly on the same View, yet will serve directly to the same purpose to be . . . a Grace and Defence of our Reformation."[12] In 1709 the Scottish Society for Propagating Christian Knowledge was founded. It was to establish 300 charity schools, most in the Highlands, by the end of the eighteenth century.

Charity children wore special uniforms, marched to church together, and were examined in public. The schools were endowed by churches, towns, private philanthropy, even workers' groups. In a typical girls' school in Lambeth, established by Archbishop Tenison in 1706, there was one schoolmistress who taught reading, writing, spinning, knitting, sewing, and religion to twelve girls aged eight to fourteen. Each girl received new clothes, a Bible, and a prayer book on entering the school. They attended from seven to twelve and from two to five o'clock in summer; from eight to twelve and from one to four in winter. Saturdays they cleaned the schoolhouse. They learned religion by means of the catechism, singing, and church attendance. All children were taught obedience to their superiors, but punishment for girls was usually through shame or ridicule, rather than through physical means. Girls also received prizes of clothing as rewards for excellence in their work.

The charity school educated large numbers of girls. In 1704 there were 745 girls and 1,386 boys in them; in 1709, 1,221 girls and 2,181 boys; in 1714, 1,741 girls and 3,077 boys. The proportion of girls was always highest in London; it averaged 2,300 girls to 3,500 boys from 1720 to 1790. As the schools spread out into the countryside, the female proportion decreased; England as a whole counted 3,911 girls to 19,348 boys in 1730. One of the problems was a lack of female teachers, despite the lower standards for them as compared with schoolmasters. They had to be good Christians, loyal to king and Anglican Church, able to teach religion, reading, and handicrafts. It was not considered essential for them to know writing and arithmetic, as the male teachers did; girls never went on to grammar schools, as did some of the boys. Female teachers received about half the salary of male teachers. Widows of clergymen filled the posts in many cases.

Most of the boys and some of the girls were apprenticed out between the ages of twelve and fourteen. Girls were more likely to be placed in domestic service, rather than in a trade. Unscrupulous masters took advantage of girls in both cases. As a result, more and more girls were kept on in the schools to preserve their morals, doing needlework to pay for their keep. Thus, in the middle of the eighteenth century, the charity school movement became absorbed into the workhouse movement, which had set up workhouse schools for destitute children under the Poor Laws after 1722. In both places the school became a miniature factory, turning out mainly textiles, in which the children were often sweated labor.

By the late eighteenth century, as the Industrial Revolution changed English society, large numbers of children were doing factory work. Education for these children was no longer simply a matter of charity, or even of orthodoxy in religion; it also seemed necessary to train them in the Protestant ethic of hard work and sober living, which would make them responsible members of society and willing, obedient workers. The answer was the Sunday School movement, started by Robert Raikes in Gloucester. In 1785 both the Anglican and Nonconformist churches set up societies to teach children reading, the Bible, and the catechism on their one day free from work. (An additional advantage was that Sunday School kept them from running wild on that day.) This movement appealed to women of the upper classes, who were urged by Sarah Trimmer in

London, and by Hannah More in the country, to become Sunday School teachers. Children learned to read, often in barns and back kitchens. But More did not teach writing, which she considered inappropriate for the lower classes. In Scotland the utopian socialist Robert Owen combined school with work for children in his factory.

By the late eighteenth century there was general recognition in England that the state should engage itself in education. But the Anglican Church insisted on a large role in any state educational system, a role the Nonconformists refused to allow them. The attempt by Bell and Lancaster to set up schools with nonsectarian religious education did not catch on. Therefore no public education existed. For poor girls, this meant that charity and workhouse schools were the best education they could receive. For bourgeois girls, education depended upon their parents' willingness to pay for an intellectual training they regarded with suspicion.

In the English colonies in America, education was regarded highly, as a means of insuring religious orthodoxy and of integrating youth into a new society. The Puritans of New England ordered that every township of fifty or more householders provide a school, without, however, stipulating the sex of the children to be taught. Girls were usually admitted only during times when the boys were not there; they were banned from all learning beyond the elementary level. Parents had the primary responsibility of teaching the basic skills of reading and writing. But here, as in England, woman's role was viewed as requiring only the learning necessary to religion, morality, and housewifery.

Dame schools, which provided training in female skills, plus moral training, existed here as in England. The common schools were attended irregularly by girls, who learned reading and sewing, while their brothers learned reading and writing. Most towns were reluctant to pay for schools for girls; too much education, as Governor John Winthrop remarked, could lead to madness in women. From 1650 to 1776 the male literacy rate in New England rose from 60 to 90 percent; that of women, from 30 to 45 percent. These figures, when compared with those of the charity schools in England earlier in that century, roughly indicate that the interest of the New England colonies in girls' literacy, proportionate to boys' (1-2), was greater than that of England as a whole (1-5), but less than that of

London (4.75-7). (There are no sources that enable us to compare the educational situation of women in England and America in the eighteenth century. Roger Thompson, in *Women in Stuart England and America: A Comparative Study*, attempts to compare the situation in England with that in Massachusetts, and finds the latter superior; but his sources are random.)

Girls received a better education in the colonies of the central Atlantic region, where both the Dutch and the Quakers brought from Europe a tradition of coeducation. The Central Europeans (Lutheran, Moravian, and Reformed Churches) also schooled some girls, but it is difficult to say how many. Pennsylvania was probably the best colony for female education, although even here there was little attention to girls beyond the primary level.

COUNTERREFORMATION IN CONVENT AND SCHOOL

The Reformation plunged the continent of Europe into a period of warfare that lasted until the mid-seventeenth century. At that point it was clear that the issues involved were not merely religious ones; but the ideological battle cries emphasized religious differences. And the Counter, or Catholic, Reformation fought back on an ideological level, which also included popular education in its arsenal. The Council of Trent decreed that there should be a school for each church, in both town and country. The kings of France, the country known as the eldest daughter of the Church, threatened by Calvinist reform, seconded the papacy with a series of decrees on the popular schooling of children.

The results of these orders were minimal. In Catholic countries it was primarily the religious orders that were to undertake the education of the people. Besides the Jesuits, who concentrated on the education of boys from the influential classes of society, many religious orders arose that devoted themselves to educating the common people in the faith. Some specifically devoted themselves to the education of girls.

One of the most widespread orders in Western Europe was the Ursuline Order, founded in Italy by Angela Merici (1474-1540).

Deeply affected by the chaos of northern Italy, which included witch burning in her native city of Brescia, Merici organized a group of twelve young women to formulate a program of Christian education to protect the morality of Brescian womanhood against what she saw as the pagan ideals of humanism. She herself was in her late fifties; thus she was able to call upon the matrons of the city for aid. The women provided an informal religious education for girls until 1536, when they became an order, with a formal rule. However, Merici's intention was that the Ursulines be uncloistered, remaining virgins and protected by the Church, but free to do their educational work in the community.

As the movement spread in Italy during the sixteenth century, it changed its character. In Parma and Venice, the order abandoned its democratic character and was open only to aristocratic women. Secular education was added to religious training. Another community in Milan chose to take the vows of nuns; by the end of the century there were 600 Ursulines there. The question of whether the order should be cloistered or not was a difficult one in all countries—in England, where Mary Ward followed Merici's formula; in France, where the Ursulines were most numerous; and later, in Belgium, the Netherlands, and Catholic Germany. By 1612 Pope Paul V ordained the order cloistered, under the Augustinian Rule; but what were called "primitive" Ursuline communities continued to form.

Frances de Bremond founded the first French Ursuline community in 1596 in Avignon. A papal bull in 1598 assigned them the duty "to remedy the ignorance of the children of the people and the corruption of morals." The date is significant, for it was also the date of the Edict of Nantes, which gave civil rights to Protestants, including the right to educate their own children. Bremond was responsible for the basic pedagogy of Ursuline schools, which was not to lead them toward the religious life, but to prepare them to be good mothers. Ursuline education aimed at strengthening Catholicism by training girls in Christian ideals, which they would pass along to siblings at home, and later to their own children.

There was at first some opposition in France to female popular education, which was considered Lutheran. But the religious wars created a demand for religious education. In 1612 Madame Sainte-Beuve founded an Ursuline institute in Paris. It was she who applied for permission to change it into a convent. Besides the usual three vows, the Ursulines took a fourth—to educate Christian women.

In Paris, the Convent of Saint-Denis alone educated more than 4,000 girls by 1657. It functioned as a boarding school for girls of the best families of Paris. The more important task accomplished by the Ursulines was the education of poor girls, about whose morals the Church was greatly concerned. Another Ursuline pedagogue, Anne de Xaintconge, modeled her school at Dole on the Jesuit boys' schools, with six classes, teaching religion, spelling, reading, needlework, manners and Christian modesty. As the order spread over France to Toulouse, Bordeaux, Lyon, Dijon, Arles, it encountered groups of women, similar to Merici's in Brescia, who had already organized to teach girls. Both primitive (not bound by vows) and cloistered Ursuline communities continued to form. Towns, clergy, and nobles preferred convents. In 1617 the Pope authorized all the bishops of France to erect Ursuline convents in their dioceses. By the mid-seventeenth century there were thirty-eight of these, besides numerous primitive teaching communities.

As a result of this mixed development, Ursuline schools taught both lower- and upper-class girls, and provided both primary and secondary education, often in the same establishment. Their aim, particularly in the boarding schools, was to reproduce the life of a family, with the nuns adopting a maternal role toward their charges. As in all convent schools, the day was minutely regulated. Girls were never allowed to be alone or in pairs, only in groups of three or more, and always under the surveillance of a nun.

In one convent, the girls rose at 6:30, tidied their rooms and breakfasted before the day students arrived at 7:30. They all lined up and went to class until 9:30 Mass. The first real meal was at 10:00, accompanied by a reading. A small sermon by the Mother Superior followed, and then lunch. After lunch there were classes until 5:00; girls would leave the main class in twos and threes for instruction in special subjects. After a short religious service, the day students left for home. After supper there was supervised recreation, games, and singing. Evening prayers ended the day, and all were in bed by 9:00.

The boarders were the paying students; the day-girls, those too poor to pay fees. Most schools taught a minimum of reading, writing, sewing, and catechism; some taught arithmetic. The poor girls were often taught a trade, such as lacemaking in Alençon, and other regional specialties elsewhere. Wealthier girls sometimes remained for a secondary education. This might include the knowledge needed to run a large household—writing business letters, deciphering legal documents, keeping household accounts, as well as young ladies' accomplishments, such as music and dancing. The most advanced secondary education included Latin, Italian, geography, and composition. About six hours a day were devoted to subject matter, including religious instruction. Boarding students helped with household tasks.

The Ursuline schools were progressive in many ways. They limited classes to about thirty-five students and provided special instruction in groups of two or three. There was even individual recitation, instead of the usual droning by rote of the entire class. Ursulines encouraged exercise in time provided for recreation. In an age in which many French people were repelled by water, they emphasized cleanliness. And in an age when beating children was normal, the Ursulines reserved it only for the most extreme cases of disobedience.

Other orders, such as the Augustinians, taught poor boys and girls. They were similar in their methods to the Ursulines. The Augustinians, the Sisters of Charity, and the Sisters of Notre Dame de la Visitation started out as dispensers of medicine to the poor, and later combined this service with education of poor girls.

Another form of convent education deserves mention, if only because it is so often referred to as a model by eighteenth-and nineteenth-century writers. This was the Jansenist school at Port-Royal, developed by Jacqueline Pascal, sister of the philosopher.

Jansenism was a Catholic sect, eventually declared a heresy, which flourished in southern France. It stressed original sin and, with an almost Protestant zeal, predestination. The Jansenists were middle class and hard working. They provided their boys with a secular education to prepare them for their work in the world. The girls, however, were taught by nuns, who prepared them only for a life of piety.

In the convent at Port-Royal, they rose at 4:00 A.M. (the youngest girls somewhat later) and said a private prayer, adoring God and kissing the ground. After a common prayer, they dressed in silence, as quickly as possible, so as "to give the least time possible to adorning a body which must serve as a field for worms. . . . " More prayers, kneeling, and confessing the sins of the previous day followed. They cleaned their rooms and had breakfast, while listening to a reading on the martyr of the day. School began at 7:00, interrupted hourly for prayer on their knees and by pious readings on the religious lesson of the day. There was also the daily office and the daily mass. The idea was that every worthy action began and ended in prayer.

The girls were exhorted to study only to please God; the work they liked the least would serve God best. At dinner they were also encouraged to eat the food they liked least, in a spirit of penitence. This meal followed an examination of conscience, a meditation, and saying grace; the girls ate while listening to a pious reading. Although games were allowed in the recreation period, the girls were made to feel it was more noble to keep studying, so the older girls took no recreation.

These girls learned to read, but their books were all religious. The general tone of the convent was hushed and pious. If a girl rebelled, individual attention drew her back into the fold. Most girls found it difficult to leave the convent for the real world, and many stayed on to become nuns. Unfortunately the attitude of total self-abnegation at Port-Royal became the model for other convents of the seventeenth and eighteenth centuries.

The teaching orders supplemented the very inadequate local parish schools—*petites écoles*. These schools were licensed by the bishop in each diocese; no one could teach without authorization. The teachers could take boarders; some of them had as many as 100 to 120, although sixty was considered proper. Besides reading and religion, the teachers tried to provide students with some vocational training. Often students were apprenticed out from the school, as in England. Girls also learned to keep house, as they were considered marriageable at age twelve. Not only were these schools inferior to those of the convents, but also parents who could afford it preferred that their children not share school benches with the lowest class of the population. Thus there was often little support among the town worthies for a *petite école*. In some areas, however, the clergy campaigned vigorously for them—particularly in the absence of schools run by religious orders. Where schools existed, strict rules concerning the separation of boys and girls had varying results. Either there was a school for boys, and none for girls; or boys attended in the morning, girls in the afternoon; or, the strictures were disregarded. In the areas where popular education was the strongest, there were many mixed schools. Sometimes, as in Germany, the regular teacher taught the boys, and his wife the girls in another room.

Many of the mixed schools were Protestant; one reason for the frequent Church decrees against them was to restrict Protestant education. When the Edict of Nantes, which had given freedom to Protestants, was revoked by Louis XIV in the late seventeenth century, some Protestant girls were taken from their families and given a Catholic education. But even though a royal ordinance of 1698 decreed that all children should go to school, it was not observed even for boys, let alone for girls. As in other countries, French parents had little interest in any more than a religious education for their daughters. A middle-class parent, Agrippe de'Aubigné, answering his daughters' request for schooling, wrote them that, for girls of their class, it had more disadvantages than advantages. He pointed out that they would lose the fruits of education upon becoming mothers anyway, for "when the nightingale has little ones, she does not sing any more."[13]

In 1724 a royal proclamation again ordered that all parents send their children to school, and further, that every parish have a male and a female teacher. Again, it was more honored in the breach, and particularly for girls, since there was a shortage of educated women to teach them. Even convent education, on all levels, began to decline in the eighteenth century. In some provinces a real effort was made to educate children, and available figures indicate a rough equality between the sexes in those areas. But the evidence is too meager to be sure. Dauphiné was one of the areas that established an unusual number of *petites écoles*; nevertheless, in 1790 only 16 percent of the women could read and write.

The city of Lyon, educationally advanced since the Renaissance, was educating 5,000 to 6,000 girls by 1791, and female teachers were numerous enough to form a religious community. Much of this advance was due to private donations for founding primary schools, which also provided vocational education. As early as 1736 there were 170 *petites écoles* for girls in Paris and 190 for boys. By the time of the Revolution each convent in Paris had a school attached, free to the poor, which taught the three Rs and some practical skills.

The education of ordinary girls in France as a whole represents the best that was available to them in Catholic countries in the early modern period. In 1690, 13.97 percent of French women could sign their marriage contracts; in 1790, it had risen to 26.88 percent. (There is, of course, some question as to what level of education a signature represents.) The only places where Catholic women had greater opportunities were in the Catholic territories of Germany, which followed the Protestants in decreeing compulsory education in the 1770s and 1780s.

Italy and Spain, hostile to any liberation of women, lagged far behind in the popular education of girls. England, like France, had relegated the task to religious bodies, with spotty results. The difference was that England, already industrializing by the eighteenth century, was concerned to socialize girls as well as boys into a new society. France, still tradition bound, was educating girls for an almost medieval piety. It was in the German territories, where education was compulsory and sponsored by the state, that the education of girls as well as boys was most widespread by the end of the eighteenth century.

Despite all of these differences, the primary education of girls in the sixteenth to eighteenth centuries was predominantly a moral education, based on some knowledge of reading, and occasionally enriched by vocational training. Where women's education was considered acceptable at all, its purpose was not the development of the mind, but of the moral character of wives and mothers.

CHAPTER III

The Lady in Salon, Convent, and School

While primary education was having its first effects on the lower classes in the early modern period, the formal education of upper-class women was deteriorating from its Renaissance level. In Protestant areas the noble or wealthy bourgeois woman was viewed as ideally a homemaker and mother, for whom an elementary education, with emphasis on religion and housewifery, was sufficient. In Catholic countries such as Spain and Italy, noble women were almost totally confined to the home; the learning provided them during the Renaissance was, in the wake of the Catholic Reformation, viewed as pagan and dangerous.

In only two countries—France and England—was there much attention paid to the education of noble and wealthy girls. In them the debate on the intellectual capabilities of women could still be heard; and individual women managed to acquire learning. However, most formal education for girls tended to emphasize the accomplishments. These rather superficial acquisitions of drawing, music, dancing, and needlework, along with foreign languages, were a degenerate version of the ideal Renaissance lady's abilities, as described by Castiglione. They were intended to provide charm, to en-

hance the girl's dowry in the marriage market. Even convent education often stressed these *arts d'agrément,* as the French called them.

France, leader of Europe in both style and intellectual matters, set
the tone for the Continent. But even the Enlightenment did not provide any immediate advances in the intellectual training of women.
Therefore the effect of Enlightenment ideas can be left to a later
chapter.

Despite the general low level of upper-class women's education in
the seventeenth and eighteenth centuries, some hopeful developments were taking place. There was some convent education of a
high caliber for the time. But more important, some women were beginning to see they needed to be educated, and to make efforts on
their own behalf. In the tradition of Christine de Pisan (Chapter I),
they took part in the *querelle des femmes,* and acquired learning
where they could.

QUERELLE DES FEMMES CONTINUES

The argument about women—their nature, intelligence, and moral
character—has a long history. Already we have seen that the French
querelle des femmes dates back at least to the twelfth century, when
the view of women in courtly love tales clashed with that of the
more scurrilous *fabliaux* (see Chapter I). Then, in the thirteenth century, the debate over the *Roman de la Rose* brought Christine de Pisan to the defense of her sex, arguing that insufficient education
caused women's seeming inferiority to men. The quarrel assumed a
more patronizing tone on both sides during the Renaissance. Some
men prescribed an education, albeit always limited in some way, for
courtly women. It also became fashionable for humanists to write
treatises for female patrons extolling women.

Much of the argument of the later works was playful; these treatises were not usually debated. But often they reiterated the point
that women, uneducated and shut up in the home, had no chance to
develop their mental abilities. Agrippa von Nettelsheim, in his treatise *On the Grandeur and Excellence of Women over Men,* argued
that women's minds had more finesse and penetration than men's;
he extolled feminine intuition. Women's field of activity, he argued,

was limited not by necessity or reason, but by the force of custom, by education, by chance, and mostly by violence and oppression.

In the seventeenth century the quarrel was renewed by the *Alphabet of the Imperfection and Malice of Women,* published in Paris in 1617—one fault for each letter of the alphabet, written in all seriousness by an expert in Church law. The book went into a dozen editions in thirty years, and aroused much reaction, pro and con. The method of argument used by both sides was to quote authorities— the Bible, the Church Fathers—and examples from history or mythology. These were traditional gambits. It fell to a woman, Marie de Gournay, to revive the argument of Christine de Pisan. Gournay was the adopted daughter of the philosopher and essayist Michel de Montaigne; although he did not approve of too much education for a woman, she was learned enough to edit his works. In 1622 she dedicated her work, *The Equality of Men and Women,* to the Queen of France. Gournay supported her argument for equality with quotations from Plato and the Bible, among others. It was marvelous, she wrote, that any women achieved excellence, since they lacked good instruction. Male and female were the same creature, with the same capabilities. The distance which now yawned between them would be filled if the female mind were developed.

Like Christine, Marie was supported by male writers, even clergymen. One Père Duboscq wrote a book called *The Good Woman* which suggested that women should educate themselves in history, philosophy, music, poetry, and rhetoric. Good books would form their judgment and show them how to attain a place in society. As interest in the debate grew throughout the century, Renaissance treatises, such as those of Agrippa, were translated into French.

The quarrel became an international one with the entry of a Dutch woman, Anne Marie von Schurmann, a linguist who knew Persian and Arabic as well as the European languages. In 1638 she produced a Latin treatise, *On the Famous Question, Whether it is Necessary for Women to be Learned,* in the form of letters to a man who lent her books but did not think all women should study. Schurmann could not agree that women should be denied "the most beautiful of all the ornaments of the world." She too pointed out that confining women to the needle and scissors was only a custom. She referred to Gournay's discourse, and argued: "It is impossible that generous souls, which are capable of everything, should be contained within the strict limits which common error has prescribed for them." She noted that Aristotle had said the ardor to know was natural to the reasoning creature, and recommended a knowledge of the natural world, of history, and of religion. The training of judgment required reading the traditional sources clarifying vice and virtue; the ancient languages were the keys to these.

But Schurmann did not intend, she wrote, to exalt her sex over his, nor to oppose studies to woman's primary duties. She also agreed that women should be modest about their learning.[1] Perhaps because she did not demand too much, Schurmann's treatise was translated into French by Guillaume Colletet in 1646 and dedicated to the King's niece, Princess Anne Marie Louise of Orléans, who of course could not read Latin.

The English translation, *Whether a Maid May Be a Scholar*, in 1659, defined "maid" as "a Christian Woman," and "scholar" as "one given to the study of Letters, that is the knowledge of Tongues and Histories, and all kinds of Learning, both superior entitled Faculties and inferior called Philosophy." It inspired Bathsua Makin, an English linguist and royal governess, who had met Schurmann, to write her own *Essay to Revive the Antient Education of Gentlewomen in Religion, Manners, Arts and Tongues* in 1673. Women, she wrote, lived useless lives. But men were as responsible for this as women because they had denied them education, lest the women be wiser than themselves. Instead of learning the foolish social graces, young ladies should have a solid classical education. "My opinion is," she wrote, "in the Education of Gentlewomen greater care ought to be had to know things than to get words."[2]

From 1630 on, there was real interest in the question of the education of upper-class women in France. The followers of Descartes' philosophy were ranged on both sides of the case. His disciple Nicholas de Malebranche, in his *magnum opus* of 1674-75, wrote that the fibers of women's brains were more delicate than those of men, causing their intellectual inferiority. Women were best at things that worked on the feelings—language, manners, taste. They were incapable of grasping abstract ideas. "They consider only the exterior of things, and their imagination has not enough force and extension to get to the bottom of them and compare all the parts without being distracted," he judged. The problem was that the least objects produced great movements in those delicate fibers and stirred up such strong and lively sensations in them as to totally fill up their brains. Thus they tended to apprehend the manner, rather than the reality, of things.[3]

The culmination of the opposite point of view was represented by Poulain de la Barre's works *On the Education of Women* (1671) and *On the Equality of the Two Sexes* (1673). Taking the Cartesian point of view, he said it was necessary to remove all the prejudices in one's head before one could arrive at truth. Doing this, one would realize that belief in the inferiority of women to men was only an opinion. No one had ever proved their basic incapacity; their abilities were merely underdeveloped, like those of uneducated men. Poulain insisted that the same range of capabilities existed in both sexes, only women had had no opportunity to develop their minds and personalities. They were given nothing but religious tracts to read; if they did manage to study further, they had to hide their knowledge. Amazingly, he noted, there were still some very intelligent women. What could they achieve if unrestricted? Since women had the same ability to learn, they had the same right to education as men. He then outlined a curriculum including science and medicine, mathematics, astronomy, law, geography, history, and philosophy.

All this might have been acceptable to at least some men of his time, but Poulain went further. If the two sexes were equal, why could women not be admitted to the great councils of State; to positions in the Church; to the judicial bench? Why could they not be ambassadors, or generals of the army? (Obviously centuries ahead of his time on this score, Poulain was also a priest who left the clergy and married.)

In a dialogue in one of his books, Poulain portrayed a young woman who asked, "How can we instruct ourselves without going to school?" The answer: "In the same way that the majority of men do who don't go to school. Whatever you wish to learn, find masters to teach you, as you do for penmanship and dancing."[4] He also advocated training women in universities, so that they in turn might educate young girls.

THE SALON AS EDUCATOR

Some women were to follow his advice after a fashion, by acquiring education informally. And, contrary to Makin's advice, they accomplished this by "getting words." The *salonière* of the seventeenth century, like the late-medieval court lady, was influential in the development of French language and literature. Unlike the medieval lady, she had no position of power in society, so she took up the *querelle des femmes*, developing it to a point where it began to resemble modern feminism. In the process she was ridiculed by men, who did not have to take her seriously. But she used her wit to surround herself with people who could help develop her mind. She made her salon her school.

And she found men willing to teach her. Bernard le Bovier de Fontenelle, precursor of the Enlightenment, introduced his women friends to the new discoveries in astronomy and physics, which were just beginning to be known amongst the educated. He wrote his *Conversations on the Plurality of Worlds* in 1686 as a series of dialogues between himself and a lady. It included, along with the typical gallantry of the salon, a short course in astronomy and a complete explanation of the Copernican system, all as scientific as it was witty. For twenty-five years Fontenelle spent several hours each day with the young Madame Geoffrin, who was to open a salon in the eighteenth century. The philosopher Jacob Grimm became the educator of Madame d'Epinay, who also presided over a salon in that century.

But in the seventeenth century, women were most active in those areas allotted them by Malebranche. At this time the French language—grammar, spelling, and usage—was still being fixed. Through their salons women became the arbiters of the use of words; they decided the precise meaning of words and enforced the use of good style in speech and writing. Men did not deny them this influence. La Bruyère was convinced that by nature women were superior at all the nuances of language. Although he did not deny women the right to education, he insisted that their skill at verbal expression was an inborn female characteristic, which rendered education superfluous.

The most famous salons gave rise to different genres of literature.

The Marquise de Rambouillet began hers, the earliest, before 1620; its greatest years were 1630 to 1648. The tradition of the literary letter began here, and was brought to its high point by Madame de Sévigné. Her letters to her daughter, in eight volumes, were models for the whole classical age. They give a picture of female concerns, particularly of the desperation Sévigné felt about her daughter's continual debilitating pregnancies. They also outline a plan of education for her granddaughter, stressing history, geography, and literature above all.

In the Faubourg Saint-Jacques in Paris, the Marquise de Sablé's entourage developed the *maxime,* best represented by La Rochefoucauld, and the *pensée,* best represented by Pascal. Attracted to Jansenism, Sablé retired to Port-Royal in 1659, where she also wrote maxims. Here she recreated her salon, which included politics, science, and moral philosophy in its discussions.

From 1654 to 1660 the Duchess of Montpensier, member of the royal family, gathered around her the personalities of the day at the Luxembourg Palace, which gave rise to the literary portrait, exemplified by La Bruyère's *Characters.* Madame de Scudéry arrived in Paris early in the seventeenth century and lived until 1701, presiding over a salon where poetry and the novel were the specialties. It was said that even her servants quoted verse. Certainly the participants in all salons arrived prepared to trade their epigrams, sonnets, maxims, and madrigals, making social life and literary life one and the same. It is recorded that one day Scudéry thanked a gentleman who had brought her a present by means of a madrigal; he returned the thanks with an epigram; she produced another madrigal. And so it went indefinitely.

Scudéry herself produced novels, including one in ten volumes called *Artamène,* or *The Great Cyrus.* It contains, among other things, a "map of the country of tenderness"—all the steps that a true lover should go through before marriage. Molière satirized this in *Les Précieuses ridicules* (1659); and it was ridiculous, considering that marriages were arranged by the parents of both parties. The country of tenderness represented the degeneration of courtly love into complete absurdity and the effort of women, in a time when they had no real power, to control the behavior of men toward them. It was, in its way, a protest against their true position.

Some of the *salonières* who were lucky enough to be independently wealthy did not get married. In novels by Scudéry and others, female characters declare that house management and children should not keep women from intellectual pursuits; some cut off their hair as a sign of independence; some even leave their husbands. In a novel written by the Abbé de Pure, who frequented the salons, a conversation on marriage takes place. One woman notes that, although the discussion might seem vain, it could be of use to their grandchildren. "Even if the only satisfaction we can hope for is to show that we are aware of our sufferings and do not merely put up with them because of stupidity or ignorance, at least we shall have done some honor to our sex and tempered its subjection."[5] The most radical proposal presented was to limit the duration of marriage to the birth of the first child. After that, the husband would get the child, and the wife her freedom plus a good sum of money as reward for her labor.

The "precious woman" satirized by Molière was one product of the salon; another was the *femme savante,* or learned woman. In *Artamène* Scudéry also took up the cudgel for female education:

> Is there anything more bizarre than to see how one approaches the education of women? One does not wish them to become coquettes, and yet one permits them to learn carefully all which is appropriate to coquetry without allowing them to learn anything which could occupy their mind or fortify their virtue. . . . Up to now, with rare exceptions, the education of girls goes no further than reading, writing, dancing, and singing. And despite that, men wish that in all circumstances of life women have a reasonable judgment that they themselves do not have. . . . In truth, I would that one took the same care to equip her mind as her body.[6]

Scudéry's criticism was well made. Most noble women did not have any education before their marriages, except in the accomplishments—music, dancing, and needlework. Cardinal Richelieu's niece, Mlle. de Brézé, did not know how to read when she married the Duc d'Enghien in a splendid wedding in 1744. She was representative of her class of women. When they entered the world of the salon, those who had intelligence and a taste for learning taught themselves to read and gathered around them men from whom they could learn through conversation.

In making her plea for education, Scudéry opposed a wise woman, Sappho, to a pedantic one, Damophile, who made a great show of her learning, used exaggerated phrases, and neglected her family duties. Sappho complained that the way women's lives were led, one would say they were forbidden to have reason and good sense, and were expected only to sleep, get plump and pretty, and do and say nothing sensible. Women should learn more, have strong and enlightened minds, appreciate works of art, talk well, write precisely, and know the world. But they should not talk like learned women. When asked why a woman should know what she dare not display, Sappho replied that it served her to understand the discourse of those wiser than she and to respond appropriately. It was not necessary to hide a knowledge of foreign languages or mythology in conversation. But a woman should not speak too much of what she knew and not speak at all of what she didn't. Scudéry wrote this work in 1653, some two decades before Molière's *Les Femmes savantes*, which dealt with the same subject—what education a highborn woman should have, and what use she should make of it. The popularity of Scudéry's book, in which her characters represented well-known *salonières*, indicates that she was expressing the ideas of her small society.

In *Les Femmes savantes*, Chrysale protests that the roast is burnt and he has no dinner because his wife reads history, discusses language, and is more interested in what happens on the moon than in her own household. In the old days, women didn't read at all; their households were their whole learning and their sewing was their book. In the same play, however, Molière had a young man say to his beloved, that although pedantic women are not to his taste, he thinks women should have knowledge of all things, provided they do not show it off—a practice he finds distasteful in men also. That women should be knowledgeable, but not *appear* so, seems to have been Molière's view, as well as Scudéry's and Sévigné's. Molière's ideal woman was educated enough to be a good companion to her husband, but not *précieuse*, like Philamène in *Les Femmes savantes* who uses exaggerated phrases and wants to dismiss her servant for vulgar expressions in speech.

Outside the salon, reading was the key for the ambitious woman. There were few to educate them, though some learned authors wrote novels in which new philosophical concepts were aired, and poems appeared on such subjects as the causes and effects of meteors. Early in the century a series of lectures on scientific and philosophical subjects was published. And in 1655 formal courses, given by celebrated scholars, were opened for both sexes as a kind of enlarged salon; between lectures there were buffet suppers and dancing. It failed, because it was open to the bourgeoisie, and the aristocracy drifted away. By the late seventeenth century bourgeois salons were imitating those of the nobility. This caused a flight into preciosity, the aristocratic women trying to distinguish themselves from their followers, and the bourgeoisie trying desperately to keep up. Molière's *Bourgeois gentilhomme* reproduced his wife's salon.

The *salonières* were a small group whose individual intellectual accomplishments were negligible. Probably their greatest contribution to culture was their cultivation of the French language, which they often carried, like Philamène, to grotesque excesses. But the salon brought to the fore the subject of women's education, not only in Paris, but even in the provinces. An account of a provincial gathering of the time quotes a woman as saying: "Why do they want to deny us the use of reason. . . . ? There is an injustice in having held our minds captive for so many centuries, and men are wrong to imagine that reason is all for them."[7] In the salon women were expressing not only the virtue of learning itself, but the relationship of learning to their position in society. The novels of Scudéry and others show that, perhaps for the first time, the claim to education by women was assuming a feminist character.

FÉNELON AND SAINT-CYR

Only a handful of noble and rich bourgeois women were able to benefit from the informal and unsystematic learning available at social gatherings. The one outstanding formal effort which was made to educate noble women in the seventeenth century was conceived in opposition to the whole atmosphere of the salon. It was meant to serve a social purpose; probably for this very reason, it became a model for the best female education on the Continent into the nineteenth century.

The late seventeenth century was a period of weakness for the

French aristocracy. The wars of the Fronde—the final effort of the nobility to defy the monarchy—had ended in failure. Louis XIV, now in control of his kingdom, kept his nobles dancing attendance on him at Versailles, while their estates declined. Aristocratic women, who had indulged in some intrigue during the wars, were the ornaments of this court life. *Bel esprit* was their forte. And it was precisely *bel esprit*—the wit of the salon—which was now attacked, in the name of a different kind of education for women.

François Salignac de la Mothe-Fénelon, who was later to be Archbishop of Cambrai, wrote his treatise *On the Education of Girls* in 1686 for the daughters of the Duc de Beauvilliers, leader of the nobles who sought regeneration of the French agrarian aristocracy. Fénelon viewed the centralization of French social and political life at court as deleterious to the nation; the nobility should be on their lands, developing the agrarian resources of the provinces, instead of frittering away their incomes and powers at court. He saw the role of women as central to his scheme for the revival of aristocratic prosperity; and he saw the social life to which noble women had become accustomed as the greatest threat to that development.

Women, he wrote, were born with a "violent desire to please." Since the doors that led men to power and glory were closed to women, they tried to compensate by developing the accomplishments of both mind and body. The *finesse* for which French women were celebrated was to Fénelon a cover for their desire to dominate. As a result the old noble customs of simplicity and wholesome family life had died out. "What is to be done," he wrote, "is to disabuse girls of *bel esprit*."[8] Society, Fénelon believed, following Aristotle, was an assembly of families. In this context the roles of noble women were as educators of the children, overseers of the servants, economic governors of the estates. The knowledge proper to women, as to men, was limited to that which related to their social functions. To raise children, a woman should know religion. To manage an estate, she should have some understanding of administration and economics. She should read and write correctly, which, he noted, most noble women could not do. Therefore she should learn the grammar of her language and be able to express herself in a concise and orderly fashion. Besides arithmetic, a knowledge of the laws of contract and inheritance of her region would be useful, provided she was led to see it was impossible for her to understand all the complexities of law. Basically, all that was necessary in that domain was an understanding of seigneurial duties and the rights of land ownership.

After learning these necessary and useful things, girls might also read books that were sober—histories of Greece and Rome, of France and its neighbors. For girls of sound judgment and modest conduct, Latin, the language of the Church, was proper, provided one did not use it to satisfy vain curiosity and show off her learning. Since women were not going to govern states, make war, or administer religious affairs, they could dispense with any extensive knowledge of politics, military arts, jurisprudence, philosophy, and theology. Italian and Spanish were to be avoided, as leading only to the reading of dangerous books; even works of poetry, art, music, and eloquence should be carefully chosen so as not to arouse romantic tendencies in girls. Fénelon warned against other aspects of woman's character—her curiosity, her desire to shine in public, her affectation, her hypocrisy, and dissimulation. Thus her education must counter these tendencies.

In *Advice to a Woman of Quality on the Education of Her Daughter* Fénelon described the girl who aspired to an education, then hid her knowledge just enough to get credit for both brilliance and modesty. He deplored women's tendency to become involved in theological disputes. It was enough for a woman to know her religion so that she could follow it in practice; she should never be permitted to reason about it.

Again, *bel esprit* was the danger. Any kind of philosophical discussion or literary elegance partook of the worldly court life that Fénelon saw as the ruination of the French aristocracy. What he had in mind was a generation of aristocratic women who would be good mothers and good managers of their husbands' estates. They should live a retired life on their lands, far from the court, where female vanity had emphasized luxury and sophistication. The basis of national prosperity was the land; women who would revive their husbands' landed prosperity would regenerate France, and save the nobility from dissipation at Versailles.

Fénelon was fortunate enough to see his ideas put into practice by a powerful woman of the day, mistress and later wife of the King, Madame de Maintenon. Maintenon had opened a small school for neighborhood children at Montmorency in 1680, and one at Rueil in 1682. In 1684 she took in as boarding students sixty girls of noble families who were in dire poverty, plus day students. Her appeal to the King on behalf of these girls resulted in the school's being established as the Maison royale de Saint Louis at Saint-Cyr, in quarters rebuilt by Mansart. It was the first state school for girls in France.

The school was expressly intended for 250 daughters of the impoverished nobility. Its original character derived from the fact that Maintenon herself was part of the salon atmosphere of the seventeenth century. She engaged to run her school an educated Ursuline who wrote religious operas and was a friend of Scudéry, Madame de Brinon. The education Saint-Cyr provided partook of both the religious nature of the Ursuline movement and the worldly, literary nature of the salon. The *Conversations* of Scudéry were used as readers and were learned by heart; one volume was written particularly for Saint-Cyr. Students acted in plays by Racine, in costume, before the court. The great playwright wrote his *Athalie* particularly for this purpose.

By 1691 Fénelon's friendship with Maintenon began to bear fruit in her conviction that these noble girls' education must be completely changed. She wrote to Brinon: "We wanted wit, and we have produced orators; devotion, and we have produced quietists; modesty, and we have produced *précieuses;* elevated sentiments, and pride is at its height."[9] There was entirely too much witty discussion and entirely too little humility. Maintenon opted for turning Saint-Cyr into a convent, against the desires of Louis XIV. In 1692 the Maison became a convent, and in 1707 the King agreed to allow the girls to wear the nun's habit.

The new Saint-Cyr was the realization of Fénelon's ideas. Maintenon intended the reform to prevent the students from having any illusions about their position in the world, particularly as they were from the poor nobility. They would be educated to be useful, sensible mothers of families; neither exalted intellectual ideas nor excessive piety would be encouraged. The girls would learn nothing that would provoke their pride of intellect. If they became bored, it would be good preparation for the simple boredom of family life. Practical household activities would be the single antidote. The philosophy and methods of educating girls at Saint-Cyr were laid down by Maintenon herself in letters to the teachers, in maxims and "conversations" she wrote for the girls to read, and in personal visits when she herself spoke with her charges.

Girls were admitted to Saint-Cyr between the ages of seven and twelve and stayed until age twenty. There were no vacations; four times a year they could see their parents with a teacher present. (This strict rule was intended to keep the girls from being infected by worldly society.) There were four classes, distinguished by the different colored ribbons worn with their black dresses. Each class was divided into families of eight to ten students, headed by a mother, or monitor. Hard seats, hard beds, minimal heating, cold water for washing, and performance of all the household tasks were intended to shield the girls from pride in their noble rank. They had, however, ample nourishing food and physical exercise, not always usual in convents.

The first class (red ribbons, up to age ten) learned to read and count, the elements of grammar, the catechism, some Bible history. The green class (eleven to fourteen years) learned also music, history, geography, and mythology. At fourteen the yellow class studied French, music, religion, drawing, and dancing. The blue class, age seventeen to twenty, ran the establishment, helping in teaching, nursing, and administering the school. All classes sewed, knitted, and embroidered all the linens and woolens of the house, infirmary, and chapel, besides their own and their teachers' clothes. They waited on tables and cleaned bedrooms and classrooms. These latter activities were considered more important than reading, which was limited to books "well chosen, suited to nourishing their piety, forming their judgment and regulating their conduct."[10]

Despite these strictures, Saint-Cyr provided a good education for the time. The girls recited dialogues written by Maintenon herself on economic subjects, such as taxation and tariffs. In language study, one exercise was the *dissertation du mot*—an extensive explication of the meaning of an abstract word such as honor, reason, civility. One of the *conversations* written by Maintenon for the girls illustrates the fine line she was trying to draw between being educated and being worldly. The subject was reading. One speaker said there were disadvantages in it for a girl, since women could only become semilearned. Another demurred: what if women were as well educated as men? The answer was that women's memories were as good, but their judgment inferior. Again it was argued that this might be corrected if women had a different education. Ah, but women have better things to do, was the rejoinder—fulfilling their duties as women. Books could help to do this by arousing piety and demonstrating examples of virtue and vice; but they should never keep a woman from her duties. These were: to please her husband, raise her children, instruct her servants, fulfill her social obligations. One pleased one's husband by studying his tastes and conforming to them, by abiding by his will rather than one's own.

One participant, Hélène, who may have represented a facet of Maintenon herself, commented that she would search for a husband who liked to read. This raises the question of whether intellectual training, however narrow, could produce only the limited results that Fénelon intended. Although always aimed at some kind of social goal, education inevitably expands the horizons of the mind and produces a certain independence, which can transcend the limits intended for it. In including this comment in her *conversations,* Maintenon may have indicated that she was fully aware of this possibility.

She was determined, however, to prepare her charges for real life. Speaking to the girls in the blue class in 1709, she pointed out to them that "obedience is the lot of our sex."[11] Women, since they are always dependent on someone, must be prepared to fit their own desires to those of the people on whom they depend. Being without fortune, destined either for marriage or the convent, they must always learn to submit their will to that of others. Among the maxims that Maintenon wrote with her own hand at the head of the girls' copy books were these:

—Learn to obey, for you will obey forever.
—Accustom yourself to the humor of others, without
  expecting them to accommodate themselves to yours.
—Obey your superiors explicitly, without wishing to examine
  whether they are right or wrong.
—The greatest ornament of our sex is modesty.

The education provided at Saint-Cyr was intended, as Maintenon put it in 1686, "less to adorn their minds than to form their reason."[12] This attitude, the sensible religious education aimed at secular life, and the useful training in the household arts, gave the school such a reputation that numerous families tried to place their girls there. It was impossible to take all the girls offered, but Maintenon was pleased to advise on the establishment of similar schools, usually Ursuline convents, throughout France. Bourgeois girls also attended these convents, whose rules were often not as strict as those of Saint-Cyr; nor was the education as good. "Instruct your bourgeois girls as bourgeoises," Maintenon wrote to the teachers at one convent. They did not have to read or write as well as ladies, but only to the level of their class. "One must preach reason to everyone equally, while applying it according to their status."[13] Just as she had taught the poor girls at Reuil to accept their position in society and function within it, so Maintenon made the distinction between even poor noble and rich bourgeois girls.

Ironically, the characteristic of Saint-Cyr education that made it universally acceptable was its bourgeois aim and method. The ethical value of work was constantly being emphasized. Manual labor was the antidote to frivolity, the cares of the household preferable to intellectual concerns. As a result of this formula, which had a universal appeal to the wealthy classes, imitations of Saint-Cyr appeared in the eighteenth century in Germany, Sweden, Denmark, and Poland. Fénelon's treatise was translated into German in 1698 by August Hermann Franke, who founded a school at Halle according to French principles, which led to other pietist schools of the same type. On the Continent discussions of female education included approving references to Fénelon through the middle of the nineteenth century.

Most of these schools were not as successful as Saint-Cyr, because they lacked trained teachers. Maintenon struggled all her life to train her Ursulines to the task; one might say she created the first teacher training school for females. But in the eighteenth century the prototype, as well as its imitators, declined to little better than the level of ordinary convents and boarding schools. There was certainly no progress made. When Saint-Cyr was closed by the Revolutionary government of 1793, the girls were still singing songs by the seventeenth-century composer Lully. The strict, practical education elaborated by Maintenon was more often practiced in convents and schools catering to girls of the upper bourgeoisie.

The first Russian school for girls of the nobility, the Smolny Institute, bore a strong resemblance to Saint-Cyr. It was founded by Catherine the Great in 1764 and remained in existence until 1917. Girls entered at six, and stayed until twenty. Every detail of their life was regulated, and the headmistress reported directly to the Empress herself. Greek Orthodox nuns were the first teachers; but later instructors were imported from abroad, and the teaching was in French. The program in the late eighteenth century was broad. In the first three years girls studied religion, Russian, French, German, arithmetic, morals, drawing, needlework, dancing, and music; in the second three they added geography, history, and housekeeping; in the third, literature, architecture, and heraldry; in the fourth, physics, anatomy, domestic economy, cooking, and citizenship.

Catherine was intent on creating the new Russian woman as well as the new Russian man. But, like Maintenon, she observed class lines. A second section of the institute, to train bourgeois girls, had a nine-year program, which emphasized domestic duties. It is not known whether Catherine read Fénelon, or was influenced by Saint-Cyr; but her religious advisor, Simon Todorskij, had studied in Halle with Franke.

SCHOOL AND CONVENT

The knowledge available to upper-class girls in seventeenth- and eighteenth-century schools normally followed no programmatic design, mainly because there was little agreement about what they should learn. While girls in convent schools could be expected to acquire at least religious training, those in secular boarding schools throughout Europe learned whatever the mistress was capable of teaching them. Hannah Woolley opened an English school in 1638, when she was fifteen; she seems to have understood Italian and known how to sing and dance and play several instruments. At seventeen she was hired as a governess, the most common means of educating girls in the seventeenth and eighteenth centuries. In later life she described the things she was able to teach:

> Works wrought with a Needle, all Transparent Works, Shell-work, Moss-work, also Cutting of Prints and adorning Rooms and Cabinets or stands with them, All kinds of Beugle works upon wyers, or otherwise, All manner of Pretty Toys for Closets, Rocks made with Shell or in Sweets, Frames for Looking-glasses, Pictures or the Like, Feathers of Crewel for the corners of Beds, Preserving all kinds of

Sweet-meats wet and dry, Setting out of Banquets, Making Salves, Oyntments, Waters, Cordials, healing any wounds not desperately dangerous, Knowledge in discerning the Symptoms of most Diseases and giving such Remedies as are fit in such Cases, All manner of Cookery, Writing and Arithmetic, Washing black or white Sarsnets [silk], Making Sweet Powders for the Hair, or to lay among Linnen.[14]

In her book *The Gentlewoman's Companion,* written in 1675, Woolley observed: "The right Education of the Female Sex, as it is in a manner every where neglected, so it ought to be generally lamented. Most in this depraved later Age think a Woman learned and wise enough if she can distinguish her Husband's bed from another's." Noting that a man saw a woman as fit merely for propagating children and doing housework, she added, "but by their leaves, had we the same Literature, he would find our brains as fruitful as our bodies." Parents let the fertile ground of their daughters' minds lie fallow, "yet send the barren Noddles of their sons to the University, where they stay for no other purpose than to fill their empty Sconces with idle notions to make a noise in the Country."[15] She begged parents at least to train their girls to run a household and manage money. But her only real solution was for parents to find better governesses. As a widow, she supported herself by selling medicines, publishing recipes, tutoring, and writing books. She also set up a training school for gentlewomen who were forced by circumstances to make a living.

The aforementioned Bathsua Makin, in the dedication of her treatise *On the Antient Education of Gentlewomen,* struck the same note as Woolley: "Women were formerly Educated in the Knowledge of Arts and Tongues, and by their Education many did rise to a great height in Learning. . . . " Now both learning and virtue were scorned and neglected. But "were a competent number of Schools created to Educate Ladys ingenuously [sic], methinks I see how asham'd men would be of their ignorance and how industrious the next Generation would be to wipe off their Reproach."[16] Her own school prospectus offered, to girls of eight or nine who could read, French and Latin, religion, botany, pharmacy and other sciences, astronomy, geography, history, and arithmetic, besides the usual accomplishments of dancing, singing, and writing.

Makin's school was a quality institution in seventeenth-century

England. By the eighteenth century, girls' boarding schools in England, like the aristocratic convents in France, had declined still further. In both countries accomplishments thought likely to attract a husband were stressed. The schoolmistresses, or nuns in France, taught the girls manners and needlework, and drilled them for lessons provided by male teachers brought in. Music, dancing, drawing, and handwriting were the preferred subjects. In both countries the girls mounted theatrical performances. At the Abbey of Blois there was an elegant theater on the premises. Princess Hélène Massalska, future Princess de Ligne, learned at the abbey school some ancient and French history, mythology, the fables of La Fontaine, and some poetry by heart, besides music and dance. But the daughters of Louis XV, returning from the famous convent at Fontrevault at age twelve, had not even learned to read.

The educational program for the better boarding schools in England consisted of religion; belles-lettres (some history, geography, biography, natural history, astronomy, poetry, painting, sculpture, architecture, travel stories); accomplishments (needlework, embroidery, drawing, music, dancing, dress, politeness); and training in manners. But few schools taught all these subjects. Except for the accomplishments, there was no universally agreed upon curriculum for the education of noble girls.

What was even worse than the lack of intellectual stimulus was the physical and psychological atmosphere of the schools. Women were supposed to be delicate; therefore they received no fresh air and inadequate food. Elizabeth Montagu remembered that her school in Kensington was dirty. Girls did not wash, bed linens were not changed; the girls slept two or three to a bed. These conditions existed into the nineteenth century. On the other hand, concern with appearance led to much tight-lacing and corseting; concern with posture, to instruments of torture. One Mary Butt did her lessons around 1780 standing in stocks with a backboard strapped over her shoulders and an iron collar. In the same period a Mary Fairfax, age ten, wore stays, a steel busk, bands that forced the shoulder blades to meet, and a steel rod up the back, attached to a semicircle under her chin. Another means of correcting posture was swinging by the chin, which was supposed to make girls grow and produce a swanlike neck.

In eighteenth-century France, the convents served also as hotels for noble women who were unmarried, widowed, or separated from their husbands. They brought their servants, their gossip, and their worldliness into the students' lives. Stories exist of revolts in convents, including refusal of obedience, broken furniture, barricades in classrooms, and ultimatums. But punishments in strict convents were bizarre. Louis XV's daughter, Madame Victoire, never recovered from the terror of being sent into the crypt alone to pray as penance. In her memoirs Madame de Campan recalled the preparations for hanging a sinner in her convent; the execution was called off only at the last moment. Even clergymen criticized the convents for lack of physical education, mortification of the flesh, failure to teach girls anything, and attempts to make nuns of their charges instead of preparing them for the real world. English critics such as Erasmus Darwin attacked the unhealthy physical aspects of boarding schools, and the fact that they placed too much stress on accomplishments. These criticisms were to become part of the Enlightenment discussion of women's education.

THE BLUESTOCKINGS

Like Hannah Woolley and Bathsua Makin, there were women in England in the eighteenth century who managed somehow to pick up an education by themselves. These women were to become known in the eighteenth century as bluestockings, when they formed a circle devoted to intellectual and literary conversation. This differentiated them from other social gatherings, in which the main amusement was gambling. The circle comprised a number of well-known hostesses, and included men like Horace Walpole, David Garrick, Dr. Johnson, and other intellectuals. The term *bluestocking* was applied to them also; at age seventy-five, Walpole expressed pride at having been one. Only later did the term come to apply only to women and to be used in derogatory fashion.

The women who joined in these circles played a similar role in eighteenth-century England to that played by the *salonières* in seventeenth-century France. They saw the connection between education and status vis-à-vis men—that women could never claim equality until they had men's intellectual training. They protested against forced marriage, as their French counterparts had, although, strangely enough, not against maternity. But they were more independent of men, relying less on their personal charm than French women; and their circles crossed class lines, as the French salons did not.

One of the forerunners of the blues was Mary Astell, who tried to get women interested in the higher education of their sex. Daughter of a merchant, Astell had learned philosophy, mathematics, and logic from her uncle and had studied Latin on her own. In 1697 she published anonymously *A Serious Proposal to the Ladies for the Advancement of their True and Greatest Interest.* It was one of a number of proposals for the establishment of colleges like Oxford and Cambridge for women. Astell did not intend to produce savants or professional women; "we pretend not that Women should teach in the Church, or usurp Authority where it is not allowed them." She spoke of her college as a "monastery," where upper-class women could retreat from the world and cultivate their minds and religious consciousness. They would not have to waste their time in social obligations. Better yet, they would not be sold into matrimony, for they would be able to choose teaching in the seminary instead of an undesired marriage.

Philosophy, Astell believed, was the study most appropriate to women, who were confined and had the solitude for speculation. Literary style was also their forte. She pleaded with women to throw off "the woeful incogitancy [sic] we have slipt into, awaken our sleeping Powers, and make use of Reason, which God has given us." It was society that had put women into a situation that "shortens our Views, contracts our Minds, exposes to a thousand practical Errors and renders Improvement impossible."[17] A benefactor, possibly Queen Anne, promised her £10,000 to fund her college. But a highly placed bishop objected to the conventlike aspect of the proposal, and the offer was withdrawn.

Thus the learned lady in eighteenth-century England was, like that of France in the seventeenth, largely self-taught. In 1752 Lady Mary Wortley Montagu (1689-1762) wrote, "Women are educated in the greatest ignorance, and no art omitted to stifle our natural reason. If some few get above their nurses' instructions, our knowledge must rest concealed and be as useless to the world as gold in the mine."[18]

A friend of Astell, Mary Montagu, like her younger relative Elizabeth Montagu, traveled throughout the Mediterranean and the Near East. She recommended for her granddaughter an education comprising arithmetic, languages (including Latin and Greek), English literature, history, geography, philosophy, drawing, and needlework.

The most intellectual of the early blues was Elizabeth Elstob, who trained herself in languages and became an Anglo-Saxon scholar. After translating a work by Scudéry in 1708, she published her translation, *An English-Saxon Homily on the Birthday of Saint Gregory*, in 1709; in 1715 she published an *English-Saxon Grammar*. Recognized as a scholar, she was unable to secure patronage when her brother died that same year; all scholarly livings were administered through the Church, and were not available to women. Reduced to destitution, she worked as a servant, as a schoolmistress, and finally, after twenty-four years of poverty, as a governess.

Such a woman was considered an abnormality in her time. One function of bluestocking gatherings in the eighteenth century was to allow women to discuss the full range of their interests. As Mary Montagu said, women had to conceal their learning as one would conceal "crookedness or lameness." In their salons they could find strength in numbers, as well as the company of learned men. Elizabeth Montagu (1720-1800), related to Mary Montagu's husband, became known as the "queen of the blues." She arranged chairs in her drawing room in a semicircle facing the fireplace, and presided over a kind of seminar each week. She herself read the classics in translation. Her essay, "Mercury and a Fine Modern Lady," included in Lord Lyttelton's *Dialogues of the Dead*, criticized the education given to girls as frivolous and immoral. In 1769 she published an *Essay on the Writings and Genius of Shakespeare*, a reply to Voltaire's attacks on the playwright. It ran into six editions before 1820 and became a classic.

Another renowned hostess was Elizabeth Vesey, who may have been responsible for the term *bluestocking*. The story is told that when she invited one Mr. Stillingworth to one of her parties, he demurred on the grounds that he did not have proper evening dress. "Oh, never mind dress," she replied, pointing to the clothes he had on, "come in your blue stockings."[19] At her gatherings chairs were arranged in little conversation groups, which Vesey visited in turn. As a proper hostess, it was her duty to keep the conversation going, using her wit and what knowledge she had. Many of these women, like Fanny Burney (1752-1840) had little formal education; but Burney taught herself to read and write, and produced novels. She reported in her diary for 1771 that Dr. Johnson had commented to Mrs. Thrale on "the amazing progress made of late years in literature by the women."[20]

It is well known that Johnson preferred a woman who could cook to one who could speak Greek. In Greek, however, he deferred to the most learned of the bluestockings, Elizabeth Carter, educated by her pastor father. Besides languages (French, Greek, Latin, Hebrew, Italian, Spanish, German, and some Portuguese and Arabic), she knew mathematics and astronomy. She also wrote music for flute and spinet. From the age of eighteen, she spent her winters in bluestocking circles. In 1730 she published a collection of her own poems; she also did translations from French and Italian literature. In 1749 she began a translation of Epictetus from the Greek. Its publication in 1758 brought acclaim from all Europe.

Hannah More, already referred to for her role in the Sunday School movement (Chapter II), was a bluestocking. Her *Strictures on Female Education* of 1779 was based on the necessity to raise public morals. Opposing the amount of time devoted to feminine accomplishments, she recommended real learning, including logic and psychology for girls. But she wanted to restrict the literature allowed to them, specifically excluding novels. This sober note differed from the *Letters on the Improvement of the Mind,* which Hester Mulso Chapone (1727-1801) dedicated to Elizabeth Montagu. The view pressed by Chapone was that women should know those things that make them capable of conversing with educated people—history, literature, natural sciences, geography, chronology, and moral philosophy. They should also write legibly and be able to do arithmetic.

One of the problems encountered by the blues in thinking about female education had to do with class. Although the bluestockings crossed class lines, there was much concern about the blurring of class distinctions and certain proprieties. This reflected general anxiety in late-eighteenth-century England that the lower classes would be educated above their station. Hannah More, who refused to teach writing in her Sunday Schools, was also concerned that aristocratic education was being offered to middle-class girls. Priscilla Wakefield elaborated different curricula for each of the social strata in her *Reflections on the Present Condition of the Female Sex* (1789). Noble girls would study languages, astronomy, natural and experimental philosophy, history. Upper-middle-class girls would concentrate on things related to homemaking; English grammar and literature, drawing, natural history, mathematics, and bookkeeping would be added to domestic skills. The lower-middle class would be confined to reading, spelling, some history and geography, arithmetic, the Scriptures, and needlework. At the bottom of the scale, reading, housekeeping, religion, and needlework would do.

By this time the discussion of female education in England had been influenced by the course of the Enlightenment. The bluestockings were, of course, limited by the intellectual milieu of their time. They had, however, made some advance on the French *salonières* of the century before. They had produced not only novels, but serious works of scholarship; they had earned the respect of brilliant men of their day. But perhaps more important, the bluestockings had begun to pull away from dependence upon men for their intellectual sustenance. They gave parties without men, and found them intellectually rewarding. After one such, More wrote: "Men were by no means so necessary as we all had been foolish enough to fancy."[21] The French *salonières* of the seventeenth and eighteenth centuries could never bring themselves to abandon charm as a backdrop to their intellectual appeal; therefore they retained the role of adorning the drawing rooms where brilliant men shone. But in England, Elizabeth Montagu could write: "We can think for ourselves, and also act for ourselves."[22] It might have been the slogan for the long course women had yet to run.

CHAPTER IV

The Enlightenment Debate On Women

Although during the eighteenth-century Enlightenment some of the worst education in history was provided for girls, the period marked a new stage in the general view of woman's nature and abilities. The basic lines of the debate on women had been laid down in the ancient world, by the Greeks and the Church Fathers. The *querelle des femmes* of the late Middle Ages had reintroduced all these arguments; but for the first time a woman, Christine de Pisan, had raised her voice in defense of her sex, suggesting that, with her mind trained, woman might stand beside man, not as an equal, but as a person of dignity and worth. These themes had been elaborated on and expanded in the seventeenth- and eighteenth-century salons. Some women were, in a slow and halting manner, beginning to sense that the true dignity of a woman lay in her becoming an independent person. Education was more than a key to the respect of male admirers; it was the key to independence and equality.

Independence and equality were fighting words in the eighteenth century. But with few exceptions, men who were willing to apply them to themselves, to colonists in America, and to black slaves, were unwilling to apply them to women. Women were inferior creatures; or, if not inferior, they were at least different. New justifications were offered for this view, but they yielded the same old results for female education. Only a few were enlightened enough to conceive of the possibility that women, properly educated, might be the equals of men.

In the heady atmosphere of the time, however, where everything was up for debate, it was inevitable that the subject should be discussed. And in an age where "enlightenment" was prized, it was inevitable that the debaters should adopt a common premise—that *some* education should be given to girls. There were three positions on the matter: women were mentally and socially inferior to men; women were equal in some abstract sense (for no one thought to give them the vote), but different from men; and women were potentially equal in both mental ability and contribution to society. Although the closing of the revolutionary era brought the most radical of these three positions, along with all radical opinions, into disrepute, statements had been made that were to be influential and even acted upon, in the future.

ROUSSEAU AND NATURE

Unfortunately the most influential writer on education was Jean-Jacques Rousseau, who laid down the program of an ideal education in *Emile* (1762). One section of this book was devoted to the training of Emile's future wife, Sophie, who was to be the ideal woman. For the woman, according to Rousseau, biology (or Nature) was destiny: "The male is only male at certain moments, the female is female all her life." [1] It was part of Nature's plan for woman to be physically weaker than man. In her weakness, woman was able to exercise control over man, particularly over his sexuality, which she could not do if she were educated to be like man. And such an education would be against Nature, which intended woman for man's pleasure and comfort.

Rousseau saw men as dependent on women for their pleasure, but women as dependent on men for everything. Therefore women had to cultivate those aspects of themselves that would acquire men's good will. (This was in complete contradiction to Rousseau's view of men, who, he believed, should not depend on the good opinion of others.) Thus the education of women should be relative to men; it should enable them "to please them, be useful to them, get them to love and honor them, raise them when young, care for them when grown, counsel them, console them, render life sweet and agreeable to them."[2] Rousseau believed that girls naturally liked to adorn themselves and their dolls. These activities would lead to training in sewing, embroidery, lacemaking, and eventually, to drawing as decoration only. (Drawing as a fine art would only interfere with their duties as wife and mother.)

It was important to show girls the utility of everything one taught them, and so reading should be delayed, and arithmetic taught first. As for religion, one waited to discuss it with boys until they were old enough to understand it; with girls, however, religion was a practical matter, and not a matter of general principles. Their beliefs should be bound to authority and not to independent judgment. Therefore it was better to teach them religion at an early age. Girls should have the same religion as their mother and/or husband. Wisdom and piety, Rousseau believed, could not be joined in a woman. The only reason she needed was the "reason of obedience." All women's learning should relate to practice, as women were not fitted for abstract and speculative ideas and the principles and axioms of the sciences. "It is for them to apply the principles that men have found."[3] It was also for women to inspire men to greatness.

Sophie's mind was not to be formed by reading, but by conversation with her parents and observation of the world around her. Mothers should strive to make girls feel dependent, because dependence was "a natural state for women." Women must always have the sense of "being reined in," which would counter their natural tendency to be fickle and carried away by feelings. Dependency and submissiveness were important lessons, because women always depend on others, and must therefore learn to subordinate their will to them.

Rousseau was scathing in his opposition to the learned woman. She would disdain her female duties and act like a man; no sensible man would ever marry a learned woman. He refused to believe that any works of genius could be produced by a woman, implying that those attributed to women had actually been produced by men. Any woman of real talent, he wrote, would have the dignity to remain unknown, basking only in the glory of her husband's esteem, taking pleasure only in her family.

There has been much speculation about how Rousseau's own unusual experiences with women affected his view of their nature and role in life. His first love was for a mother figure; the woman he lived with and who bore his children was simple and illiterate. In any case, his view of women was the traditional one, based on "the nature of things," though with some few differences. He believed that girls' bodies should be exercised in the fresh air when they were young and that all education should follow the logical development of learning and of the child's natural interests. But his interpretation of the natural implied no equality for girls and no opportunity for real intellectual development.

Rousseau's ideas were taken up by the German philosopher Immanuel Kant. In his *Observations on the Beautiful and the Sublime* (1764), he wrote that women had a different kind of mind from men. The male mind was suited to abstract speculation; it produced a profound understanding. The female mind, however, experienced the most delicate sentiments; its understanding was aesthetic. Any extensive learning would destroy women's natural advantage over men. In his later *Anthropology in Its Practical Aspect* (1798), he set up a series of oppositions between the male and the female; the womanly was the weak and passive, the manly the strong and active, and so on. Like Rousseau, he emphasized that woman's very weakness was the means by which she ruled man.

Later German writers took up the same theme. Goethe wrote that even the most educated women had more appetite than taste. We love everything in a woman except intelligence, he said, unless it is brilliant, or unless we already loved her before it was evident. The poet Friedrich Schiller sang the glories of woman, but found them in her beauty and charm. Carl Wilhelm von Humboldt, in his work *On the Difference Between the Sexes and its Influence on Organic Nature* (1794), found men more enlightened, women more emotional. A combination of the two—man's strength, fire, and vivacity, with woman's steadiness, warmth, and sincerity—was the height of human fulfillment. Friedrich Fröbel, originator of the kindergarten movement, saw man as plus, expansion, day, white, reason, understanding; woman as minus, contradiction, night, black, sense, feeling. He recommended that both sexes should be educated, but in different ways. The Swiss pedagogue Johann Heinrich Pestalozzi considered mothers most important in children's first education; he thought it necessary to attend to girls' primary education and also develop female teachers for all young children. Male teachers would teach subject matter, appealing to the intellect; but females were specially endowed to develop the child itself, by appealing to the feelings.

Rousseau's ideas tended to restrict the content of female education and the development of women's self-esteem throughout Europe. Hannah More, in her *Essays for Young Ladies* (1777), cautioned girls to restrain themselves, to give up public expression of their own opinions, even if they were right. "It is of the greatest importance to their future happiness," she wrote, "that they should acquire a submissive temper and a forbearing spirit."[4]

The famous *idéologue* and physician P. J. G. Cabanis opposed public education for girls on the basis of their weakness. "To impose on these frail organs wearisome tasks" would be "to outrage Nature with the most dastardly barbarity," he wrote. It was dangerous to expose women to the perils of a life that their physical constitution could not support without being denatured. Scholarship might obliterate "that exquisite sensibility which constitutes, so to speak, their essence."[5] He agreed with Rousseau that rather than enabling women to share man's power, education would result in their losing the advantage over men that nature had given them. Cabanis opted for training in the home completely supervised by the mother.

Indeed, one of the strongest effects of Rousseau's ideas was to encourage education of girls in the home. Convents in France and boarding schools in England had both acquired a bad reputation by the late eighteenth century, and so families reverted to educating girls at home. In France, particularly, women published works on how mothers should train their girls. Most of them believed in some intellectual training for girls, but differing in many respects from that of boys.

A SEPARATE AND DIFFERENT EDUCATION

The group that adhered to the belief that women were different from men but also worthy of intellectual development was the largest and most varied of the period. In the famous *Encyclopedia* of 1756, under the heading *Woman*, Desmahis wrote that women differed from men as much in mind and feeling as they did in face and body, although education could modify their natural dispositions. Men in general had force, majesty, courage, and reason; women grace, beauty, finesse, and sentiment. The end of the article stated that any praise of strong mind or character in a woman almost always implied that she was ugly. Voltaire, in his essay on girls' education showed a preference for maternal education at home, remarking that the only thing learned in convents had to be forgotten in the rest of life, and that *bel esprit* was to be avoided. He believed that women were as intellectually capable as men, but preferred them to shine by exercising their feminine qualities. Certainly a woman should not abandon her female duties to cultivate knowledge. But he praised his mistress, Madame du Châtelet, because she had gained a reputation for being learned without seeking it.

Almost all men thought men's education unsuitable to women, even those who thought women capable of it. Charles Rollin, whose *Treatise on Studies* (1726) was influential in France and England, felt that girls should not learn Latin because, unlike men, they did not need it for their functions in the world, unless they were to be nuns. He disapproved of reading plays, which would make girls wish to go to the theatre; but he approved of educating girls in religion and history as well as in the domestic arts, provided they did not make a show of their learning. Madame de Lambert, who opened her eighteenth-century salon at the age of sixty and entertained such literary lights as Marivaux, wrote in her *League of Women:*

> They tell us in the cradle: You are not capable of anything, don't concern yourself with anything, you are good for nothing but to be prudent; they told it to our mothers, who believed it and repeated it to us. . . . What other resource did they leave us but the miserable function of pleasing? Our coquetry comprises all our wealth.[6]

Her *Advice of a Mother to Her Daughter* warned that the usual roads to glory and power were closed to women, and so they tried to attain these goals by charming men. As an antidote she recommended a program of ancient and French history, philosophy, one's own language, and Latin. Other modern languages, for example Italian, were potentially harmful to morality, as was most poetry. The study of science, she felt, led to pride; but it was preferable to romantic novels.

The Comtesse de Miremont, whose seven-volume course on girls' education (1779-89) bore the royal seal of approval, believed that girls' training must be distinct from boys'. Women were not destined to learn anything in depth. The study of religion and the accomplishments was to be enriched by the three Rs, grammar, geography, history, and natural science. Women should never appear learned, the Comtesse wrote, but should know enough "to understand everything, be bored with nothing, make an astute comment, and enjoy the knowledge of others."[7] Madame Puisieux, whose *Counsels to a Friend* (1755) was also admired in England, did not recommend too much study for girls, since it was unsuited to their sex; and she advised girls to keep whatever they knew to themselves. It was not appropriate for women to talk about politics or religion. For women, "the art of pleasing is the greatest of arts,"[8] Puisieux admonished. But girls who were not beautiful could ornament the mind. Puisieux recommended French history, language, music, and reading—the *Fables* of La Fontaine, the *Pensées* of Pascal, the *Caractères* of La Bruyère. Most important was speaking and writing one's own language well.

Another work, popular on both sides of the Channel with those interested in home education for children, was *Adèle et Théodore* (1782) by Madame de Genlis. It is the tale of a baron and his wife who leave the city to bring up their two children, age six and seven, in the provinces. Adèle's English governess (whom she has had from the age of six months) comes along. An Italian drawing teacher and a maid who is excellent at needlework complete the ménage. The baroness and Adèle are together for the entire day, which includes religious observances, household duties, reading and reciting, examining maps and pictures, drawing lessons, counting, and music. The house is decorated with tapestries depicting scenes from history and mythology, which the children eventually learn. It contains collections of minerals and shells; the plants in the garden are labeled.

At the age of twelve Adèle will have very little formal knowledge. Her mother has withheld the great literary works, which are to be the prize for maturity. At age thirteen the education of both children is enriched by a trip to Italy. Here the baroness adopts a young girl for Adèle to bring up under her guidance, as preparation for motherhood. At age sixteen Adèle takes complete charge of her own apartment in the house, paying bills and doing the housekeeping. By eighteen she is well read in sacred history, English, and the French classics. She is then allowed to read selected moral novels. She also knows music, arithmetic, geography, and history. She is married at age eighteen and a half, but continues her education.

During all this time the two children share only drawing lessons and meals. Théodore, under the guidance of his father, does more extensive reading than Adèle, because he also reads while Adèle sews. He knows Latin, and reads books on law and politics. He learns no music, however.

Madame de Genlis noted that since girls were born for a monotonous and dependent existence, they should not study anything that would influence their imagination or swell their head. "Genius is for them a useless and dangerous gift."[9] Any love of knowledge for its own sake would tear them away from the simplicity of their domestic duties. They were destined to run a home, to depend on a master who would demand both good counsel and obedience, so they needed patience, prudence, and good judgment above all. They should, however, be familiar with all kinds of knowledge, enough to converse agreeably; they should learn the female accomplishments. They should have a taste for reading, but not for showing it off, and they should know how to love without being demanding.

Madame de Genlis and all the women who advocated maternal education at home were influenced by Rousseau, in that they saw girls as different from boys by nature and therefore destined to be educated differently. Few of them, however, were willing to limit a girl's intellectual life to the same extent as Rousseau. A girl's distinctive education was dictated by the different life she was to lead; but this did not necessarily imply her inferiority. Elizabeth Hamilton, whose *Letters on the Elementary Principles of Education* appeared in 1801 and was popular in France, expressed this idea strongly. It was absurd, she said, for women to claim equality in terms of talent and career. Equality had nothing to do with similarity. Unfortunately, men claimed superiority for all the things men customarily did, and so honor and esteem had become connected with knowledge. Women were foolish enough to accept this evaluation and demand to do the same things. (Hamilton's observation is applicable to historical studies today, where for the first time importance is being accorded to areas of society where women play primary roles.) Madame de Lambert presented a different argument in her *Reflections on Women* (1728): Men deemed women intellectually inferior because they were more feeling creatures; but there was more than one road to truth, and woman's instinctive certainty was in some instances superior to men's logical reasoning.

While Rousseau and his German disciples clearly saw women as intellectual inferiors, they tried to sugar-coat this pill by emphasizing women's personal influence over men. The separate-and-different group were willing to narrow the intellectual difference between men and women through education, but they still insisted on the difference between the sexes and on the necessity to preserve peculiarly female qualities. The importance of the family in society required them to make sexual distinctions; yet in an age where equality was becoming a slogan, they drew back from the admission that separate was not equal.

EDUCATION FOR EQUALITY

As the Enlightenment reached its more radical stage, the belief grew that education was a solution to the inequities of society. Claude Helvétius, in *On the Mind* (1758) took up the idea, derived from Locke's psychology, that the mind developed according to the sense impressions it received. If, then, all children received the same education they would be equal, since the mind was a blank to begin with. The new society envisioned by Enlightenment philosophers thus awarded an important role to education.

Nevertheless, only one *philosophe* extended this concept to women. The Marquis de Condorcet believed in the unlimited progress of humankind. This would take place through increased knowledge of the world, and through education, which would gradually erase what seemed like natural inequalities. In his essay "On Public Education," he maintained that instruction should be the same for women as for men. Since all education aimed at exposing truths and developing proofs for them, it was hard, he wrote, to claim that one sex had more right to it than another. Even if a complete education was too extensive for women, who were not called to public functions, they should certainly share it in their early years. But he added that women disposed to higher education should have it, except for programs preparing for professions reserved for men. And in his *Lettres d'un Bourgeois de New Haven à un Citoyen de Virginie* (1787) he indicated that all professions should be open to both sexes. He particularly mentioned medicine as a field where women's aptitude was equal to that of men.

Condorcet gave four reasons why women should share the education given to men. First, for the sake of male equality; poor boys, who could not afford tutors, could never become equal to rich boys without educated mothers to help them with their lessons. Second, for the sake of equality within the family; lack of instruction for women produced inequality between husband and wife, between brother and sister, between son and mother, undermining family unity and maternal discipline. Third, for the preservation of knowledge acquired by husbands when boys. Husbands could not only share it, but also extend it, with an educated wife. Finally, for the sake of simple justice; women had the same right as men to public education.

Condorcet was probably the first man in history to declare that society owed an education to all women, as well as to all men. Further, he believed that the two sexes should be instructed in common, by teachers of either sex. He did not approve of education at home, which vitiated equality by preserving class distinctions. This applied to girls as well. "It would be dangerous," he wrote, "to preserve the spirit of inequality among women; this would prevent it from being destroyed among men."[10]

The educational projects presented to the different governments of France during the Revolution all provided for primary education for both sexes. But most of them made a sharp distinction between the two, stating clearly that the lessons provided for girls were intended to prepare them only for domestic and family life. Only Condorcet's plan stipulated equal numbers of teachers for girls and for boys. Unfortunately, no system of national education resulted from the chaos of those years. Later supporters of popular education used Condorcet's other arguments, but it took almost 100 years for them to rediscover his reasoning on education for women.

In England the call for equality through education was not left to men. The anonymous "Sophia" who wrote *Woman Not Inferior to Man* in 1739 may have been the same Lady Mary Wortley Montagu who advised women to hide their learning. The book said women were slaves, who had achieved less than men only because they had been given less education. It argued that women should be allowed an independent role in society. They could become doctors, lawyers, teachers, even soldiers, if they were not limited to household duties and were given a good education. It even implied that, foolish as they might seem in their present state, women were innately superior to men in some respects.

Catherine Macaulay Graham, author of an eight-volume history of England, discussed the position of women in her *Letters on Education* (1790). Dismissing Rousseau's view of the inferiority of women, she noted that men's superior physical strength had been used in the past to destroy the rights of women and reduce them to slavery. Women's present condition, though perhaps somewhat improved, was also artificial. They were raised, she noted, according to "a false notion of beauty and delicacy"; thus they were physically weaker than necessary. But the main source of their weakness was their education. "All the higher parts of rectitude, everything that ennobles our being and that renders us both innoxious [sic] and useful, is either not taught, or is taught in such a manner as to leave no proper impression on the mind."[11] As long as society retained the idea of male superiority, she wrote, there would be no good education for either sex.

Graham's remedy was physical and mental coeducation. Girls should do the same physical exercises as boys; they should study the same subjects; they should be friends with each other. She then went all the way and demanded that women should have political rights, reasoning that if men and women were equal in the sight of God, then they should be equal in this world.

The *Letters on Education* were reviewed that same year in the *Analytical Review* by a remarkable woman, Mary Wollstonecraft. At that time she was thirty-one years of age, unmarried, and experienced in the misery that can result from woman's position as man's dependent. Her own father and also the father of her dearly beloved friend Fanny Blood had failed to provide for their families. Her brother-in-law was, as she saw it, responsible for her sister's complete breakdown after the birth of their child. Wollstonecraft had left her own home at nineteen to become a lady's companion, returned to nurse her dying mother, and settled with the Blood family where she joined the women's herculean effort to maintain the household through their needlework. When called upon to aid her sister, she had removed her from her husband's house, determined to preserve her from his influence. The sisters and Fanny Blood had opened a school. But Wollstonecraft had lost her dear friend, first to marriage, and then to death during childbirth. When her school failed, she had taken a position as a governess, and had written her first book, *Thoughts on the Education of Daughters* (1786), in which she decried the uselessness of accomplishments, and maintained that women should be "taught how to think." She also began to write novels, which led to the courageous decision to make her living as a writer.

Wollstonecraft's own education was informal. Taught to read, probably by her mother, she was fortunate in encountering men who tutored her and lent her books. She was also lucky in her friendship with a publisher who printed her works and employed her to write for the *Analytical Review*. One of her books was a translation from the French, another from the German, so she must have studied languages. In 1790 she wrote a political polemic against Edmund Burke's *Reflections on the Revolution in France*, called *A Vindication of the Rights of Men*, which revealed in its social criticism, an extensive knowledge of the injustices prevalent in England in her time.

With the exception of the work she reviewed, however, there is no indication that Wollstonecraft was familiar with any writings before her time that dealt with the position of women. Therefore her ground-breaking work, *A Vindication of the Rights of Woman*, was the result not of scholarship but of experience as a woman in a man's world. In this way she was both the heir of Christine de Pisan and the source of modern feminism.

Throughout the *Vindication* Wollstonecraft was concerned with the education of women. Virtue in women, she wrote, was supposed

by many to result from innocence; actually women were kept ignorant in the name of innocence. "In fact, it is a farce to call any being
virtuous whose virtues do not result from the exercise of its own
reason."[12] The education provided for women rendered them weaker, more artificial, and more useless members of society than they
would otherwise have been. Because of their dependence and domestic duties, "women of strong minds" (like Wollstonecraft herself) were able only to snatch at knowledge, not to study anything in
depth.

And what was the main thing a woman was taught? To be pleasing
to men. First of all, it was assumed that she had a natural tendency
to coquetry. Then she was told that beauty was a woman's only
asset. Women were taught accomplishments, and encouraged to feel
rather than to reason. Their only power, they were assured, was
their power to charm men. Here Wollstonecraft specifically attacked Rousseau, analyzing Sophie's education. She pointed out
that women not capable of reason were not capable of educating
their children. Even Rousseau admitted that after six months of
marriage the transports of passion were over and the couple settled
down to be friends, so:

> According to the tenour of reasoning, by which women are kept from
> the tree of knowledge, the important years of youth, the usefulness of
> age, and the rational hopes of futurity, are all to be sacrificed to ren-
> der woman an object of desire for a short time. [13]

Taking up Rousseau's argument that educated women would lose
their natural power over men, she replied: "This is the very point I
aim at. I do not wish them to have power over men; but over themselves."[14]

This is the key passage of Wollstonecraft's work. It is the first
clear statement of a concept only imperfectly glimpsed by the *salonières* and only tentatively expressed by the bluestockings: that the
defects and the miseries peculiar to women arose from their state of
dependence upon men, and that education was a step toward independence. Wollstonecraft wrote:

> If all the faculties of a woman's mind are only to be cultivated as they
> respect her dependence on man; if, when a husband be obtained, she

have arrived at her goal, and meanly proud rests satisfied with such a paltry crown, let her grovel contentedly, scarcely raising her employments above the animal kingdom. [15]

She described female weakness "that loves, because it wants protection; and is forbearing, because it must silently endure injuries; smiling under the lash at which it dare not snarl."[16]

True, men seemed to be superior in bodily strength. But let girls be allowed to exercise as boys did in their youth "that we may know how far the natural superiority of a man extends." And as for moral superiority, "It is vain to expect virtue from women till they are, in some degree, independent of men." [17] Of course women were cunning, mean, selfish. As long as they lived by their personal charms, they could not possess virtues that required exertion and self-denial.

Wollstonecraft believed that upper-class women were the most affected by dependence.

> How many women thus waste life away the prey of discontent, who might have practiced as physicians, regulated a farm, managed a shop, and stood erect, supported by their own industry, instead of hanging their heads surcharged with the dew of sensibility. . . . How much more respectable is the woman who earns her own bread by fulfilling any duty, than the most accomplished beauty![18]

A woman thus capable would not have to marry for support; and if she was forced to earn her living it would not be only on a menial level barely above a prostitute's. The best position open to women, that of governess, was still considered a degradation (here she spoke from personal experience).

This did not mean that women must work outside the home—Wollstonecraft considered the role of wife and mother important—but to be a good mother, one must have sense, "and that independence of mind which few women possess who are taught to depend entirely on their husbands."[19] Women could fulfill their domestic duties well only if their minds were exercised over a wider range than the household.

Her solution was a system of national education, in which boys and girls would be instructed together in public schools. The primary school, for ages five to nine, would be open to both sexes and all classes. They would learn reading, writing, arithmetic, natural history, the elements of religion, history, and politics. There would be open space and ample time for exercise in the fresh air. Vocational schools would train the lower classes over nine years of age for various trades; the upper-class and superior students would attend secondary school. Girls would not be confined to needlework, but would be taught political and moral concepts and learn the principles of anatomy and medicine. "It is likewise proper only in a domestic view, to make women acquainted with the anatomy of the mind, by allowing the sexes to associate together in every pursuit,"[20] she wrote. All education should be coeducation.

Her idea was not that all women go out into the world but that they be capable of doing so.

> Would men but generously snap our chains, and be content with rational fellowship instead of slavish obedience, they would find us more observant daughters, more affectionate sisters, more faithful wives, more reasonable mothers—in a word, better citizens. We should then love them with true affection, because we should learn to respect ourselves.[21]

The *Vindication* brought fame to Wollstonecraft, in both the positive and the negative sense. But many women turned their backs on it. Hannah More wrote to Horace Walpole that she would not read it. "To be unstable and capricious, I really think, is but too characteristic of our sex; and there is, perhaps, no animal so much indebted to subordination for its good behavior as woman."[22] Unfortunately More was typical of most intelligent women. The work survived to become a bible of nineteenth- and even twentieth-century feminism. Its immediate impact on women's education, however, like that of Condorcet's works, was almost nonexistent.

POST-ENLIGHTENMENT DEVELOPMENTS

The Enlightenment had some effect on the course of women's education in the late eighteenth century and first decade of the nineteenth. The reaction against the French Revolution, however, tended to discredit Enlightenment thought, which was believed to have produced republicanism. Thus the ideas on women's education preserved from the period tended to be those of the most reactionary school of thought.

One of the most impressive results of enlightened ideas for women's education was the extensive curriculum mandated for the Smolny Institute by Catherine the Great in 1764 (see Chapter III). But this program was reduced at the turn of the century, returning to a nine-year course emphasizing religion and needlework, thus making it resemble its model, Saint-Cyr. Girls' schools on this model, aiming to produce good Russian wives and mothers, spread to many towns. Coeducational primary education was introduced by Catherine in 1782, providing religion, reading, writing, counting, drawing, and calligraphy. From 1786, in larger towns, secondary schools teaching grammar, arithmetic, history, geography, mechanics, physics, sciences, and architecture were open free to both sexes. Graduates of secondary schools often became primary school teachers. At Catherine's death in 1796, however, only 176,730 pupils had been educated in all, thirteen times as many boys as girls; and more than half of the girls came from the environs of St. Petersburg. The problem was again the parents, who particularly objected to coeducation. The situation declined at the turn of the century; girls were now admitted only to primary schools run by the Orthodox Church. By 1855, only 10 percent of the Russian children in schools were girls.

In Germany, also, the Enlightenment encouraged education for girls, but only for their roles of wives and mothers. Schools for upper-class girls tended to imitate Saint-Cyr. Those like the Antoinette School in Dessau, founded in 1786, advertised that they aimed not at an intellectual education, but rather at training girls to benefit the household and community. Needlework figured largely in the curriculum. In German Catholic states, Ursulines and other orders provided convent education. In 1811 the Prussian minister Stein urged that women teach in girls' primary schools. Since German teachers in state schools were civil servants, however, women could teach only in private schools, except in states where the authorities recognized the need for them. Even here, they taught only practical female subjects and religion, as assistants. (Although in theory the program for both sexes was the same in the people's schools, in practice the girls often learned less, or different things.) Since there was no official status connected with teaching for women, few heeded the call to that vocation in state schools.

The German philosopher Schleiermacher, in his pedagogical writings of 1826, pushed for an education for women more like that of men—not so that they could participate in the larger world, but so they could serve as the understanding companions of men who did. The belief that women's nature was different from men's pervaded the German intellectual scene. Even Elizabeth Gleim, who founded girls' schools and believed that women should acquire independence through working (she founded an Institute of Lithography in Bremen), believed that women were psychically different from men. She wrote in her *Education and Instruction of the Female Sex* (1810) that education should develop the finer aspects of women's nature, such as appreciation of the true and the good.

Education for women that emphasized feeling over intellect was the norm in Germany into the 1860s. It could be interpreted broadly or narrowly. One school director divided his curriculum into four parts: subjects to waken the religious and moral sense (religion, singing, nature studies, history); subjects to waken and shape the sense of beauty (German, writing, counting, singing, needlework); subjects to shape the intellect (German, arithmetic); and subjects related to women's future position in the world (German, arithmetic, writing, needlework, modern languages). Sometimes such subjects as city architecture, higher mathematics or "practical information" were conceived as essential.

In France, there were literary salons, where women like Madame Lambert learned what they could through conversation with the great men of the day. They also took advantage of such publications as the *Encyclopedia* to extend their knowledge. Besides this work, whole series of educational books were created for them. The *Historical Library for the Usage of French Women*, part of a larger series for the general public, published in 1779, provided a complete course in history from ancient times. The *Universal Library for Women* was a ten-volume work, edited by scholars; it included Voyages, History, Literary Melanges, Theatre, Novels, Moral Philosophy, Mathematics, Physics and Astronomy, Natural History, and Arts. The King's sister owned the series, which was widely accepted. Outlines of reading were published for women, usually confined to literature, history, moral philosophy, and the arts.

Women also went beyond the salon to educate themselves. The *Journal of Women*, founded in 1759, was directed by women from

1764 and under the protection of Marie Antoinette from 1774. A monthly, it had four sections: poetry, new books, plays, and diverse notices. The last was to insure that women could be *au courant,* not only of literary but also of the latest scientific developments, such as inoculation. These written sources gained in importance in the years before the Revolution, as the salons became political rather than intellectual centers under such hostesses as Madame Necker.

The Revolution caused chaos in female education, since all nuns, noble women, and those associated with them were excluded from teaching by the revolutionaries. Fired by the slogans of freedom and equality, women presumed to petition revolutionary governments. Even before the Estates-General met in 1789, women of the Third (lowest) Estate petitioned the King, since they had been given no political role: "The women of the Third Estate are almost all born without fortune; their education is much neglected or very faulty . . . " wrote the anonymous author of the petition, who went on to say that girls learned only the Mass in French and vespers in Latin. The ugly got married; the pretty became prostitutes. "We ask to be enlightened, to have vocations, not to usurp the authority of men, but to be more esteemed by them; so that we have the means to live secure from poverty." Addressing the King directly, the women pleaded that he "establish free schools where we can learn our language in its principles, also religion and morality: that both of them be presented to us in all their grandeur, entirely stripped of those little practical aspects which reduce their majesty." They also asked, however, to be taught the virtues of their sex—"sweetness, modesty, patience, charity."[23] As for the accomplishments, they felt women could learn them without being taught. They asked to be delivered from their ignorance so as to give their children a sane and reasonable education for citizenship. A patriotic society called the Friends of Truth, founded by women and devoted to education of poor children, proposed to set up schools for girls, taught by women, in the poor quarters of Paris. The plan was similar to that of the English charity schools; they hoped that their pilot project would be adopted as a model by the new revolutionary government.

In 1791 the "Motion of poor Javotte" to the National Assembly complained that while there were many free schools for boys, where they were taught useful things, there were few for girls, who learned only the catechism. Many of the feminists of the revolutionary period emphasized the importance of education for the "rights of women." They gained no hearing from the revolutionaries, except for inclusion of women in primary education projects, none of which went into effect. After the fall of Robespierre, nuns could teach again, in secular dress; and under Napoleon, some of the convents reopened. But Napoleon, who spoke of women's "weakness of brain," included nothing for them in his national system of secondary and higher education. "Nothing is more hateful than a woman who reasons," he said of Madame de Staël.[24]

He did appoint Madame de Genlis to inspect the primary schools of Paris, which she found in a terrible state. She was able to correct some of the abuses. A Mlle. Sauvan started a school at Chaillot, which turned out teachers for these primary schools. Boarding schools, opened in Paris by Madame La Maison-Neuve, who wrote an outline of education for girls, began the renewal of upper-class girls' education. But the frivolity and accent on accomplishments, which had marked pre-revolutionary boarding schools, returned in full force.

The model boarding school of the period, set up by Napoleon for female relatives of Legion of Honor holders, was in the tradition of Saint-Cyr. It was headed by Madame de Campan, who soon after the fall of Robespierre had opened a school in a Paris suburb attended by relatives of Napoleon's wife Josephine. The Legion of Honor school was intended to operate on the principles laid down by Fénelon and Maintenon, now laid down by Napoleon himself. The girls were to learn just enough to make them good wives and mothers in upper-class Napoleonic society. The goals of Madame de Campan, an admirer of Fénelon, were:

> To form the judgment of women, so that they can usefully be consulted on the interests of the family, so that they can appreciate the education, the great tasks and valorous exploits of their husbands, so that they can recognize their [husbands'] true superiority; so that they can satisfy them through their spirit of order, charm them through their sweetness, and know how to distract them through their talents.[25]

Campan considered religion and morality sufficient education for girls of the common people, but reading, sacred history, geography, spelling, penmanship, history, drawing, music, dancing, and needlework were prescribed in the Legion of Honor schools. As at Saint-Cyr, the girls kept and administered the school and sewed its linens and clothing. There was great emphasis on competition—not in intellectual pursuits, but in moral virtues such as submission, tenderness, order, cleanliness, care of younger girls, politeness, goodness to servants, for which prizes were awarded. The Legion of Honor schools inspired the best girls' boarding schools in Europe in the nineteenth century, as Saint-Cyr did in the eighteenth.

In early-nineteenth-century England all education was still under private and religious sponsorship. In 1811 the National Society for Promoting the Education of the Poor in the Principles of the Church of England took over the charity schools and increased the number of children educated there. The Royal Lancastrian (later, British and Foreign School) Society responded by founding undenominational schools. Numerous other private organizations tried to fill the gap caused by the failure of the government to take a hand in education.

The conditions which had long been deplored in English boarding schools—poor physical arrangements, lack of serious education, and emphasis on the accomplishments—persisted into the mid-nineteenth century. In the United States also, a type of secondary education had been established for upper-class girls, which differed from the English in that they were usually day schools. The purpose was much the same, however—training young ladies in the accomplishments, French, and domestic arts. As private, moneymaking enterprises, they tried to offer whatever subjects there was a demand for (thus they have been called "adventure" schools). Unfortunately, there was little demand for solid education for girls. As early as the American Revolution, however, at least one woman was thinking along the same lines as Wollstonecraft. Judith Sargeant Murray did not publish her essay "The Equality of the Sexes" until 1790, when it appeared in *Massachusetts Magazine*, signed only "Constantia." She asked if it were possible that Nature had given one sex mental superiority over the other. Certainly it was not apparent in young children. But "how is the one exalted and the other depressed, by the contrary modes of education that are adopted! The one is taught to aspire, the other is early confined and limited."[26] Murray maintained that while women should not be educated to neglect their female duties, a responsible housewife should have wider mental horizons than her cooking and her sewing.

Benjamin Rush, doctor and scientist, speaking to the students of the Young Ladies Academy in Philadelphia in 1787, called for a female education suited to society. In a society of equality (for men) women should be educated to instruct their sons in liberty and government. Therefore English, geography, history, biography, music, and religion should be part of the female curriculum. There was no thought, however, of educating women to be independent of men. The valedictorian of the same academy in 1794 said:

> Anticipating soon to be called upon to fill their various domestic stations in society, [the students] will, it is possible, never more be required, or never more have the opportunity of delivering their sentiments in public.[27]

By and large, the influence of the Enlightenment was not conducive to enlightening the female mind. Political equality for men, even where partially achieved, did not lead to belief in equality for women. Girls' education was either neglected or woefully inadequate up to the mid-nineteenth century. One reason was that the leaders of society dealt mainly with ladies of leisure, who seemed silly and brainless, with few exceptions; another, that the most radical Enlightenment ideas on all subjects were repudiated in the wave of reaction following the Revolution.

Of course, lower-class women had been working beside men for centuries, overlooked by the movers and thinkers of society. The gradual industrialization of Europe was to make national leaders realize that women performed necessary economic tasks, and so draw them to consider the importance of at least a primary education for women. This process had already taken place in the first industrial country, England, in the charity school and Sunday school movements.

The spread of industrialization and the centralized nation state that fostered it was to affect the primary education of girls in the nineteenth century. The slow spread of Enlightenment ideas among women themselves was to culminate in their participation in all levels of education.

BREAKING DOWN THE BARRIERS:
THE NINETEENTH CENTURY

During the nineteenth century all Western nations moved toward universal education, free and compulsory, for girls as well as for boys. Interest in popular education was tied to two factors associated with that period—industrialization and nationalism. Where the industrial revolution had taken place, education was regarded as necessary to prepare people to operate in a highly complex society, and give them the skills and discipline required by mechanization. As a by-product, it was hoped that schooling would ameliorate the social problems brought on by urbanization—vice, crime, abandonment of children, prostitution. We have already seen that the charity school movement in England, the first nation to industrialize, had begun to adopt these aims.

In all the Western nations, increased centralization, delayed until the latter part of the century in Germany and Italy, required training in good citizenship. The best way to inculcate national values into all classes was to provide some knowledge of national history and literature. Even before unification, Germans stressed national values, particularly after the Napoleonic occupation had aroused German nationalism. Service to the state had been part of the German tradition, particularly in Prussia, since the early eighteenth century. In nations where the gradual extension of democracy brought more citizens to participate in government, a literate, educated electorate was deemed necessary. This factor was less important for women's education, since in no country did women receive the vote before the twentieth century. Training women for their responsibilities as citizens was seen as enabling them to be good mothers of future male citizens.

In some cases, industrialization was more relevant than nationalism to the position of women. On the one hand, it situated the important economic activities of society outside the home and removed upper- and middle-class husbands into the public sphere. The woman's role was reduced; no longer an economic helpmeet, she was left to be a housekeeper. The upper- and middle-class woman became the Victorian housewife in every nation of the West. Her education was seen only in relation to that task, so good secondary and higher education for girls was slow in arriving; its development depended to a great extent on women's own efforts.

On the other hand, industrialization brought the working-class woman out of the home and into the factory. The old concept—that an education in religion and domesticity was adequate for lower-class girls—was now clearly outworn. The tendency was therefore toward equalization of primary education for the two sexes. Some women in highly industrialized societies were also trained as primary school teachers. Teaching came to be viewed as a normal and proper extension of their domestic, child-tending role. It released men for commercial and industrial work. Since these activities were more highly valued in society, teaching, although considered "respectable," was relatively poorly paid by the time women began to take it on.

Nineteenth-century revolutionary movements also affected the position of women. Throughout the century French women participated increasingly in mob actions of a revolutionary nature. Socialist theories, even before Marx, pointed to women as one of the groups exploited in capitalist society. And in any country where a more democratic system was attained through revolution, as in France and Italy, it was considered necessary to wean the women away from the old society through education.

Considering all this, it would be logical to conclude that the education of women came sooner and progressed faster in the more industrialized and more democratic nations. Unfortunately this was not always so. The records of the different countries are highly idiosyncratic, reflecting the imprint of past conditions, national differences, and religious traditions. Authoritarian, bureaucratic governments, as Russia showed in freeing the serfs, can often accomplish things more quickly than freer societies. On the other hand, they can also prevent things from happening, as Germany showed in keeping women out of universities.

Europe began the century, after the defeat of Napoleon in 1815, in a tide of reaction, which was more pronounced the further east one looked. But far to the West, the United States, having gained a new stability, was cutting the umbilical cord tying her to Europe and was beginning her hundred-year flowering as the land of opportunity. Less burdened with tradition than her European sisters, she was to surpass them in providing educational opportunities for women.

In discussing the changes that took place during the century, I have chosen to move from East to West. This is merely a geographic progression, since some eastern nations outdid some western ones in various aspects of female education. In general, however, there is more government control and later industrialization in the East; eventual governmental control of education combined with Catholic religion in the center; more local and private initiative in education in the West. In all countries there is irregular development on all three levels of education for women—primary, secondary, and higher.

All countries provided some primary education for women in the nineteenth century. The important questions to be answered are: Was it provided for all by the state? Was it compulsory? Was it free? Unless all three answers are affirmative, it is unlikely that a majority of girls received an education, given the poverty in many families and the prejudice against educating girls. The same questions are relevant to secondary education, which tended to remain a class education. With respect to higher education, one is confined to recounting how the brave and determined few stormed the bastions of intellectual privilege. The relevant question then is: Were these few educated women given positions in society consistent with their education?

The answers to these questions are not always clear. But certainly the nineteenth century was a time of rapid movement in women's education. The next three chapters outline that development in the major nations, first in primary, and then in secondary and higher education.

CHAPTER V

East of the Rhine: Germany and Russia

Both Germany and Russia had primary education at the beginning of the nineteenth century. In both it had been established by autocratic government decrees; its purpose was to produce useful and obedient subjects. Beyond that, the differences were great. Early in the eighteenth century, primary education for both sexes had been declared compulsory in most German states (see Chapter II). At that time the only primary schools in Russia, established by Peter the Great, did not include girls or peasant boys. It was Catherine the Great who, inspired by the Enlightenment, envisioned universal education.

By the end of the eighteenth century coeducational schools in country towns taught religion, reading, writing, counting, drawing, and calligraphy. They were open to all except serfs, but only a minuscule number of girls actually attended. Under Catherine's successors in the early nineteenth century, most of the schools were Church schools. Girls were confined to them until 1825. Nicholas I decreed that all state and crown villages maintain them for boys as well, but of the millions of Russian children, fewer than 100,000 attended in 1855, and only 10 percent were girls.

After the serfs were freed, an 1864 statute encouraged elementary schools for all classes, religions, and sexes, to be founded by district and municipal councils, local landlords, or village communities. They were to be under control of the Ministry of Education. The most common type of school that resulted from this statute was founded by a *zemstvo*, or district council—a three-year school for both sexes, with three teachers and a priest. These schools added to the old Church school curriculum such subjects as nature study, geography, Russian history, drawing, and singing. Some town schools added extra years, but these were not coeducational. The girls' schools emphasized hygiene and needlework, and usually charged fees.

The government offered special positions in the military for educated men so as to induce boys to attend these schools, but there was no such inducement for women, and many girls' parents believed that only nuns should be educated. The fact that schooling was not obligatory, and that parents were either taxed for the maintenance of the school or charged some tuition, worked against girls' education.

By the end of the century, however, local interest in education was high. Sunday and evening classes and libraries were opened in some districts for adults. This interest dovetailed with the late arrival of industrialization in Russia. The Prechistensky School for Workmen was founded in Moscow in 1897. Here 200 teachers, including high school girls, middle-aged women, and university professors, taught about 1,000 workers a year without charge. In St. Petersburg, Countess Sophie Panina set up a "People's Hall," which provided educational services to working-class families. Besides classes for children and adults, there were reading rooms, day nurseries, a theatre and concert hall, and a savings bank. The 1897 census, the only comprehensive census before the Revolution, showed 13.1 percent of Russian women to be literate. In urban areas as many as 33 1/3 percent of the women could read; in rural areas, fewer than 10 percent.

By 1910 popular interest in education had grown to the point that almost 100,000 children had to be turned away from primary schools for lack of space. It is not known whether preference for entrance was given to boys. But there was still a great deal of prejudice on the part of parents against schooling girls. Of children age eight to eleven in the year 1911, 72.7 percent were attending school—over 6 1/2 million children—but of these only 32.1 percent were girls, despite the fact that the Duma (Russian Parliament) had passed compulsory education laws.

The German situation was superior because of state compulsion. The Prussian *General Code* of 1794 read: "The instruction in school must be continued until the child is found to possess the knowledge necessary to every rational being"—a true Enlightenment statement. In the early nineteenth century, however, families often fulfilled this obligation by sending girls to religious schools, where spirituality was emphasized over intellectual pursuits. This accorded with the Romantic view of the special and different nature of girls. Upper-class girls attended private schools, which stressed practical domestic training. In some areas where public primary schools had been coeducational, girls were now separated from boys and given female teachers. In Austria, where Maria Theresa had decreed schools for both sexes in 1774, girls attended the boys' school if there was no second school, but they sat on separate benches, and learned feminine subjects. However, the Austrian decree required six to seven years of school for both sexes, or proof of literacy.

When industrialization arrived in Germany after midcentury, the compulsory character of education preserved German children from the worst aspects of child labor. There were attempts, as in England, to circumvent the laws by giving factory children lunchtime lessons and Sunday schools. But the government considered primary education essential to national well being. Laws against child labor were passed early in the German states; in 1853 a Prussian law forbade children under twelve to work. All German states decreed compulsory schooling for both sexes, from age six or seven to age fourteen in the latter half of the century. Furthermore, they began to subsidize the schooling of those who could not afford school fees. In 1871, the Germanies, excluding Austria, were united into a German Empire, under Prussian leadership. The traditional Prussian concern for education thus infused every area; there were even attempts under Bismarck to secularize the education of the southern, Catholic states, where girls still attended convent schools.

Thus Germany, where state control was exerted most efficiently, had by the end of the nineteenth century the most literate population in Europe, including its women. Industrialization does not account for Germany's success in education. As early as 1846 Prussia had an average public school attendance of 1,235,448 boys and 1,197,885 girls. The same situation existed in other Protestant countries. In the same year Holland was educating 179,760 boys and 140,657 girls. Denmark decreed compulsory education for both sexes in 1814, conceived of primarily as vocational education for the poor. Although true universal schooling in Denmark came much later in the century, more than half the children in state primary schools were girls. These developments came decades before the country's industrial era. Therefore we must attribute the growth of primary education in these countries mainly to the Reformation tradition of literacy, heightened by the national awareness resulting from the Napoleonic Wars.

SECONDARY AND HIGHER EDUCATION IN GERMANY

Although there was great hostility in both Russia and Germany against any higher education for women, the prejudice was more firmly rooted in Germany, where the difference between the sexes was supported by extensive theory, and where, in Prussia at least, the emphasis on militarism devalued women. German women's campaign for higher education in the nineteenth century was conducted mainly against male society.

Secondary education in Europe was a class education; its institutions included the elementary curriculum, so that its students did not mingle with the lower classes, who were confined to primary schools. Thus it is often difficult to tell what level of education was offered at a school. The German Middle School, for instance, included and surpassed the education provided by the people's school, while remaining a primary school. In Baden, however, the Middle School became a secondary school in the nineteenth century. Another difficulty in assessing girls' education lies in the fact that European secondary education includes subject matter that would be considered part of higher education in the United States. Thus it is difficult, particularly in girls' schools, to tell where higher education began, particularly as it was usually first offered as an extension of the secondary school curriculum. For these reasons, secondary and higher schools for girls must be treated together.

Almost all secondary schools for girls in nineteenth-century Germany were founded by private initiative. Some dated back to the Enlightenment; many were inspired by Saint-Cyr or the French Legion of Honor schools. Usually opened in cities by interested upper-class groups, they gradually became an accepted category of public education, ranking with the "modern" secondary course for boys, while substituting housework for Latin. Although the state government held aloof from this movement, a common type of school began to emerge, in which girls attended until age sixteen, and learned, among other things, German literature and two foreign languages. The Louisa School, founded in Berlin in 1838, had over 800 girls in nine classes, divided into an upper and a lower school. The curriculum included religion, natural history, diction, German, French, English, Italian, geography, history, arithmetic, physical sciences, penmanship, drawing, needlework, singing, and gymnastics. By 1877 it had sixteen men and eleven women teachers.

Clearly secondary education for girls could be of high quality. But how many girls received it? We know that in 1820 there were twenty-two public secondary schools for girls in Germany; in 1821-40, thirty-four; in 1841-60, forty-seven. In 1846 in the state of Prussia alone, secondary education was being given to 48,302 girls in public schools. The private schools must be added to these figures. But there were no standards for female secondary education, and one cannot assume that all schools paralleled the Louisa School. One group that can be pinpointed is the girls who trained for teaching positions. In 1811 Prussia founded the first normal school, for girls age eighteen to twenty-two, with a three-year course. Private secondary schools gradually began to add a year, and then more, of teacher training. The Augusta School, founded in Berlin in 1832 for girls sixteen and over, provided two years of advanced education and a third year of practice teaching.

The German states were interested in educating girls beyond the elementary level only for the purpose of providing primary school teachers. Even then, the important part of teacher training for women was religion. Females were expected to teach only those areas natural to women, such as character building and needlework. State examinations were set up, notably in Prussia; but Prussia did not provide a system of normal schools. As hundreds and thousands of middle- and upper-class women flocked to teaching, private schools for girls added special courses in pedagogy. These were usually two-year courses, but many took the examination after one year.

Because of the states' lack of interest in teacher training for girls, the education given as preparation for teaching was tailored, not so much to primary school teaching, as to teaching in private secondary schools. The result was that girls desirous of becoming teachers often received a more advanced education than they would have if there had been state normal schools, and did so until the end of the century, when some states established normal schools to provide female teachers specifically for primary education.

Although the number of women teachers in Prussia increased sevenfold from 1861 to 1891, while that of males only doubled (the situation was similar in other German states), male teachers continued to predominate in girls' schools. In 1895 there were still only 13,700 women to 74,500 men teaching in Prussia; in Germany as a whole there were 66,000 woman teachers to 151,000 men. Despite their relatively small numbers, these female teachers formed a nucleus of educated women who were to be the core of the German Women's Movement (*Frauenbewegung*).

Unlike the women's movements of other European countries, the German campaign for education, civil rights, and access to all types of employment was led by unmarried women, mostly schoolteachers. The All-German Women's Association, founded in 1865 (before German unification), was composed of teachers in the girls' secondary schools, widows and spinsters who taught young children in dame schools, and governesses. Middle class, often reduced to teaching by poverty, excluded in favor of males from well-paid positions in state schools, many of them were bitter. Their difficulties were compounded by emigration, which left a surplus of women in Germany—a surplus that Bismarck's wars was increasing. Female education and access to civil service posts were high on their agenda.

In 1870 the Germanies were united under the leadership of Prussia. The traditional Prussian interest in education caused the new nation to occupy itself with the instruction of males. It was left to municipalities to provide for women. By this time there was general acceptance, in urban areas at least, of the need for girls' secondary education. There was also some recognition that female teachers should have the same training as male. In ten years 130 new secondary schools for girls were founded. In order to develop some fixed program for these schools, private and public school headmasters met at Weimar in 1872 and founded the German Association for the Secondary Education of Girls.

This organization, which met regularly thereafter, represented the upper classes—petty nobility, civil servants, and rich bourgeoisie. It was the bourgeoisie and civil servants who, while they still saw woman's place as in the home, recognized the implications of Germany's shift from agriculture to industry. In the long run, men were going to move out of the teaching field for more lucrative positions, and surplus women would take their place. The education of these women would have to be improved.

The curriculum elaborated by the Association included French, English, German literature, history, geography, mathematics, natural history, physical science, penmanship, drawing, singing, gymnastics, and religion. In some schools Italian, dancing, and mythology were added. Needlework was a common subject, since it was believed that it trained women in patience and made them stable.

Most German states began to classify girls' secondary education along with boys', Prussia being a notable exception. A description of a girl in a private secondary school in Bonn in 1883 gives us a glimpse of a fairly solid education. Six days a week, four hours a day, were devoted to classes in French grammar, literature, and conversation; German reading, literature, composition, and grammar; English reading, composition, grammar, and literature; general and German history; arithmetic; geography; natural science; pedagogy; and religion. In the afternoons she did drawing, needlework, and gymnastics. A woman in her village had tutored her for entrance to the school. When she matriculated she had known English perfectly, and some French. Her notebook contained four compositions she wrote during the year. One dealt with an ode of the German poet Klopstock; she noted his religious enthusiasm, but found him too sentimental (her teacher warned her against personal judgments). In the second, an essay on Antigone and Ismene in Sophocles' tragedy, she defended Ismene. The third was an imaginative work about what colors signify to people, and the fourth a theme on the critical writings of Lessing. The teacher's comments showed that he considered her ideas a bit too independent.

Besides the secondary schools for girls, a kind of higher primary education was added to the elementary school in many areas. For grown women, adult education courses offered mathematics, accounting, penmanship, writing of business letters, drawing, geometry as applied to needlework, painting, merchandizing, and hygiene, as well as languages, history, and geography (this was a typical curriculum in Stuttgart, 1878-79). Clearly women were being trained for the lower positions in the commercial world also.

Meanwhile, although the public subscribed to the local societies of the Association, every advance in curriculum for girls' schools was viewed with alarm by some. A school inspector at Halle urged:

> Let us reject science from the school, in the largest sense of the word: it is repugnant to the feminine nature. Man pursues the real, woman is content with the appearance. Science does not admit sentiment: it flatters only the reason: it provides not faith but doubt; it would destroy one of the most charming traits of the feminine character: her naiveté.[1]

A representative to the Prussian Parliament complained in 1882 that they were teaching girls such useless things as physics, chemistry, anatomy. He was sure that under such a heavy program the beauty and intelligence of women would give way. We need not bluestockings, he maintained, but housewives.

During the late 1880s and early 1890s the Women's Movement began to put pressure on the government to end the predominance of male teachers, trained by the state, in girls' schools. They presented to the Reichstag (Parliament) a series of petitions seeking reform of girls' secondary education, access for women to higher education, and replacement of male teachers by females in girls' schools. The arguments used to support these petitions were presented in accompanying memoirs and published articles, typified by those of the movement's leaders, Helene Lange and Gertrud Bäumer. Both women postulated a specific female nature, but denied that the German system of educating women produced it. One's nature developed organically, like one's physical body, and not through some mechanical principle imposed by a male pedagogue. Attempting to direct this organic principle was analogous to binding Chinese women's feet, Lange maintained in "The Organic versus the Mechanical Principle in Women's Education." German and religion, in particular, should be taught by women who understood the female mentality. In this work Lange indicated that mathematics and science might be left to male teachers, but elsewhere wrote that women should teach women wherever possible. The important thing, as Bäumer noted in "The Problem of Women's Education," was that the old German admonition to "be a real woman" should be interpreted: "Do not deny your Nature." To the leaders of the German Women's Movement this meant that, just as men educated boys to be men, women should educate girls to be women.

This was the basic demand of the 1888 petition to the Reichstag, which included two motions: that women play a greater role in the middle and higher ranks of girls' education, particularly in the teaching of German and religion, and that the state establish normal schools to train woman teachers for the higher classes of female secondary education. A pamphlet written by Lange accompanied the proposals, and strongly opposed the influence of Rousseau in German women's education: "Just as the male sex must take the task of its formation from the hand of nature to its own, in order to achieve its destiny, so must the female sex take the task of its formation from men's hands into its own, in order to attain its destiny."[2]

In other writings Lange questioned the value of demanding for women the education given to men, which she considered pedagogically unsound for both sexes. But she recognized that women were not then well educated enough to teach at the higher levels of secondary schools. Therefore she demanded higher education for women—not in annexes to existing male institutions, but in separate facilities. In 1890 she organized the All-German Woman Teachers Association to press for more education for women teachers. (Pauline Herber had already organized the women in Catholic states into the Association of German Catholic Woman Teachers, which later produced women active in state governments and the German Center Party.)

In 1890 the Association for the Secondary Education of Girls unanimously voted for the proposition that women teachers were indispensable in the upper classes of secondary schools. They asked the state to establish an examination for them. At the same time the All-German Women's Association was exerting pressure for entrance of women into the universities. In the eighteenth century isolated women had gained entrance, and even degrees, from German universities. Now many faculties moved to deny entrance to women where their statutes did not make exclusion clear. All of them either refused or failed to respond to women demanding entrance. Women who had received sufficient secondary education were encouraged by the All-German Women's Association to attend those universities abroad that were open to women by 1890.

By this time Lange and other sympathetic persons had already canvassed the possibility of setting up private courses in higher education for women—a solution that had already been tried in other European nations. In 1889 the *Realkurse* for women opened in Berlin, in rooms donated by the Charlotte School, with money donated by private sources and the Women's Association. These courses prepared women for the baccalaureate degree given by the modern school for boys; however, since it was a state degree, women could not obtain it in Germany. Some women obtained a baccalaureate degree later by taking examinations in Switzerland. (The European baccalaureate corresponds, roughly, with the two-year associate's degree in an American university.)

The first German state to respond to the campaign for women's higher education was Baden, which established a classical secondary school in Karlsruhe in 1893. The same year Lange, administrator of the Berlin *Realkurse*, raised it to the level of a classical school, which was necessary preparation for university entrance. Admission to the *Realkurse*, at age sixteen, required passing an examination in the subjects taught in the regular girls' secondary schools. The goal was the state degree. Lange described in her memoirs how the first examination in 1896 was a test for both students and teachers. Six young women passed the test and became the first in Germany to hold the coveted degree; of these, three later became medical doctors; four out of the six were later married. The first degree in the Karlsruhe school in Baden was awarded in 1899. Similar schools for girls were founded in Leipzig, Breslau, and Hanover; famous names in the German academic world joined the campaign for women's higher education.

In Prussia, the government delayed recognition of secondary, let alone higher, education for girls. All the petitions of the late 80s and early 90s were denied, both by parliament and universities. The government's sole positive response was to add a three-year course in history and German to the Victoria School in Berlin. Finally, in 1894, the Prussian Ministry of Education issued regulations for secondary girls' schools, as well as for training and examination of woman teachers. Girls' schools were still not recognized as on a level with boys'. (Actually, they were not. In 1905 a speaker at the Association for Girls' Secondary Education remarked that they differed from elementary schools only in that the teaching was inferior and they massacred foreign languages.)

The program the government set up provided for nine years, instead of the ten years in the better existing schools. The Ministry of Education gave the excuse that nine years of study was the maximum a girl's health could take. The hours per week ranged from eighteen in the lower grades to thirty in the last five. History, beginning only in the fifth year, was to be used to evoke patriotic sentiments (less time was devoted to history than to needlework). As for female teachers, the old examinations for the primary level were enlarged to include testing on a major subject, which would gain their entry to secondary teaching. And to satisfy those who wanted further education for their girls, courses outside the regular nine-year cycle could be taken on a voluntary basis.

At this point (1896) there were 196 secondary girls' schools in Germany. Of the 128 in Prussia, only four were founded by the state, the rest by towns or private organizations. There were also twenty-four schools in the rest of northern Germany and forty-four in the south. All but six were founded in the nineteenth century. Fifty-three schools had courses beyond the basic nine-or ten-year program, and local women were enrolled in them as well as advanced students. In these schools, 1,551 men and 1,369 women taught 57,918 girls. At the same time there were about 160,000 boys enrolled in secondary education in Prussia alone.

Now began the fight for entrance to the universities. Already there were some breaches in the dike: in 1892 "adequately prepared women" were allowed into the mathematical-natural science section of Heidelberg University; in 1899 the University of Giessen opened its legal and philosophical faculties to women. There was much discussion of a women's university, since, as one professor wrote, the suitability of men and women studying together was questionable. The matter came up in the Prussian parliament in 1898. The arguments used against the presence of women in male universities were that it was shameful for the women and unwholesome for the men, and that knowledge would suffer from women's inability to study seriously.

Lange pointed out that of the approximately 1,000 female secondary school graduates, half were unsuited to university careers and the other half were mostly destined to teach. Most were totally unprepared for the necessary entrance examinations. The actual number who would enter the universities if allowed would cause little difficulty. This seemed to be the position of an increasing number of universities, which were beginning to allow women full matriculation: Baden in 1900, Bavaria in 1903, Wurtemberg in 1904, Saxony in 1906, Thuringia in 1907, Hesse in 1908. Finally in 1908 the Prussian Minister of Education gave in and issued a decree recognizing women's higher education and allowing full matriculation in Prussian universities. There was one limitation—women could be excluded from specific lectures for various reasons with the agreement of the Ministry—a provision that was not dropped until 1918.

Germany was the last western nation to open the doors of its universities to women. Other Protestant continental nations had been more progressive: the Swiss first, with Zurich in 1864 and Bern in 1873; the Scandinavian countries in the 1870s; the Netherlands in 1875. In these countries, however, secondary education for girls remained a class education unsupported by governments, and charging fees. The Netherlands had only twelve girls' secondary schools in 1893, but it allowed girls into forty coeducational schools. In 1866 the Swedish parliament refused to subsidize girls' secondary education as it did boys', although it did sponsor teacher training for women to almost the same extent as for men. The situation was similar in other Scandinavian countries—great interest in primary, little in secondary education for girls. At the same time, these countries were willing to open their universities to women who qualified for entrance. Why did Germany hold out?

In the period when women's advanced education was a question throughout Europe, Germany lay under the influence of Prussia, the state under which it was to be united. The peculiar nature of the Prussian state was its high degree of organization on every level of activity. The business of the society, its religion, its education, and its welfare were controlled through an extremely efficient and hierarchical civil service, and had been since the eighteenth century. This was one reason why, once decisions were made favoring primary education, they were implemented more effectively in Prussia than in any other European nation. The other important characteristic of the Prussian state was its militarism; from the eighteenth century on, it had made its way as a great power through the might of its army. In every upper-class family, there was ideally at least one civil servant and one member of the armed forces. In a society based upon militarism, women tend to be devalued as the weaker sex. In a society where all important functions are performed by state officials, there is little room for women in the public sphere, unlike societies where women can operate informally in important matters such as health care, education, and charity. Because every important position in the education system was a civil service position, any training that would allow women to fill these jobs was a threat to the official male world. Since most higher education led to professional positions in the state, it was considered unsuitable for women in a period when female participation in political life was not accepted.

By the end of the nineteenth century, however, Germany was a highly industrialized nation. Positions that had seemed so important to men, particularly in the educational field, now yielded less income and prestige than posts in industry and commerce; and so it became more possible to yield them to women.

SECONDARY AND HIGHER EDUCATION— RUSSIA

As previously noted, secondary education for girls in Russia stemmed from the efforts of Catherine the Great. The wives of emperors who followed her patronized the Smolny Institute. By 1828 five new state schools (institutes) for girls and three private ones had been opened in St. Petersburg and Moscow. Under Catherine, the emphasis had been on French culture. Now the preferred language was German. The programs were reduced from their broad Enlightenment base; religion and needlework were now the main subjects. In 1846 a government department was created to oversee the schools, still patronized by the empress. The curriculum was broadened somewhat, and Russian became the primary language.

The institutes, all boarding schools, were conceived and run on strict class lines. Girls were placed according to whether they were noble or bourgeois, and according to the level of the nobility their fathers occupied. Private schools for merchants' daughters arose when fathers were willing to contribute to their support. This broke down the system somewhat, to the extent that some day students were being accepted by the institutes by 1853. The class character of the institutes, however, prevented them from developing into a national system of girls' secondary education, at a time when there was much discussion of the subject. By the time the institutes were taking poor girls on scholarship (1862), another system was developing.

The Russian institutes shared many of the disadvantages of English boarding schools and French convents. In the Ekaterinsii Institute, for poor noble girls, 1,500 rubles were spent annually on embroidery materials, while there were only eleven books in the library. Dancing instructors were paid four to five times the salary of mathematics instructors. In 1842 Gogol, who lectured at an institute, wrote in *Dead Souls:*

> In Russian boarding schools for young ladies three things are looked upon as the foundations and pillars of all human virtues: the French language—indispensable for domestic happiness; pianoforte playing, as an agreeable means of entertainment; and the art of housewifery, by which is meant skill in embroidering purses and other objects wherewith to surprise a fond husband. Our modern period in Russia has been particularly inventive in perfecting this method of education.[3]

Examinations were public, often attended by the emperor himself, and consisted of the students' parroting sections of basic textbooks they had committed to memory. The students were deprived of intellectual training and not allowed to visit their parents—one woman complained in her memoirs that she did not see her parents for seven years from age eight. Institute education hardly prepared girls for life in the real world.

Outside the institutes, secondary education for girls was negligible until the reign of Alexander II. The Crimean War, a debacle for Russia, stimulated discussions of the country's backwardness. The pedagogue N. I. Pirogov published an essay in 1856, pinpointing women's education as crucial to the future character and attitudes of Russian children. The Tsar instructed the Minister of Education to prepare a statute on secondary day schools for girls. In 1858 the official plan received his approval. The first girls' secondary day schools under the 1858 plan had either a three- or a six-year program, but by 1870 many had been transformed into schools modeled after the gymnasium for boys. The girls' gymnasium provided an eight-year program, corresponding roughly to fifth to twelfth grades in the United States, but with the broader curriculum of European secondary education, that is, more literature, history, geography, and languages, taught in a six-day week. It was still not at the level of the boys' classical secondary education, as it stressed science and modern languages over Greek and Latin.

The institutes also set up day schools in the 1870s, emphasizing modern languages and the accomplishments, and adding a two-year extension course in pedagogy. By 1911 the institutes were teaching 16,298 pupils, 41 percent from the nobility and civil servant class, 15 percent merchant, 38 percent lower middle class, artisan, or peasant, and 4.8 percent clergy, foreigners, et cetera.

The gymnasia were more numerous. They were organized by private groups or municipalities, and largely supported by them, receiving only small government subsidies. Only thirty-two girls' secondary schools were fully maintained by the state. After 1875 there were two levels of school—the gymnasium (seven or eight years), and the progymnasium (five or six). All had to conform to state standards; many offered more subjects than required, thereby approaching or equalling the best secondary schools for boys. Required subjects for the gymnasia were religion, Russian, mathematics, Russian geography and history, general geography and history, natural science, physics, calligraphy, needlework, and calisthenics. Optional subjects included French, German, Greek, Latin, drawing, music, choir, dancing, and hygiene. The last four years could be taught only by people with university degrees. Priests taught religion.

As early as 1881, 45 percent of the secondary school enrollment in Russia was female, a percentage only topped at this time by the United States. The 1911 census showed 678 state and private girls' gymnasia in Russia and 105 progymnasia, with a total of 259,079 students. The nobility contributed 23.8 percent, the merchants 10.5 percent, the lower middle class 35.8 percent, the peasants 20 percent. Russia's was the first state-supported secondary education for girls in Europe. Although secondary education was not compulsory and the schools usually charged fees, poor children were admitted free. By the end of the century the level of education was quite high. To these must be added the institutes, and secondary schools for daughters of the clergy run by the Holy Synod, which taught 21,131 girls in 1912, most of whom became primary school teachers. In 1914 there were 380,306 girls in secondary education in Russia, including gymnasia and progymnasia.

The extra years added to secondary schools for teacher training provided a form of higher education. And women were not automatically denied entrance to Russian universities. Soon after Moscow University opened in 1755, women obtained permission to attend physics lectures, and in the early nineteenth century some women attended lectures in Russian literature, archaeology, history, art, physics, and mathematics. There were few of them, however, since the lectures were given in German, for lack of Russian professors. During the reaction under Nicholas I no women appeared in the university classrooms.

The Women's Movement in Russia is usually considered to have begun in 1859, when women began to audit university lectures in St. Petersburg in large numbers. By 1866 the movement had spread to other universities and women equalled men in some classes. There were few objections, either by students or professors. Russian women argued successfully that in a backward nation, the education and employment of all was essential to the nation's progress. Not that opposition was absent; even some of those who had enthusiastically supported secondary education for women drew the line at higher education and professions. Women were refused entrance to Moscow University on the ground that it would be "a sacrilege of the temple of learning." But few professors were opposed to having women in their classes. The trouble came from the government, which tended to view the universities as a disruptive force in society. The admission of women seemed likely to exacerbate the continual warfare between state and academe.

Thus Russia was the first European state to recognize officially the "woman question" in higher education. A revision of university statutes in 1861 by the Ministry of Education raised the question; university councils were consulted. Where women had been attending, St. Petersburg, Kharkov, Kiev, and Kazan, for example, the councils favored including them in higher education. Aside from the traditional argument for educating women—their role of mothers— they took the progressive stance that women had a right to equal educational opportunities. The Moscow Council declared, however, that women were fit to be only wives and mothers.

Unfortunately, Moscow won. Women took part in university riots during the autumn of that year; one was arrested; and so when the new statutes were published in 1863, women were barred from universities. It was Russian women seeking higher education abroad who helped persuade the University of Zurich to be the first university to admit women for degrees in 1864.

Meanwhile the manifesto freeing the serfs, with land, had been issued in 1861. Its effect upon upper-class families was great; no longer could they count on an income from serf labor. As a result, many moved to the cities (the urban population of Russia had nearly doubled by 1870). But some women, whose families could no longer support them on their shrinking income, came to the city alone. Some became "emancipated women" and joined revolutionary circles; many sought only some means of making a living.

In St. Petersburg they found an incipient women's movement, gathered around three women. N. V. Trubnikova, daughter of a Decembrist revolutionary, was interested in social action. In the circle she collected around her in the late 50s were N. V. Stasova, daughter of an architect, and A. P. Filosofova, daughter of an aristocrat. They organized societies to find work and accommodations for poor women. Dining halls and dormitories, child care and vocational training were among the Trubnikova circle's activities. But the members became divided between the radicals, who felt that philanthropy was not enough, and the liberals, who tried to avoid repression by a government that viewed all social action as revolutionary activity. The circle survived through the 50s only as a liberal society of thirty-six women editors and translators providing work for upper- and middle-class women.

This kind of work, besides teaching and midwifery, was all that was open to upper-class women. For the lower class there was only factory and domestic work. Faced with the rush of women to St. Petersburg in the 60s, the Trubnikova circle decided the key to the problem was professional education for women. "Thus, here in Russia," Trubnikova declared in 1867, "on the one hand, there are many women looking for work, on the other, a total lack . . . of school teachers, doctors, rural pharmacists, horticulturists, all kinds of specialists. All these facts show that specialized education [for women] is not a fantasy but a true, a real need."[4]

In 1867 the circle originated a petition for university-level courses for women, and acquired 396 signatures. The St. Petersburg professors agreed, even giving lectures in private homes before official permission was received. At the same time, 100 women in Moscow requested courses in the sciences. The campaign was followed with interest in England. Josephine Butler corresponded with Trubnikova, and John Stuart Mill sent a letter of approval. But the idea was vetoed by Alexander II himself and by P. A. Shuvalov, head of the secret police. Government officials argued that university courses for women were premature, since they were insufficiently prepared for them. All that was allowed was public lectures, open to women.

Moscow and St. Petersburg women immediately presented projects for university preparatory courses. In 1869 the Vladimirskie and Alarchinskie Courses opened in St. Petersburg, attended by 767 women (some came to single lectures only). The few men who attended soon dropped out, and the courses became known as Women's Courses. The program was gradually expanded to include university-level courses in history, literature, law, and the sciences. Professors donated their services and opened their laboratories and libraries to the students. The Moscow Lubianskie Courses provided a secondary education and added new courses each year. The first year drew 190 students of different ages and education—sixty-five to study physics; forty-two, mathematics; thirty-one, Russian history; twenty-four, general history. Each year the popularity of the science courses grew more evident, and more mathematics, physics, astronomy, and mechanics courses were added. By 1872 the program was equal to the physico-mathematical faculty of the university. The humanities and arts students then moved to the newly formed Guerrier Higher Education Courses.

The Lubianskie Courses were organized by the students, who selected the professors to teach them. Gradually the faculty was consulted in matters of curriculum. A financial committee to handle funds was elected by the student body, whose meetings were lively and whose majority decisions were accepted by all.

The Guerrier Courses were also initiated by women, with the aid of history professor V. I. Guerrier and the rector of the university. Set up as an experiment in 1872, it was the first women's school officially recognized as giving higher education for women. Originally a two-year course, it offered ancient and medieval Russian history, ancient and medieval European history, history of England, of the French Revolution, of the Reformation, of ancient civilization, of art; in literature, ancient Russian philology, German literature, Shakespeare's sonnets, eighteenth-century literature, nineteenth-century literature, outstanding works in western literature; also astronomy and hygiene. At the end of the second year the students petitioned for a third; later the courses were extended to four years.

In 1876 the Tsar issued a decree permitting higher education for girls in all university towns and providing for pedagogical courses at all girls' secondary schools, normal schools for primary school teachers, and the establishment of women's commercial, technical, and industrial schools. D. I. Tolstoy, Minister of Education, supported the decree and women's efforts to open higher courses because the expanding primary and secondary schools needed teachers and because the government feared that the women's movement would become revolutionary unless given some satisfaction. (Russian women in Swiss universities joined the emigré radical community, following the anarchist Bakunin and populist leaders.)

Following the decree, Kazan opened a school for girls' higher education with two faculties—sciences and arts—which survived extensive harassment by local officials. Kiev, where lecture courses had opened in 1871, established a school modeled on the Guerrier Courses in Moscow. At Odessa and Kharkov bureaucratic red tape foiled all efforts. There was still a strong feeling that the only higher education appropriate for women was pedagogical training.

The Lubianskie and Guerrier Courses in Moscow, along with the courses at Kazan and Kiev, became the first accredited four-year Russian universities for women, equal in instruction, curriculum, and requirements to the male universities. They were joined by the Bestuzhev Courses in St. Petersburg, founded by the Trubnikova circle and administered by Stasova. Two faculties—historico-philosophical and physico-mathematical—were staffed by the outstanding professors of the capital. The Bestuzhev School was the only one of the five to survive the lean years of repression of women's higher education, which began in 1886.

In 1881 radical populists assassinated Tsar Alexander II. This opened a period of reaction in Russia, and universities were among the first institutions to feel its weight. In women's higher education, where, with the exception of the Guerrier Courses, the students had considerable control over their schools, there had never been any student disturbances; but this saved them for only a short time. In 1886 the faculties were ordered to take no more students, and to shut down by 1889.

By this time the Lubianskie Courses had taught 1,973 students; the Guerrier Courses, 2,064; the Kazan Courses, 576; the Kiev Courses, 1,098. In St. Petersburg the Vladimirskie Courses had merged with the new Bestuzhev faculties. The financial backing for these courses was good enough to tide them over a period without new students, and they decided to hold out, hoping for permission to continue. The government wished to limit women's higher education to teacher training; but through the intercession of highly placed people, the Bestuzhev Courses were allowed to continue under strict government supervision. For eleven years they were the only school of higher education for women in Russia.

In Moscow the property of the Lubianskie Courses was given to the Society of Women Tutors and Teachers. This society offered its members "Collective Lessons" to supplement their education. There were no restrictions and only a small fee for membership, so many women besides teachers joined to take the night courses. Gradually the teachers became a minority and 1,300 students were attending by 1897. Free from government control, this society also ran a pedagogical school and had a student government. The students refused to take part in any university demonstrations. According to one, they "understood only too well, that this School was altogether an oversight; that the Government endured it temporarily, probably until there was some pretext to close it."[5]

The pretext came in 1900, when permission was given to open one school for higher education for women in Moscow. The approved school, however, the Moscow Courses of Higher Education, required a secondary-school certificate, which many of the students did not have; it was more costly than the Collective Lessons; and it was limited to 100 students, fifty in the liberal arts and fifty in the sciences. It was to be administered by Guerrier (of the old school of that name), and there would be no student participation. Old Professor Guerrier was patronizing and had a limited view of women's scientific education. The students resented him; when two of them were dismissed, others resigned, endangering all hope of an education for themselves. The matter was solved by inducing the other professors to take a hand in administering the school.

After the revolution of 1905, the government was forced to relax its stand on many fronts. "Temporary regulations" for higher education allowed universities autonomy and student organizations. The student body of the Bestuzhev School in St. Petersburg jumped from 557 in 1904 to 5,785 in 1911. A law faculty was added in 1906. All shades of the political spectrum had chapters at the school. Radical speakers such as Alexandra Kollontai were in great demand.

Towns all over Russia reorganized higher education for women— twenty schools in eleven towns between 1905 and 1910. Some, like Kiev, had as many as six faculties, including law and medicine. Some of the old normal schools for teacher training, which had developed a three-year curriculum after 1870, now extended their program to four-and-one-half years, and became schools of higher education.

The education provided in these schools was on a high level.

Professors from the regular universities who taught in them found the women eager to do rigorous work, and provided it. When the law faculty was added to the Bestuzhev School, the women noticed that a lecturer in financial law treated girls more leniently than men in examinations. They convoked a special meeting and sent a delegation to the professor requesting that he not favor the women. He agreed.

Women gravitated toward science and mathematics courses in particular, and toward medicine (see Chapter VIII). This may have been because at the end of the nineteenth century, industrialization was spreading so quickly in Russia that the demand for scientifically trained people was greater than the supply. Women were able to find positions in the ministries of agriculture and transport, and in the state bank. There was a tremendous need for doctors in rural areas. As for the traditional job, teaching, posts were granted to women in the higher classes of girls' secondary schools in 1901; in boys' schools, in 1913. Women comprised 60 percent of the teachers in primary schools in 1914, as opposed to 25 percent in 1897.

In 1913 women were first granted degrees in higher education. Four schools were raised to university status: the Moscow Courses, which became the Women's University of Moscow; the Bestuzhev Courses, which became the Women's University of Petersburg; and the faculties at Kazan and Kiev.

In comparing the two politically reactionary societies east of the Rhine in the nineteenth century, we find Germany a leader in primary education for women, Russia in higher education. Since Germany's lead dates back to the eighteenth century, both countries can be said to have achieved their greatest progress under autocratic governments. Democratization, unless it includes women's suffrage, seems to have little to do with the status of women as reflected in their education. Germany was certainly further along the road to democracy than Russia in the nineteenth century, yet women's demands for higher education were denied again and again. One must therefore look elsewhere to explain Russian women's phenomenal success in gaining educational equality with men by 1914.

It has been noted that the Russian Women's Movement concentrated on securing educational and employment opportunities rather than on civil and political rights. With the exception of the few radical women who joined revolutionary movements, most women worked within the system for these limited goals, which they sought by petitioning the government. They were willing to do so because legally both sexes in Russia were nearly equal. All rights under autocratic government are limited. But in Russia women, like men, had the right to own property, the right of inheritance and trusteeship, and near equality in marriage (married women were allowed to work only with their husbands' permission).

These rights dated back to the tenth and eleventh centuries, when Russian women were more educated than men and acquired near equality in law. Many western European women were still fighting for them in the nineteenth century. The few political rights Russian male property holders had—electing members of municipal and district assemblies—could also be exercised by female property holders casting ballots through male delegates. When the university councils were consulted in 1861 on the question of higher education for women, they pointed out that excluding them would contradict the Russian legal system, since "women under our laws enjoy the same civil rights as men." Women could not, however, hold public office.

Therefore the main distinctions between men and women in Russia lay in the fields of education and employment. And here, in the nineteenth century, they had an invincible argument—Russia's backwardness, which must be eliminated by every available means, including the education and employment of women. This was not a plea for female emancipation, but a patriotic goal, which gained the support of a large portion of the educated classes. As Russia moved into the modern world, even local district councils in rural areas recognized the need for trained professionals. They established schools, and opened careers to women, particularly in health and education.

The zeal to "make Russia anew," which dated back to Catherine's desire to transform Russian society, and even to Peter the Great, took on an urgency that accounts for the liberal atmosphere prevalent in most of women's higher education. Professors and students together were embarked on a great work, a common progressive endeavor. Professors gave their time, unstintingly and often without remuneration, to establish women's courses. The crucial factor was probably the freeing of the serfs in 1861. It resulted in intensive urbanization and a need on the part of upper-class women for jobs, which matched the need of the country for trained people.

Of course, in an autocracy, the final decision on everything new rests with the government. The greatest gains in women's education were made under Alexander II, who was convinced by D. I. Tolstoy, his Minister of Education, that education was necessary to the advancement of Russia and a means of keeping Russian women away from revolutionary movements at home and abroad. He was not in the slightest interested in women's emancipation. The Tsar was pressed in the opposite direction by the secret police, who viewed all change as revolutionary; this side was to win temporarily in the reaction of the 1880s following Alexander's assassination. What autocracy can give, autocracy can take away.

The industrialization of Russia at the end of the century renewed the struggle. By that time there was a general awareness in Russian society of the need for a highly educated population. After the 1905 revolt the Tsar was forced to back down in many areas, including women's higher education. The Russian women's victory was due to prior conditions and the pressing needs of Russian society. To the Tsar, however, it may have seemed that Tolstoy had been right when he sighed, "What a woman wants, God wants."[6]

CHAPTER VI

The Catholic Countries: France, Italy, and Spain

In France, Italy, and Spain the tendency had always been to allow the Church to educate women, or at least to have a primary role in whatever formal education they received. As in the Protestant countries, girls were presumed to need different education from boys; but the emphasis was not so much upon the positive female virtues to be inculcated, as on the major sin to be avoided. The possibility that exposure to knowledge might compromise a girl's chastity was considered serious enough to warrant severely limiting her education. The convent was the best solution, shutting her away from the world and insuring that literacy would not lead to such license as reading novels. Strict surveillance, common in boys' schools also, was carried to an extreme with girls. No aspect of a girl's life or thoughts was allowed to be private; girls must never whisper to each other so that the teacher could not hear. Girls were raised to be dependent, pious, and chaste. A religious education, provided by orders of nuns, fulfilled these needs for Catholic girls well into the nineteenth century.

There was one difficulty, however, which each of these countries encountered as its political system became more liberal. Having suffered greatly in the anticlerical atmosphere of the French Revolution, the Church remained wedded to the old regime of absolute monarchy. Reduced in political power in the modern world, it continued to exert a moral sway over the faithful through its influence on the education of both sexes. Liberals and republicans in Catholic Europe soon realized that it was essential to their cause to wrest the ideological control of the masses away from the Church. As the suffrage widened, it was also necessary to see to the education of more and more citizens.

These two factors account for the growth of popular education in the nineteenth and twentieth centuries in these countries. The second was not applicable to women, who were never expected to have the vote. Even the first was not seen as relevant to women until late in the nineteenth century in France and Italy—much later in Spain. At that point it coincided with the beginnings of industrialization; but all these countries remained essentially agricultural well into the twentieth century. The extension of women's education was primarily related to the extent to which each society had freed itself from Church influence.

France was the leader in this process, which she completed in the early twentieth century. Italy followed at a distance. Spain has still some steps to take before her women become part of the modern world. Therefore the focus of this chapter will be mainly on the French experience.

PRIMARY EDUCATION

In 1815, with the final overthrow of Napoleon, the Continent settled into reaction, as legitimate rulers were restored to their thrones and aristocrats prepared to enjoy things as they had been in the "good old days" before the Revolution. To most, this implied restoration of the influence of the Church, since it supported a hierarchical society. Even to the liberals, shaken by the events of the Terror, the Church seemed to be the guarantor of social order. Throughout the century, whenever France was torn by riot and revolution, education was vested in Church hands. Primary education, not included in the Napoleonic education system, returned to its pre-Revolutionary state—local parish schools, which sometimes included girls at times when the boys were not in attendance, sometimes had separate facilities for girls. The government ignored girls' schools, except to put them under surveillance of local committees of the Ministry of Education in 1820. They did not appear in the first educational statistics of the century, made in 1829.

In 1830 the French revolted against the absolutist Charles X and put his cousin Louis-Philippe on the throne. The rebellion had its anticlerical aspect; when it was over, the liberal winners turned their attention to primary education. In 1833 a law on the subject was presented to the parliament by François Guizot. Originally it included a whole section on girls' education; but on the advice of his colleagues, who said the bill would never pass because the cost of educating girls would be too great, Guizot limited it to male education. At this point there were a little over a thousand girls' schools in the whole country.

In 1836 the Guizot law, which mandated boys' schools for every commune, was applied to girls' schools, in the sense that government aid could be given to them. Over 1,000 new girls' schools opened in the next three years. But the law did not succeed in putting even one school in every commune, since the initial funds had to be raised locally; two schools were too much to expect. And there were still strict rules against coeducation, considered "worse than ignorance" by almost everyone. (As late as 1866 a school inspector spoke of the necessity of separating children "who have reached the age of evil instincts.") A survey taken in 1835 showed that in the countryside girls were not thought to need schooling. Only certain communes, where the benefit could be seen immediately, welcomed girls' education. (In one fishing village two girls' schools existed because the men wanted their wives to be able to sell the fish and keep the books.)

By 1840, even the government saw the need for some schooling for girls. The Minister of Education reported to the King that girls' primary education should spread along with that of boys, particularly for the lower classes. Five teacher training schools were set up for females. There were also some state schools for girls, teaching the three Rs and vocational skills. But suggestions for a law on female education came to nothing. And despite constant pressure on the communes, the Guizot law did not bring universal education to France for boys, let alone for girls. Even the standards set up for existing girls' schools in 1836 were almost useless, since nuns, who taught most of them, were exempt from the standards laid down for teachers.

In 1848 another revolution, establishing the short-lived Second Republic, raised thoughts of education for all. A Josephine Bachellery called upon the Minister of Education to provide public education for women, to teach them "the sacred dogma of the rights of all and the great duty of human solidarity in the triple principle of liberty, equality, and fraternity."[1] This they would pass on to their republican children. This was exactly what the republic had in mind—universal education for both sexes. But it fell afoul of a new Napoleon, and a new Empire—the Second. Under the Second Empire the Church had complete control over all primary education. Despite the fact that the Falloux Law of 1850 required a girls' school in every commune of over 800 inhabitants, by 1866 there were still only 42,457 schools for boys and 28,214 for girls. For the girls, however, this was a 100 percent increase over 1837.

In 1866 another school survey was taken. In the second-richest department of France, with thirty-three communes numbering over 800 inhabitants, there was not a single girls' school. And this was not an isolated case. The situation was attributed to three things: indifference to the value of public education, particularly for girls, on the part of families; the cost to the commune of establishing a second school; the opposition of the clergy. The following year the Minister of Education, Victor Duruy, presented a bill to the parliament requiring one girls' school in every commune over 500. Duruy was to be the first Establishment spokesman for women's education.

The Empire toppled in 1870, during the Franco-Prussian War, giving way to the Third Republic, France's longest-lasting government since the Revolution. Republicans, underground since 1852, had long been planning for this moment; and part of their plans had been universal education, under the control of the state. It took about ten years for the republicans to gain control of the republic from the monarchists. Then, in 1881, they passed the Ferry Law providing free, secular, and compulsory primary education for children of both sexes, from ages six to eleven.

The law was bitterly opposed by those who thought that religious education was the only proper education for women. But as one republican had put it in 1867, "We are not thinking of making revolutionary women. We wish to make them intellectual companions of their husbands. One of the great misfortunes of the present society is the greater and greater separation which is being established between men and women."[2] In other words, French men were turning to republicanism, while their wives were still being educated by a Church devoted to absolute monarchy. This was the reason behind the extension of primary education to women. Civic education was a basic part of the curriculum.

But the law could not be strictly enforced, because there were too few trained teachers. Normal schools for the purpose were set up in each department, but the stock of teachers grew slowly. Even by the turn of the century most of the female teachers in the primary school system had acquired their education from nuns. There is also evidence that the compulsory aspect of the law was not enforced. In the first decade of the twentieth century, 10,000 draftees a year were found illiterate. If this was true of the males, it is likely to have been true of females as well.

The process was similar in Italy. In 1859 the unification of nothern Italy created a conservative constitutional monarchy, opposed by the papacy. The Casati Law of that year, like the Guizot Law in France, provided for primary education that was not compulsory. In 1877 Italy, now one nation, made education compulsory, but did not enforce it, particularly in the south. In 1904 a stringent enforcement law began to produce results; by 1907, 93 percent of all children age six to twelve were in school. As in France, salaries for female teachers were well below those for males.

In Spain girls received hardly any education. The primary schools for girls were vocational for the most part; often the teacher was almost illiterate herself. The 1900 census showed 63 percent illiteracy among all ages in Spain; one can presume a much higher figure for women. In both Italy and Spain convents provided a basic education for upper-class girls.

SECONDARY AND HIGHER EDUCATION

The early nineteenth century represented no advance over the Enlightenment in the matter of women's education. Madame de Rémusat, wife of the famous liberal, represented the vanguard of opinion, when she wrote in her *Essay on the Education of Women* in 1821: "Woman is on the earth as the companion of man, but nevertheless she exists for her own sake; she is inferior, but not subordinate." Although women had no place in politics, Rémusat maintained they had a right to knowledge because they were capable of it. As a liberal, she looked forward to the time when every French man would be a citizen and when every French woman would bear two titles "no less noble"—wife, and mother of a citizen. She believed women had the same faculties as men, but to a smaller degree, and deserved the chance to exercise them. The ideal women's education would not alarm husbands: "One must always see in the young woman one is raising the future companion of a being from whom she cannot exist independently."[3]

Except, perhaps, for the home training to which Rémusat's book was directed, the education of girls was at a low ebb, since most schools for girls of the upper classes were so poor that the state made no distinction between primary and secondary for them until 1837. Then the standards for regular boarding schools and institutes were established in the department of the Seine and copied in numerous other departments. Except for modern languages, still considered essential to young ladies, the boarding schools provided a fairly elementary education. The institutes added more history, literature, composition, ancient history and geography, and cosmography.

It was not until after the 1830 revolution that women themselves expressed much interest in advanced education. In this period there was a flurry of female activity, if not of feminism. Periodicals for women were published as early as 1832 *(The Free Woman, The New Woman, The Women's Tribune, The Journal of Women)*. The Utopian Socialist Movement, whose different sects supported equality for women in varying degrees, was often instrumental in raising female consciousness on women's issues. Charles Fourier believed that women should have an education equal to men's, but weighted toward the arts, while men's would be heavy on the sciences. The communist Cabet called for equal education for the sexes, without allowing women a role in public life. Saint-Simon believed in full equality of the sexes.

Saint-Simonism was one of the influences that prompted Eugénie Niboyet, the wife of a lawyer, to start a periodical, *Le Conseiller des Femmes* (The Counselor of Women), written mainly by women in Lyon in 1833. Its goal was "the amelioration of women's condition in all social ranks." Among the projects it began was the Atheneum, a society formed to provide books, discussion groups, and courses of study for women. *Le Conseiller* hoped to develop the intellect, talent, and aptitudes of women as individuals, and was popular with the bored bourgeois housewives of Lyon who bewailed their confinement to home and lack of education in articles in the periodical. But *Le Conseiller* also gave thought to working women, many of whom had come from rural areas to work in the silk weaving industry and were floundering in the chaos of unfamiliar living and working conditions. *Le Conseiller* urged the creation of schools for poor girls, which would teach them how to cope with a harsh life. It established day care centers (two for each sex), where workers' children learned the three Rs, health and hygiene, and religion.

When Niboyet left for Paris in 1835 the periodical closed down, and as far as one can tell, so did its projects. Not a feminist publication, it advocated different education for the two sexes, on the basis of different capabilities—more intellectual in the male, more affective in the female. The goal of girls' education was to make them better wives and mothers. This reflected somewhat Fourier's idea of the couple as a social unit embodying complementary functions, although Fourier envisaged the two sexes practicing the same profession together.

Later Saint-Simonians and other Utopian Socialists had a more radical view of women's roles. This was represented by the paper *Gazette des Femmes* (The Women's Gazette), run by Madame Poutret de Mauchamps and published in Paris from 1836 to 1838. The Utopian Socialists looked ahead to a new society in which all would be productive, women working alongside men. All would perform the same functions, each in relation to his or her own sex; but there were thought to be special feminine qualities by which women would benefit all humanity. The *Gazette* published petitions demanding equality for women in commerce and entrance to all professions. It urged parents to send their girls to attend courses at the university and the Collège de France. In 1838 de Mauchamps deposited a petition in the French parliament demanding access for women to courses and examinations in medicine and pharmacy and licensing of qualified women as physicians and pharmacists. The Utopians argued that there were certain problems in both medicine and law peculiar to women, which should be handled by women.

The Utopians insisted, not only that women be educated, but also that they be taught by women. Actually, the most successful women's secondary education of the period was the public courses taught by men. They were open to young women, who usually attended with their mothers, taking a variety of serious and frivolous subjects. One such school was Abbé Gaultiers', which opened on Saturday mornings for six months of the year. The first hour was history; the second, French; the third, geography, cosmography, and arithmetic. The lessons consisted of questioning the students on assignments read at home during the week. The mothers, many of whom helped their daughters study, listened and took notes. This novel method often educated the mothers as well as the daughters. In the 1830s and 1840s the number of these courses grew, until 2,000 girls were enrolled in them in Paris by 1846.

In 1847-48 Ernest Legouvé, a proponent of legal rights for women, gave courses at the Collège de France on "The Moral History of Women" in which he called for better female education. In 1848, Madame de Bachellery petitioned for girls' secondary education as well as primary, and laid out a plan for female normal schools. By this time there was some opposition to the overwhelming predominance of male teachers in secular girls' schools and in the public courses. It was claimed, though, that woman teachers, however high they ranked in devotion, were incapable of stimulating the students' minds or of inspiring confidence.

While most female education returned to Church control under the Second Empire, state teacher training for women proceeded rapidly. Many women, cut off from other kinds of secondary education, enrolled in normal schools, as they were the only schools open to women that provided proof of the attainment of an advanced level of knowledge in the form of a certificate to teach. Courses also flourished, particularly in Paris; and because of the stringent official requirements for men who wished to teach girls during the Second Empire, women began to take them over. Many of the courses prepared girls for the elementary school certificate, and private normal schools prepared them for the state teaching examination in greater numbers than the public ones.

The level of education received in all these schools was seldom beyond the elementary. The best of them were considerably inferior to boys' secondary education. This was deplored by some republicans, and even by liberal clergy, most notably the Archbishop of Orléans, Msgr. Dupanloup.

In a didactic work, *The Studious Woman* (1867), the archbishop maintained that after her duties to God, to her husband, to her children, to her household, and to the poor, woman owed some duties to herself—namely, "to cultivate her mind and elevate her soul by habits of intellectual work wisely measured and ordered." This would not detract from, but only add to, her ability to fulfill her other duties. Piety was not enough; it must be informed by intelligence. Dupanloup went on to talk about the influence of women in society and the family, which made their education important. He complained about superficial education in the accomplishments, and praised the model of Saint-Cyr in the seventeenth century.

Pointing to the empty lives led by so many upper-class women, Dupanloup urged them to fill their time with learning. Although he did not eliminate any subject from consideration, he felt literature— of a serious nature, of course—was most appropriate. History, biography, some knowledge of law, even a touch of science, were recommended. He carefully discriminated between the learned woman who went too far with education, and the studious woman who used knowledge to mature her judgment and reason.

It is in the archbishop's plea for educated women that one finds, clearly stated, a socioeconomic argument: women who don't take life seriously prevent husbands and sons from being sober and productive members of society. Wealthy men give up careers at their wives' behest. Sons are raised to be social successes rather than active and productive citizens. Foolish women, who know nothing of society's needs, contribute to the idea that work is demeaning, so that even the masses are infected by it. But work is the salvation of our generation. "As long as the women know nothing, they will want nonworking men. And as long as men do not choose work, they will want ignorant and frivolous women."[4]

Dupanloup spoke for education of women in all classes of society. His argument was echoed in other countries where industrialization was taking place. A Belgian spokesman for women's higher education maintained that upper-class youth was dangerously idle and women would regenerate society. Education would make women see wherein lay the true dignity of man, and admire only men who led an active life in the world.

Victor Duruy, Minister of Education, took up the cause of women's education as a necessary part of raising the general level of French schooling. In the debates on the primary education law in 1867, he made the point that advanced education of girls was essential to the success of industrialization in France. Higher primary school programs and vocational courses should be established for working-class girls, a solid secondary education for upper-class girls. Duruy tried to enlist the sympathies of the Empress on the matter.

Duruy intended to attach girls' day schools to existing *lycées* (classical secondary schools) for boys. Orléans was one of the few towns which seemed favorable to such an experiment, but when plans were announced, it was Msgr. Dupanloup himself who threatened all-out war. Young girls of sixteen could not, he insisted, be educated by secular, but only by ecclesiastical authorities. Education by the state might lead them to doubt their faith, and encourage a spirit of independence. They might even be taught by unmarried professors.

But Duruy persisted. He created a secondary curriculum emphasizing scientific and literary studies, excluding Greek and Latin, and culminating with examinations and diplomas. Well-to-do families would pay fees, part of which would be used for scholarships for poor girls. Otherwise, Duruy left it to the municipalities to engage the local professors and run the schools. By emphasizing local control, and by recommending that mothers and governesses accompany the students to class, he hoped to head off the opposition.

Associations were formed in Paris and other cities to facilitate the new program. But in Orléans, Msgr. Dupanloup was preparing the first of four polemical pamphlets against Duruy. He attacked the proposed schools as leading to the moral degradation of French womanhood; and he attacked Duruy as a freethinker who wished to destroy religion in France. Clearly the archbishop feared that if the Church lost its monopoly on the education of women, the "dechristianization" of France, already widespread in the male community, would run its course unchecked.

Some of the clergy tried to mediate the quarrel. Then the pope intervened. In a papal brief he pictured an antireligious conspiracy seeking to corrupt French society through secular education, particularly of women. If women were deprived of their "native prudence," if they were distracted from "the care and duties proper to them," the social order would be totally destroyed. This brought a goodly portion, although by no means all, of the higher clergy to Dupanloup's cause. Conservative newspapers called for Duruy's removal from office. On the other hand, the agitation brought some anticlericals to the support of women's education. Schools were established in thirty-nine cities in the first year.

In Paris the schools were a notable success. Empress Eugénie sent her two nieces, and the Minister of Foreign Affairs sent his daughter. The majority of the students and teachers were Protestant, which gave the schools an even worse reputation in the eyes of the Catholic clergy, who intimidated the faithful and kept them away from the schools.

There were objections besides religious arguments to secondary schooling for girls. It was said that women needed no more than an elementary education, that education would create liberated women, that it would ruin domestic happiness. An official in Lyon protested to Duruy that in areas like his, where most women were more intelligent than their husbands, it was necessary to keep the women at home, for the sake of family stability. Girls attending the schools were attacked in the press and by anonymous letters. Duruy was forced out of office in 1869, and the number of schools had declined to ten by 1880.

By 1882, however, 109 secondary school diplomas had been awarded to women, most of them in Paris, and some of them to non-French (English, German, and American) girls. And this first official effort at secondary education for girls laid the groundwork on which the French Third Republic would build.

In 1879 a law provided for a normal school for women in every department. A superior normal school for training the personnel of these schools was established at Fontenay-aux-Roses. Then a bill was presented to the French parliament by Camille Sée for the regular secondary education of girls. Defending the bill, he pointed out that in France the father spoke to the child in the language of reason, the mother in the language of superstition, because women were uneducated. "France is not a convent, women are not in this world to become nuns. They are born to be wives and mothers."[5]

Some republican newspapers saw his point; it was time to end the difference between husband and wife—he educated by the Republic, she by the monarchist Church. The doors of knowledge must be opened to women. "It is only then that one will no longer see women marching toward the past while we march toward the future!"[6] But even many republicans were not enthusiastic about a program of education for women approaching that for men. There were doubts that women were capable of scientific studies, and suggestions that a curriculum of specifically feminine subjects would be preferable. On the one hand, radical newspapers complained that secondary education would be useful only to the bourgeoisie; on the other hand, they acknowledged that it would provide teachers for working-class children and might decrease competition between middle-class and lower-class seamstresses by educating bourgeois girls for other positions.

Conservative opponents appealed to natural law: instead of teaching women to appreciate their inferior but important role, such education would bring them to demand that men share their superior role. This would reverse the laws of nature, and abandon the conditions of an orderly society as laid down by the Church. There was also the nature of women to be considered:

> The French young woman, raised under the vigilant protection of the family, had been preserved carefully from a masculine education and the brutalities of science. She grew up . . . in a poetic ignorance of the mysteries of things. . . . A state education . . . will prove to them, scalpel in hand . . . that there is neither God, nor Devil, nor duties, nor justice, nor virtue. . . . They will teach them everything, even rebellion against the family, even impurity.[7]

One of the big debates in parliament was over the provision to make many secondary institutions boarding schools. According to French pedagogical theory this was considered necessary to a complete education. Sée predicted that otherwise the convents would compete successfully with the new schools, as they had with Duruy's. But the opposition, as well as the potential cost of boarding schools, was too great; the law required only day schools. As one speaker pointed out, boys have to learn to live away from home, but girls do not.

Sée insisted that the state did not intend to produce women lawyers, and certainly did not envisage political rights for women. But he pointed to women's influence in the home and to the influence of the Church on them. "Who would doubt the Republic if all the women were Republicans?"[8] he asked. This brought questions from the opposition as to the wisdom of raising women's expectations through an education that could not lead to a professional career. The old objections to learned women who would neglect their household duties were raised again.

Nevertheless, the bill became law. It did not provide a secondary education equal to that of men. There was no Latin and Greek, both required for entrance to the universities. The science courses were more elementary than those of males (fifteen hours as opposed to fifty-five); the philosophy course was confined to ethics. French literature and history were emphasized. Courses in domestic economy and hygiene were added. Even so, there was much concern voiced about overloading women's delicate brains; all the old clichés about the intellectual differences between the sexes were aired.

The girls' program did not lead to the baccalaureate degree, which in France opened all doors to university education and status. This degree was confined to men only by custom, not by law. It had been sought by an informally educated woman, Julie-Victoire Daubié, in 1861. Having passed the examination in Lyon with honors, she was refused the degree by the Minister of Education. Even if she had received it, she could not have enrolled in the university. Only in medicine was the tradition somewhat relaxed (see Chapter VIII). But the rising numbers of girls in secondary school—from 10,000 in 1882 to 21,200 in 1900—began to create pressure for a secondary education leading to careers. (In 1900 there were 84,500 males in secondary schools.)

In 1902 the baccalaureate degree for males was altered to include three new programs. Beside the traditional classical degree were placed a Latin-modern language degree, a Latin-science degree, and a science-modern language degree—all to be equivalent. In 1907 a group of girls from a private secondary school in Paris, the Collège Sévigné, presented themselves for the Latin-modern language examination after a two-year special course in Latin. Eighteen out of nineteen received the degree. Other private schools began to do the same thing; the state schools were now under tremendous pressure. Parents were willing to pay for after-school courses in Latin, which opened the baccalaureate examination. The government, however, did not upgrade women's public secondary education until well into the twentieth century.

The only area in which women entered the professions in large numbers was primary school teaching. In 1889 there were 60,000 women primary school teachers; in 1912 there were close to 70,000, which was 15 percent more than the number of male teachers. As in Germany, the industrial revolution provided men with more lucrative and prestigious positions, and so primary school teaching was opened to women. Their salary was about 200 francs less a year for the same work, which also helped to break down prejudice against them.

The big question raised by female secondary education in France was that of entrance to universities. The Collège de France opened its courses to women early in the century. Some of the faculties outside Paris were open to women in the 1860s. In 1864, when women petitioned for entrance to the Sorbonne, they were given open courses, but not matriculation. In 1867 a woman student named

Mlle. E. Chenu registered for courses in the Faculty of Sciences at Paris; she was not followed by another woman until 1875. In 1871, Daubié, who had finally been given her bachelor's degree in Lyon, registered at the Faculty of Letters in Paris. There are no records from that time until 1884.

The establishment of secondary education for women made it necessary to offer higher education to female candidates for teaching. But the University at Paris drew almost as many foreign women as it did native French, particularly from Russia. Even by 1893, women, including foreigners, were only 10 percent of the students in the Faculty of Letters. Male students demonstrated—with shouting, stamping, rotten eggs, and obscene songs—against the increasing female presence in their classes. The French women decreased in numbers, to become fewer than the foreign women at the turn of the century.

One problem was that state secondary education did not then prepare women for the baccalaureate degree essential to university entrance. Private education and tutoring were the only recourse. In 1905 only twenty-six women received the degree. In 1919, spurred on by the severe loss of manpower during the war, a commission recommended the establishment of a separate women's baccalaureate degree. A storm of protest from feminist organizations, plus the pending reform of male secondary education, postponed action until 1924. The delay in making this degree easily accessible to women accounts for the small number of French women in universities before World War II.

As French women began to obtain the baccalaureate in small numbers, they enrolled in the universities, most of them in the Faculty of Sciences in the late nineteenth century and in the Faculty of Letters in the twentieth. Although the Law Faculty was opened to them in 1884, very few women took advantage of this before the turn of the century, when they were finally allowed to practice in the courts (they still could not hold judicial positions). The prestigious École Normale supérieure remained closed to women until after the war. But Marie Curie, the world's most celebrated woman, was named professor at the University of Paris in 1908, replacing her deceased husband.

* * *

In Italy the Casati Law of 1859 decreed that women teachers be in charge of girls' schools; however, secondary education to train them scarcely existed. Napoleon had founded some establishments in Italy similar to the Legion of Honor Schools. Six of these were under government supervision in 1860, while most of the private schools were run by religious orders. During the 60s northern cities—Milan, Turin, Bologna, Venice, and Rome—established secondary schools for girls, which were placed under the Ministry of Education in 1871. Normal Schools were established in Rome and Florence during the 70s. Nevertheless, a bill presented to the Italian Parliament in 1870, which would have required a girls' high school for every province of Italy, was never even discussed by that body. Pachietti, who championed the bill, remarked, "The enemies of education for women are legion."[9]

Even had this not been so, there were certain problems. Fees would have to be charged, with scholarships for poor girls. There was a lack of secular teachers. Like the French, Italian educators believed that only boarding schools, providing constant surveillance, gave a good education. The government, however, did not wish to make use of nuns—as in France, Church and State were at war. The unification of Italy in 1870 took the Papal States and Rome out of the Pope's hands, and so he refused to recognize the legitimacy of the new government. As the only pool of teachers for boarding schools consisted of nuns, most secular schools for girls were day schools, established by provinces, cities, and private associations, mainly in northern Italy.

Classical and technical high schools were opened to girls in the 70s, but Italians disapproved of coeducation for adolescents. In 1891 there were only 1,498 girls in these schools; in the same year there were 124,733 girls in private secondary schools (mostly religious) and 15,894 in normal schools. Since only five years of primary education was the entrance requirement for normal schools, they can hardly be considered secondary. Their students were mainly women of the lower classes, who attended them to gain access to primary school teaching—one of the few types of work open to Italian women, and miserably paid.

Most women's secondary education was acquired by middle- and upper-class girls and prepared them to be wives and mothers. Generally Italian women were uninterested in education, except for some in the north, according to Signora Zampini-Salazar, Italian representative to the Chicago Women's Congress of 1893. The bourgeoisie, she reported, refused to take advantage of the opening of boys' schools to girls; they still preferred the convents. Even in Rome the women's clubs were "mentally moribund." The conservatism bred by the Church was more pervasive in Italy than in France, where the tendency to leave women to the Church was fought by the republican establishment.

In Italy there was no law denying university attendance to women—some had attended in the eighteenth century—but for most of the nineteenth women were no longer accepted. Then, in 1876, women who could pass the entrance examinations were allowed into all faculties, including medicine and law. But the bourgeoisie was opposed to coeducation at this level also, and there were no women's universities. A few women became the exception to the rule and studied literature, philosophy, or mathematics at universities; but the woman who acquired a degree in law or medicine was prevented from practicing in both fields. Generally, the attendance of women at universities was severely limited, not only by the prevailing mores, but also by the weakness of girls' secondary education.

In Spain the few secondary schools were private, usually under religious auspices. A brief move in the 1880s toward founding more of them had petered out by the end of the century. At that time the government attempted to take control of education from the clergy, but the effort ended in failure. The education of girls remained severely limited and determined by the Church.

By royal decree in 1882 women were forbidden to attend Spanish universities. Ten years later the Queen Regent reversed this decree, but only twenty women took advantage of the opportunity. They concentrated on medical studies, where they were allowed to acquire doctorates. But there was even more prejudice in Spain against women's attending classes with men than in Italy.

Of the three countries, France was clearly the leader in nineteenth-century women's education. She was more democratic and more industrialized than the others, and these were undoubtedly important factors. One cannot, however, ignore the different influence of the Church in the three nations. Spain, the most backward, was still in the grip of a traditional monarchy with clerical support; the Church directed her educational ideals according to the traditional patterns. Italy as a nation had broken with the papacy, but her society was still more traditionally Catholic than that of France, and women's education could still be left under religious auspices. French republicans, however, were actively anticlerical and determined to eliminate Church influence from education and thus from the society. The schooling they provided for girls in this cause eventually opened all levels of French education to women.

CHAPTER VII

The Way of Free Enterprise: England and the United States

Unlike the governments of Continental Europe, the governments of England and the United States long refrained from any subsidy and control of education in their countries. In the United States all powers not specifically designated in the Constitution as national were relegated to the individual states, each of which followed its own course in education. In England, although the need for government involvement in education was recognized by the late eighteenth century, the split between the established Church and the Nonconformists prevented any unity on educational questions. Unlike Germany, where each state had its own religion, England was heterogeneous. In the nineteenth century the growth of new evangelical sects, notably Methodism, complicated the situation even further. On the other hand, the evangelicals' campaign, which called for all to be uplifted, intensified the push for universal education, and the evangelicals added their own schools to those already existing.

In both countries, then, education developed mainly through the efforts of local government and private institutions. Thus it is difficult to determine in this chaos of schools how much education was directed to females, particularly to females in comparison with males. In both countries it was not until the twentieth century that free and equal primary education was mandated for all children.

PRIMARY EDUCATION

At the end of the eighteenth century in both countries dame schools, sometimes supported by low fees, sometimes town subsidized, taught both boys and girls. The curriculum varied according to the skills of the teacher, who was usually a local widow or spinster forced to make a living by teaching. Ideally, children aged four to seven learned the alphabet, spelling, reading, writing, and their numbers. Needlework, often the area of the teacher's greatest competence, was included for girls. In both countries fewer girls attended than boys. In New England, dame schools prepared boys to enter the town schools, usually closed to girls until late in the eighteenth century. In the nineteenth century, some American towns began to offer equal primary education for both sexes.

In the cities, an elementary education was given to poor children of both sexes in charity and workhouse schools run by the National Society and the British and Foreign School Society in England, and by the Society for the Propagation of the Gospel in the United States. For the middle class there were boarding schools in both countries which taught a primary education plus whichever accomplishments for girls were in demand. None of these schools was entirely free. In 1820 John Pounds, a shoemaker in Portsmouth, England, started the ragged school movement, for children who could afford no school fees. Spurred on by Methodist evangelism, the Ragged School Union was educating over 17,000 pupils by 1848.

Early in the nineteenth century a number of proposals for a national system of education failed to pass in the English Parliament. But in 1833 the government began to subsidize school building by the two Societies. In 1839, following a survey by a Select Committee on the Education of the Poorer Classes, a committee on education was formed in the Privy Council. But the schools did not improve. In the years 1845 to 1850, 45-49 percent of English women could not sign the marriage register, as opposed to 31-33 percent of the men. Ten years later, 57 percent of the British army was still illiterate.

In 1858 a Royal Commission was established to study popular education. After a three-year survey, it reported that primary education was totally inadequate even for those who received it. The girls could barely read, could not write or spell, and could only rarely do arithmetic. Not only that, they did not even learn needlework. The report covered 1,895 schools, half coeducational, 10 percent infant, 22 percent boys, and 18 percent girls. It included the testimony of one Mary Carpenter, who ran the ragged schools of Bristol, describing the condition in which poor children arrived at the school. The Commission decided that free schools were essential.

Yet religious rivalry still prevented moves toward a national system of education for England. Instead, the government set standards—the three Rs as a minimum, plus needlework for girls—and encouraged the different schools to compete for state grants. Of course, boys' education was the greater concern; and the requirement of needlework for girls could only cut down the amount of time spent on other studies.

One of the reasons many Englishmen were willing to leave education of the masses to Church sponsorship was that they felt the Church would be most efficient in inculcating the poor with the necessary qualities—belief in hard work and obedience to their betters. (Not until the late nineteenth century was the connection made between illiteracy and crime.) In 1864 Parliament turned down a compulsory education act; one school inspector predicted that any attempt to enforce it would cause rebellion. In 1870, of the children age six to ten, one million were unschooled, only 700,000 attending school. The proportions were worse in the ten to twelve age group.

Political events, however, dictated a change. The Reform Bill of 1867 enlarged the suffrage to include all householders. "We must educate our masters" was a slogan with meaning.

A compromise bill was passed in 1870, providing for election of local school boards in districts without a school. The board would establish a school, either by voluntary means or through a compulsory local tax. It would decide what religious character the school would have, or whether it would be nondenominational; it would set fees and decide if attendance was to be compulsory.

In 1876 Parliament voted compulsory school attendance in all districts without board schools, leaving the principle of local determination where elected boards existed. By a law of 1880 all boards had to make a rule of compulsory attendance. But it was not until 1891 that state grants to the districts made it possible to waive tuition for poor children; primary school education in England became completely free only in 1918. As a result, laws on compulsory schooling were not strictly enforced.

The first American state to try compulsory education was Massachusetts in 1852. But parents who could plead poverty were excused, and there was little compliance. In the 1870s, many states passed laws on compulsory schooling, few of which were rigorously enforced. The South lacked such laws into the twentieth century. Most states at that time did not even have laws forbidding children of school age to work during school hours, as did Massachusetts. Financing of schools varied in different areas of the country.

The questions of compulsion and payment are important for the education of girls. Without compulsion many parents did not send any children to school, preferring them to work. If education was considered important, boys were more likely to be sent to school than girls; this was even more true if fees had to be paid.

A typical curriculum of an English girls' school at the end of the century, when girls attended from age five to age eleven or twelve, was: the three Rs, plus two subjects out of five (English, geography, history, sewing, singing), plus one subject out of five (algebra, chemistry, domestic economy, French, cooking). The standard in arithmetic was lower in girls' schools than in boys' schools, and the time spent on sewing and cooking meant that other subjects were often neglected. Almost half the children in school were girls. The number of certified female elementary schoolteachers had risen to 60 percent, from 48 percent in 1869. But as in other countries, their paycheck lagged behind the male teachers' by about a third. The majority of primary schoolteachers were of working-class origin.

Attendance at school remained low in England and the United States. With the absence of child labor laws and neglect of black children, the United States had the worse record. Children under the age of twelve were forbidden to work in England in 1901; children of twelve had to have a certificate of physical fitness and proof of a certain standard of primary schooling before being allowed to work. Halftime compulsory attendance at school was provided for working children age twelve to fourteen.

Certainly one must view the record in primary education of the two wealthiest countries in the world as spotty at best. Presumably more liberal and democratic than Continental nations, they did not evidence the will to educate all their people until much later than Continental countries. The greater freedom—freedom to neglect children's education—affected girls at least as much as boys on the primary level, and probably more. As for attitudes toward education for girls beyond the primary level, the liberal nations showed no more liberal attitudes than the rest.

SECONDARY AND HIGHER EDUCATION — ENGLAND

Interest in women's secondary education was at a low point in nineteenth-century England. It was considered more important for a young woman to be pious than intelligent. A few women tried to campaign for girls' schools in the 1830s. The *Quarterly Journal of Education* called for a sound system of women's education from 1831 to 1835. One Catherine Sinclair dedicated a book on the subject to the new Queen, Victoria, who unfortunately was no more interested than other English women. And most women believed in their own inferiority. Mrs. William Ellis, author of *Daughters of England* (1843), urged women to be as content with their mental inferiority as with their physical weakness.

Nevertheless, many a middle-class English woman was, in the uncertain heyday of industrialism, forced to earn a living as a governess—the only respectable position available to her. Most were themselves uneducated. In 1844 the Governesses' Benevolent Institution opened a residence for governesses between jobs and was swamped with applications. In an effort to train them, Reverend F. D. Maurice, professor at King's College, began a series of evening lectures in 1847. Women crowded into these classes, which educated many of the pioneers of good secondary education for girls—Dorothea Beale, Frances Mary Buss, Sophie Jex-Blake, and Elizabeth Day. One of the Queen's ladies-in-waiting, a Miss Murray, raised money to put the lectures on a permanent basis. In 1848, lodged in a house on Harley Street, they became, officially, Queen's College for Women.

Queen's College was a secondary school, but a good one. It

offered English, theology, history, geography, Latin, mathematics, modern languages, natural philosophy, music, fine arts, and teacher training. It was the seedbed of English women's movement into higher education, although it never attained that status for itself. It inspired Elizabeth Reed, then over sixty, to plan a second college in London, which would eventually win full title as an institution of higher education for women. Lectures by professors at the new, un-denominational University College opened in Reed's home in 1849. Twenty years later Bedford College was chartered. But Reed did not live to see women granted full degrees.

Meanwhile, Queen's College provided the personnel for a renaissance in girls' secondary education. In the 1850s Buss founded the North London Collegiate School (a day school) and Beale took over the Ladies' College at Cheltenham. Although the female accomplishments such as French and music were retained in the secondary curriculum of the new schools, they were taught thoroughly. The programs of the Buss and Beale schools emphasized literature, history, art, ethics, religion, and philosophy.

But the older schools remained in the majority. They were to be attacked by Emily Davies, whose main interest was preparing girls for university education. The daughter of a clergyman, Davies envied her brothers their Cambridge education, which prepared them for careers. She joined the women's movement, edited the *English Woman's Journal* for a time, and founded the Society for the Promotion and Employment of Women. She wrote an article in 1857 on medicine as a profession for women for the National Association for the Promotion of Social Science; in 1864 she wrote one on girls' secondary education (she did not presume to read either of these before the Association herself, but entrusted them to male readers). In 1862 she had persuaded Cambridge to open its local examinations to girls. The Cambridge examinations established the basic requirement for university education, and Davies wanted to use them to set standards for girls' secondary schools. When eighty-three girls took them the following year, many failed mathematics.

In 1864 a Royal Commission began to investigate secondary education. Davies convinced the commissioners that they should look into girls' schools also. The commissioners called Davies, Buss, and Beale to testify. Davies wrote:

We are not encumbered by theories about equality and inequality of mental power in the sexes. All we claim is that the intelligence of women, be it great or small, shall have full and free development. And we claim it not specially in the interests of women, but as essential to the growth of the human race.[1]

Buss told the Commission that most of the girls she admitted to the North London Collegiate could hardly do simple arithmetic at age thirteen to fifteen. All the women complained about the deficiencies of girls' primary education and advocated training for secondary school teachers. They recommended allowing girls to take the boys' secondary examinations. The Commission also gave heed to a paper by Davies arguing that endowments originally made to provide education for both sexes were being used mainly for boys' schools.

The Commission report was thorough and fair. It concluded that girls' schools were characterized by "want of thoroughness and foundation; want of system; slovenliness and showy superficiality; inattention to rudiments; undue time given to accomplishments, and these not taught intelligently or in any systematic manner; want of organization . . ."[2] It pointed out that the few good schools proved girls as capable of learning as boys, and it recommended a girls' school in every town of over 4,000 population, with a broad secondary curriculum.

The Commission also noted that endowments for boys' schools, exclusive of the great ones such as Eton and Harrow, amounted to £177,000 a year, as compared with £3,000 for girls' schools, the latter providing only elementary instruction for the lower classes, while the former offered excellent advanced education. It recommended that a fair share of endowments go to girls. The Endowed Schools Act of 1869 acknowledged the women's claim to that fair share and set up the Endowed Schools Commission to administer the funds. (At that point twelve girls' schools educating about 600 girls were receiving 2 percent of the total endowment.)

The report also suggested that higher education be opened to women, which was Davies' aim. In 1871 Maria Shirreff Grey, who had published *The Intellectual Education of Women*, founded the National Union for the Education of Women of All Classes, which was joined by 300 persons interested in female secondary education. The National Union formed the Girls' Public Day School Company, which raised capital to run girls' schools on a business basis. Thirty-four of them existed by 1890, serving girls of all classes and denominations who could pay reasonable fees. On account of the fees, in practice the girls served were upper-class girls. These high schools, as they were later called, were modeled on the North London Collegiate School. They taught the three Rs, plus bookkeeping, grammar and literature, French and German, physical science, drawing, singing, and calisthenics. The final year prepared students to take the university examinations. The National Union also founded a Society for the Training and Registration of Teachers in 1877, to train secondary school teachers.

The day schools became pilot projects for other independent schools, which received aid from the Endowed Schools Commission. Girls' boarding schools began to imitate Cheltenham Ladies' College and the better boys' schools, with more stress on mathematics and science. Although there were no national standards for secondary education, the opening of the Cambridge, and later the Oxford, local examinations to girls raised the academic level of girls' schools. In the 1880s some endowed schools, forced to provide for girls as well as boys, became coeducational to avoid the expense of building separate schools. This caused some furor, and occurred only in smaller country towns. Girls were beginning to achieve educational equality with boys. But secondary education for both sexes still required tuition payments, and in practice more scholarships were available for boys.

During the 1890s primary schools were adding more advanced education to their curriculum; but as in France, there was little transfer from one system to another. The Bryce Commission on Secondary Education (1894), consisting of fourteen men and three women including Buss and Beale, recommended coeducation and equal education for both sexes. A Royal Board of Education was created in 1899. The 1902 Education Act provided for secondary education for both sexes at public expense in day schools established for all classes by the local authorities. At this point some of the private schools entered the national system.

Although more and more of the state-endowed schools became coeducational, for economic reasons, the trend to single-sex high schools continued. As a result equality of secondary education was not usually practiced. The Board of Education report of 1908 recommended full equality of opportunity for girls, with an education as good as that of boys. But local authorities considered mathematics and science unnecessary for girls, and so where the schools were not coeducational, little was offered to them. Fewer girls attended than boys. In 1907 to 1908 there were 79,002 boys and 68,853 girls in secondary schools; in 1913 to 1914, 113,615 boys and 96,578 girls (the proportion of boys actually increased a little). But even though secondary education was neither compulsory nor free, now lower-class children predominated in the publicly supported high schools. In 1913, 64 percent of the boys and 60 percent of the girls entered from primary schools, indicating that, in an industrialized society, the value of education was recognized by parents of modest means, for girls as well as boys.

HIGHER EDUCATION — ENGLAND

In England it was accepted that women would engage in girls' secondary education; they did so with great fervor. Buss wrote: "As I have grown older, the terrible sufferings of women of my own class, for want of a good elementary training, have more than ever intensified my desire to lighten . . . the misery of women, brought up 'to be married and taken care of,' and left alone in the world destitute."[3] Women of the kind Buss pitied could find positions teaching, but the quality of the education they provided depended to a great extent on their access to higher education. Graduates of Queens College and other good secondary schools formed the core of a new and dedicated cohort of teachers. (Sometimes class intruded. When Sophia Jex-Blake, a graduate of Queen's College, was offered a post as mathematics tutor there, her father objected to her taking wages normally paid to a lower social rank. She accepted the position without salary.) There were also some normal schools for women, most of them founded by the Anglican Church, some by other religious institutions; but by the 1880s there were still only sixteen of these.

It was through trying to solve the problems of female unemployment that many such as Emily Davies had become involved in women's education. To her the final goal was a true higher education for women equivalent to that of men. The opening of the Cambridge local examinations to girls was only a first step.

Davies' campaign to that end was not simple, for many women, including Beale, did not approve of girls' openly competing with boys. Indeed, it was years before the lists of those who passed included girls' names. But Davies was convinced that if special examinations were given to girls, as some recommended, the principle would be established that women's education should be inferior to men's. It was necessary to bring girls' secondary education to the level of boys', and to open university courses to women. These two goals she saw as interdependent.

Another group of women, led by Anna Clough, was not interested in university education for women so much as in improving the qualifications of female secondary school teachers. They were more willing to accept special women's examinations. Cambridge established a women's examination in 1869 with particular emphasis on qualifications for teaching. In later years it was opened to men, and became known as the higher local exam.

In 1869 five women from the Davies group rented a house near Cambridge and persuaded interested professors from the university to give them lectures. After a year of work, all five took the first examinations for the bachelor's degree and passed them. By 1873, three of the women had passed the examinations for the classical tripos, with honors. Meanwhile a subscription had raised money to buy a site for a building, which was incorporated as Girton College in 1874. An American student reported that, during the erection of the college building, students and professors frequently laid stones with their own hands.

The first students worked without tutors at lessons given by Cambridge professors. Half of them intended to become teachers. By 1890, the student body numbered 100, and the college had tutors, like other university colleges. By 1887, 127 women had passed the bachelor's examinations—thirty-four in classical philology, thirty-six in mathematics, one in mathematics and history, twenty-two in natural sciences, two in natural science and philosophy, fourteen in philosophy, eight in history, one in modern languages, one in theology; twenty-nine more had passed the higher degree, the tripos. A Miss Ramsay, age twenty, passed the classical tripos with highest honors in a class by herself—something never attained by a man at that time.

In 1871 the group of women led by Clough, reluctant to compete with men, founded a college in Cambridge for girl students. It moved to Newnham in 1875 and was incorporated as Newnham College in 1880, with Clough as principal. Newnham girls were encouraged to take only the first college examinations; but by 1885, 80 percent of them were also preparing for the tripos. By 1890 Newnham served over 100 students.

For the first ten years girls of both colleges were examined unofficially by Cambridge professors dedicated to the cause of women's education. The results were also unofficial; they did not lead to university degrees. Davies conducted an unending campaign to secure the degrees to which the girls' examinations entitled them. But a degree would have given women voting rights in the university, which was anathema to the "old grads." For ten years they gathered from far and near to vote down the proposal, which was favored by a large number of the Cambridge faculty. In 1880 Miss C.A. Scott's performance in the mathematics tripos attracted widespread attention and a demand that she be given the degree; she did not get it. But in 1881 the university began to post women's examination results with the men's. Women often headed class lists, but were not formally given degrees. It was not until 1921, the year Davies died, that women were officially granted Cambridge degrees, from which voting rights had been severed. In 1948 they were finally given degrees on equal terms with men.

The story at Oxford was much the same. Schemes for lectures by university professors were mounted in 1865, 1873, and 1878. The movement there was led by Anne Rogers, who won the highest grade in classics in the 1873 local examinations. In 1884 the first university examinations were opened to women; all classes and examinations were opened in 1894. Four colleges—Lady Margaret Hall and Somerville College (1879), St. Hugh's (1886), and St. Hilda's (1893)—were opened to prepare women for the teacher's certificate. After 1894 they prepared women for regular degree examinations. They had no formal relationship with Oxford, although the women's names appeared on the examination lists and ranked along with the men. Oxford also withheld the degree from women until 1920.

The opposition to higher education for women claimed that too much studying would make them lunatics. Davies, writing in the *Victoria Magazine*, asked, "Why should simple equations brighten their intellects, and quadratic equations drive them into a lunatic asylum? Why should they be the better for three books of Euclid, which they are required to master at Queen's College, and 'stupefied' by conic sections and trigonometry?"[4] This particular exchange concerned admission of girls to University of London examinations. Not a traditional university, London opened all its degrees to women in 1878. Several colleges were founded to prepare them for examinations. The lectures, laboratories, and libraries of the university became coeducational, by vote of all the faculties except the medical (see Chapter VIII).

Women were able to acquire academic degrees at Victoria University in Manchester from its founding in 1880. Not all courses were open to women, and there was a residence requirement. Universities in Wales, Scotland, and Ireland were granting degrees to women by the end of the century, although not always equivalent to male degrees. St. Andrew's University in Scotland offered a Lady Literate of Arts degree (L.L.A.). The numbers of women in English universities remained small. But the ivy gates had been forced open.

In one area, teacher training, English women moved ahead of men. The Maria Grey Training College, founded by the Women's Education Union in 1877, emphasized methods of teaching as well as content. Cambridge University's extension courses for secondary school teachers became the Cambridge Training College for Women in 1885. Other universities did the same. The movement grew, so that by 1914, of the 175 normal schools in England, 167 were for women. The number of these schools, established without government activity or support, reflects the fact that, while women were enthusiastic about preparing for teaching, the government was slow in providing grants for teacher training. When the 1902 Education Act set standards for secondary schools, it required only a proportion of teachers in each institution to have teacher training; in fact, men without teacher training held the best posts in secondary schools.

A survey of teachers in public secondary schools in 1914 shows a higher number of women (29.7 percent) than men (27.9 percent) with both university degrees and teacher training, 52.3 percent of the women and 71.6 percent of the men with a degree but not teacher training, 47.4 percent of the women and 37.5 percent of the men with teacher training but no university degree. Of those with teacher training only, 8 percent of the men had a secondary education, compared to 47 percent of the women.

As for university teaching, it was open to women in women's colleges, but even there they competed, usually unsuccessfully, with men. In coeducational universities a woman had to be exceptional, as only a handful were, to acquire positions. The few full professorships held by women were in women's colleges where the professors had participated in the founding and the first difficult years.

English women had some advantage over Continental women in access to universities before 1914, but few seized this opportunity. Not only was higher education of girls considered unimportant by society at large, but also the government failed to require a level of secondary education which would prepare them for it. A Parliamentary report on German girls' education estimated that in 1897 a larger proportion of girls was receiving a quality secondary education in Germany than in England. This was due to the fact that, while British schooling had traditionally developed under private auspices, education had long been accepted as the responsibility of government in Germany. Although women's education was not eyed with official favor in Germany, once compelled to accede to the principle, German bureaucracy was quick to set up and enforce academic standards in girls' secondary schools. The English government failed to do this. Thus in Europe, the key to high-quality advanced education for girls seemed to be action on secondary schools taken by national governments. This was not to be the case in the United States.

SECONDARY AND HIGHER EDUCATION
—UNITED STATES

American women were pioneers in women's education earlier than European women, perhaps because coeducation was more common in the New World than in Europe. In 1818 Hannah Mather Crocker published *Observations on the Real Rights of Women.* She cavilled at some aspects of Wollstonecraft's call for complete female independence; but she maintained that "the powers of the mind are equal in the sexes . . . and if they received the same mode of education, their improvement would be fully equal."[5] The following year De Witt Clinton, Governor of New York, received Emma Willard's *Plan for Improving Female Education.*

Willard, teaching with her husband in a coeducational academy in Vermont, felt that girls were deprived by prejudice of good postprimary schooling, particularly in mathematics and science. She concerned herself with the problems of standards and teaching methods for girls' secondary education. Thinking along the same lines as Davies would in England, she sought permission to sit in on the entrance examinations for the University of Vermont, in order to learn how they evaluated the secondary education of their male applicants. She was refused. Determined to provide training for girls in subjects not usually considered part of the female curriculum, she studied on her own, one by one, all the fields of mathematics and geography. When she had mastered a subject, she would teach it to another woman teacher. In this way she hoped to formulate a systematic course of studies for girls in fields unfamiliar to them.

Her *Plan* for an endowed school for girls was presented by Clinton to the legislature. When they refused to subsidize it, she pressed it on the wealthy citizens of Troy, New York. In 1821 the Troy Female Seminary opened with a curriculum including mathematics and sciences, as well as domestic science. It was the first endowed secondary school for American girls and became famous for its public examinations and training of teachers.

The idea of housewifery as a science was adopted by Catherine Beecher, who raised money by subscription for the Hartford Female Seminary in the 1820s. She planned to provide an alternative to factory work for the surplus women in the East resulting from male migration west. She looked to professionalization of domestic work; many of her books dealt with the technical training and rounded education necessary to a good housewife. She also shared Willard's interest in training teachers, and founded pilot normal schools at central points in the West. These were joined with placement agencies, which found positions for the surplus women of the eastern seaboard.

In 1836 Harriet Martineau, in *Society in America,* had seen only seven occupations open to women: teaching, needlework, keeping boarders, working in cotton mills, bookbinding, typesetting, and housework. In 1852 women composed 2/3-3/4 of factory employees, mostly in eastern mills, and at the lowest pay. Beecher was right in her assessment of the need for alternate employment. In 1852 she organized the American Women's Education Association to establish women's schools. The only remaining school it founded is Milwaukee-Downer College, once Milwaukee Normal Institute and High School.

The pioneer phase of American women's education in the early nineteenth century was completed when Mary Lyon founded Mount Holyoke. After years of teaching in district schools and academies, Lyon worked out a plan for a seminary for teachers in New England. It was to be available to all classes at low cost; the students would handle the domestic tasks; and the curriculum would be broader than mere preparation for housewifery or teaching. At first keeping in the background while a male committee failed to raise the capital, Lyon finally stepped forward with her green velvet bag and toured New England herself, seeking money and causing many a raised eyebrow. She was also seen proselytizing among the mill girls, offering them hope of another way of life.

Lyon collected enough money to found the Mount Holyoke Female Seminary in 1837. The students were sixteen years or older, with preference given to teachers. Fees fluctuated with expenses, and were much lower than in the female academies, which had provided the only secondary education heretofore open to girls. Students were tested upon arrival in grammar, United States history, geography, arithmetic, and selected texts. They faced a three-year program that constituted a true secondary education—English, geography, ancient and modern history, biology, chemistry, mathematics, philosophy, geology, religion, music, French, and gymnastics. Domestic science was practiced to keep down fees, but not taught. During Lyon's life about 1,600 girls attended Mount Holyoke, and left, with great religious fervor, to become teachers, missionaries, and housewives.

Lyon agreed with Willard and Beecher that secondary education for girls should teach a selection of basic subjects well—with thoroughness and continuity from year to year—rather than offering the twenty to forty subjects in the academies' catalogs, parcelled out to a few teachers (academies continually enlarged their offerings to include every subject a prospective student, or her parents, might desire).

The seminaries, structured along the lines of Mount Holyoke and the Troy Female Seminary (renamed Emma Willard), gradually replaced the academies. The best of them had entrance requirements and provided an excellent secondary education. Although many were church connected, they stressed moral philosophy over religion as such. The usual program was three years, and many of them still included the accomplishments in the curriculum.

While pioneer efforts were opening these private schools, cities were beginning to offer secondary education for girls in tax-supported institutions. The high school movement in the United States was as varied in its approach to education as were the different regions of the country. It began in Massachusetts, which decreed in 1827 that every town of 500 families offer public instruction in United States history, bookkeeping, geometry, surveying, and algebra. Larger towns of 4,000 families were to offer in addition general history, rhetoric, logic, Latin, and Greek. Response was slow; in 1840 there were sixteen high schools in the state. In 1852 Massachusetts made school attendance compulsory for all children between the ages of eight and fourteen, for at least twelve weeks of the year, six of which must be consecutive. This was the first compulsory school law in the nation.

How did all this affect girls? The original high school act touched them hardly at all, since these schools were intended for boys. The city of Worcester, however, had already established a girls' high school in 1824, the first in the nation. When Boston followed suit the next year, it was swamped with applications, and closed after two years rather than try to deal with the demands upon it. The example of Worcester was also followed by New York, where a high school for girls was founded in 1826. The compulsory attendance law was ineffective, since it contained many exemptions, including inability to pay. Therefore, without a publicly supported high school accepting girls in a town, there was no compulsion for parents to send them to school.

In the cities of the nation many girls were extending their primary school education until age sixteen or seventeen, wherever teachers were willing to offer them advanced work. Unlike boys, middle-class girls had few opportunities for suitable employment. Wherever the numbers were great enough and the city fathers willing, advanced primary education broke away to form separate schools on the secondary level, with programs widely divergent from city to city.

Girls' high schools aimed mainly to produce "fit wives for educated men," and limited their curriculum accordingly. At the opening of the New York Female High School, the speaker, John T. Irving, after emphasizing the importance of women's education for future generations, added, "I would not wish to be understood as advocating their attention to any abstract branch of science. Such knowledge is not necessary for them."[6] The subjects considered important for girls were English, French, geography, arithmetic, geometry, astronomy, and domestic science.

Although eastern cities (perhaps more influenced by Europe) generally tried to establish separate schools for girls, the coeducation of primary schools extended into the high schools of the West. Coeducation provided girls the opportunity to take more science and mathematics, less religion, philosophy, and modern language training than was considered ideal for them, and to take the advantage of the added year when three-year schools adopted four-year programs (a more common development in schools attended by boys).

Before the Civil War high schools were confined to cities. In 1857 they existed in eighty cities. There was little uniformity of curriculum even within individual states. The best offered English, humanities, algebra, geometry, natural sciences, Latin, and sometimes Greek. Programs ranged anywhere from one to four years.

After the Civil War high schools burgeoned across the country, including rural areas; sometime in the 1880s they surpassed private schools in pupils. The earliest reliable statistics, in 1890, show that there were 202,963 pupils in public high schools, representing less than 1 percent of the population. Some of the private schools, teaching 94,391 children almost equally divided by sex, were also subsidized by public funds. Unlike the situation in Europe, this high school elite numbered more girls than boys, despite the fact that the secondary school curriculum was oriented almost entirely to university entrance. One reason was the lack of compulsion. The middle-class boy as well as the lower-class one left school to take a job, while his middle-class sister remained in school until ready for marriage. In 1890, 57.6 percent of the pupils and 64.8 percent of the graduates were girls.

Turn-of-the-century educators attributed this to the fact that adolescent girls were more precocious than boys, who did not like to compete with them. This, along with the traditional arguments for a distinctive female education, was used by those opposed to coeducation. In the pragmatic United States, however, the added costs of separate education were the determining factor, and coeducation became the rule, rather than the exception.

Another factor favoring the presence of girls in high schools was related to the expanding need for primary school teachers, as states adopted compulsory education laws. The entrance of women into teaching was slow. Massachusetts opened some normal schools to train teachers as early as the 1830s; New York, Connecticut, Pennsylvania, and Michigan followed. But in 1850 two million American children received no education whatsoever, and a petition presented to Congress for free normal schools for primary teachers was tabled. As in other countries, high schools began to add a year or two of teacher training to their curriculum, thus opening the door to a possible vocation for women. State normal schools also multiplied after midcentury, and by the end of the Civil War women in them outnumbered men. Some had even acquired civil service posts in education. A Massachusetts committee hiring a county superintendent of schools reported: "As there is neither honor nor profit connected with this position, we see no reason why it should not be filled by a woman."[7]

As local education costs rose in the 1870s and 1880s communities that had previously preferred male teachers discovered that women, who earned about 60 percent of male salaries at best, were appropriate teachers of children. They were gentler, more patient, tender, and motherly than men. Teaching was now recognized as women's natural profession, as Beecher had said. (Also, as she had noted, women were more likely to settle for underpayment in teaching than in more debilitating factory work.)

By the 1890s the evils of women's preponderance in the schools were being decried in educational circles. The schools were being "feminized"; this was added to the previous reasons for the male dropout rate. By 1907 one educator was declaring it "monstrous" for boys to be receiving most of their intellectual and moral education from women. In 1903, when girls were still 60 percent of the high school graduates, educators were warning that too much education could lead to invalidism in females.

It was just as impossible in the United States as in Europe to consign all women to housewifery, motherhood, and teaching. Caroline H. Dall, in her *College, Market and the Court,* demanded for women "free, untrammeled access to all fields of labor" on the ground of sheer subsistence. She also pointed out the alternative—prostitution. "For lust is a better pay master than the mill-owner or the tailor."[8] The percentage of women over age ten who were gainfully employed rose from 14.7 percent in 1880 to 23.4 percent in 1910. Domestic jobs for these women declined; clerical and industrial jobs increased.

Private schools sprang up to train women for these new positions. Nurses' training (See Chapter VIII) gained impetus from the experiences of the Civil War. Schools of industrial design for poor girls were established in Philadelphia and New York. The new telegraph system provided jobs for women; Cooper Union in New York set up classes in the 1880s to train them. High schools as well as private schools instituted commercial courses to train girls for office work.

The report of the Douglas Commission on Industrial and Technical Education in Massachusetts of 1906 reinforced this trend. Not only was there now a demand for public vocational education in the country, there was a concomitant denigration of "literary education." The latter was pinpointed as the weakness of the American school system by Theodore Roosevelt in his annual presidential message to Congress in 1907. Although he spoke only in terms of males, girls' education was also affected. Cooking and sewing courses, labeled in turn housewifery, domestic science, home economics, were considered vocational, and qualified for federal subsidies. Commercial training for girls received no such grants.

Thus in its first effective role in girls' education, the federal government opted to prepare them for unpaid housekeeping rather than paid jobs. At the same time literary education was attacked as unsuitable for girls. A school superintendent in Pennsylvania insisted in 1907 that it was necessary to weigh Latin against cooking, solid geometry against dressmaking, and algebra against household duties.

This debate on the function of the high school took place in the first decade of the century, when there were still only 10,213 high schools in the country, 30 percent of them with only three teachers, many with one-, two-, or three-year programs. The results were more ominous for girls than for boys. The high school of the twentieth century came to provide vocational, industrial, technical, and economic training for males, in addition to college preparation. For girls the main advance was the commercial, or "business," curriculum to prepare secretaries.

The public high school of the nineteenth century had never aimed at equipping girls for colleges and universities. But the principle of coeducation had already moved past the high school level. Oberlin had opened as a coeducational college in 1833; the first women's bachelor degrees were given in 1842. Coeducation at Oberlin was established, not for the sake of women, but so that men at the college might have a more wholesome and realistic view of women than those at all-male schools. But even as a corollary to male education, coeducation was a boon to women. Antioch College, founded in 1853, also took women.

The great advances in coeducation were made by the state universities. Some of them in the West attached female academies to their branches, which led to coeducational universities later. These were known as colleges; many secondary private schools in the East took this rubric and began offering some form of "higher" education, usually of dubious quality. Certainly they were unable to offer an education equal to that of men's colleges.

By the midsixties Iowa and Wisconsin, by the early seventies Michigan, Maine, and Cornell Universities had admitted women to degree programs. Other state universities and land-grant colleges followed suit. But the old universities of the East resisted the trend. As a result, the first exclusively women's colleges aiming at true higher education arose in that area of the country. Vassar, founded in 1860, was the first endowed women's college.

Recognizing the insufficiency of its students' previous training, Vassar used its preparatory department to raise their level of education. Not wishing to train women in exactly the same way as men, it modified the curriculum. In chemistry, for example, it taught practical subjects such as culinary chemistry, toxicology, and treatment of leather. Wellesley College, which opened in 1875, also had to make good use of its preparatory department to raise its academic level. (Wellesley was the first college to have women presidents from the beginning, and a faculty composed entirely of women.)

Smith College opened in the same year. Unlike the others, it insisted upon the same entrance requirements as the best men's colleges, and had a comparable curriculum. It opened with only fourteen students. The last of the first four "sisters," Bryn Mawr, was founded in 1880 and offered graduate degrees in 1885.

Sophia Smith, who endowed Smith College, saw the opening of higher education to women as a panacea that would redress the wrongs done to women, equalize their wages, increase their influence for reform in society. Clearly it was not all as easy as that. Opposition to higher education for women came from academe itself. Edward Clarke of Harvard College published a book called *Sex in Education* in 1873, in which he argued that higher education would destroy the ability of American women to bear children, by overtaxing them at a critical stage in their adolescent development. Martha Carey Thomas, later president of Bryn Mawr, recalled that she was terror struck by a similar work, fearing that attending college would make her "a pathological invalid."

Others argued that women would be unsexed by too much education; it was unfeminine and almost obscene for a woman to seek it. Thomas, who went to Germany to acquire her doctorate in 1879, learned from a relative that family friends did not ask after her, as she was considered to have disgraced her parents. The women's reactions to such attitudes were usually healthy. "A Maiden's Vow," a poem by Alice Miller, expresses their derision: "I will avoid equations/And shun the naughty surd,/I must beware the perfect square,/Through it young girls have erred,/And when men mention Rule of Three/Pretend I have not heard."[9]

In 1888 Mount Holyoke joined the ranks of quality women's colleges. By 1891 there were over 10,000 women in college, but in the U.S. Commissioner of Education's report of 1895, only sixteen of the 158 women's colleges were distinguished as being equivalent to men's colleges. Three-quarters were in the North Atlantic region. Over 50 percent of the teachers in women's colleges were female; however, some of them had not been educated in a college. The report covered 415 colleges in all, of which 256 were coeducational in some or all departments. By 1907 there were 110 women's colleges, of which only 32 percent were considered by the Commissioner to be offering true higher education.

Few women college graduates entered professions in the nineteenth century, though some acquired professional training from schools that did not require higher education as a prerequisite.

Through most of the nineteenth century legal training was acquired by clerking in the office of a lawyer admitted to the bar, which effectively eliminated women. There were a few law colleges. Ada Kepley won her degree from the Union College of Law in Chicago; the University of Pennsylvania opened its law school to women in 1881, and graduated Carrie Burnham. But it was not until the 1890s that law schools, and therefore opportunities for women to get legal training, began to burgeon. By 1900 there were ninety-four of them, enrolling 12,365 men and 151 women. But the elite schools—Harvard, Yale, Columbia, Washington and Lee, University of Virginia—resisted pressures to take women. (Yale conceded in 1918; Virginia in 1921; Harvard only in 1948.)

Not even a law degree gave access to the bar. Common law did not allow women to plead in the courts, although some exceptions had been made in the colonial period. Women were refused admission to the courts for this reason, and on the grounds that a married woman's contracts were not binding in common law; that access to courts would open judicial and executive positions to women; and that women in court would endanger the delicacy of the female sex.

Many women trained in law acquired renown as writers and editors. Myra Bridwell founded and edited the *Chicago Legal News*; Catherine Waite, the *Chicago Law Times*. Only by a state-by-state process of antidiscrimination laws were women enabled to practice law as a profession. By 1920 there were 1,738 women lawyers.

There was, however, some graduate education open to women in the 80s and 90s. In 1882 the University of Pennsylvania opened its graduate school to women. Bryn Mawr offered graduate education from its beginning; by 1900 it had given forty-four master's degrees and eighteen doctorates. Columbia in 1890, Yale in 1891, Brown and Chicago in 1892, and Harvard in 1894 opened graduate education to women. In 1900, 312 men and thirty-one women received Ph.D. degrees in the United States.

The women's college movement provided an advanced education to many women, and a true higher education to a few. The movement rose out of the need for secondary school teachers and also out of the belief that education would raise women's status in society. Women's colleges, however, were imbued with the traditional view that women were equal but different from men. The elite colleges providing education equal to men's colleges contributed to higher status for women, but true equality of intellect was better proved by coeducation, in which women competed with men in the same classroom.

Although some state universities opened as coeducational institutions, most of the quality schools, particularly in the East, would not accept women. Harvard and Columbia both refused to consider the matter, agreeing only to affiliation with Radcliffe and Barnard. The less well endowed universities of the West, although just as much opposed to accepting women, could not as easily afford to turn them away. In the depression of 1873, the University of Chicago, faced with bankruptcy on the one hand and pleas for coeducation on the other, decided to allow women entrance. This solution to financial crisis was adopted by other western universities, notably Stanford.

As female enrollment climbed to almost 50 percent in coeducational schools and as the economic picture brightened, Chicago tried, and actually succeeded for a while, segregating its women in a separate junior college. It was believed that, given the choice, men would choose an all-male college over a coeducational college. John

Dewey and others spoke out against education by sex, and separate but equal proved too costly; so coeducation was reinstated. Throughout the first decades of the twentieth century, women made up over a third of the students in higher education, most of them in coeducational institutions.

The fact that higher education in England and the United States was not subject to government control meant that women's access to it was dependent on public opinion. The fact that it was not subsidized by government meant that women's access was subject to economic conditions. Both factors favored American women over their British cousins. Traditional social attitudes confined higher education to a very few British women in the early twentieth century, whereas receptiveness to new ideas pervaded the still young United States. The class nature of British education limited the number of universities in existence, while they multiplied across the Atlantic. Those in existence in England were well endowed, and did not need to seek a new clientele in times of economic crisis. In the United States, there was little pattern to the proliferation of higher education, because of regional differences and local, rather than federal, control. In general, large coeducational state universities developed in the West, while private one-sex colleges predominated in the East. But interested individuals and groups were able to found both separate-sex and coeducational colleges, granting degrees, in all parts of the country. Although the quality of these schools varied, it was in their very number and variety that women found opportunities for higher education that were unavailable to English women.

CHAPTER VIII

Medical Education for Women

In almost all societies, past and present, women have played some role in medicine, because they have always tended the sick and aided each other in childbirth. For much of the past, male care of women in childbirth has been considered either improper on the one hand, or unworthy of male talents on the other. But women have seldom been confined to caring for other women in labor. Ministering to the body has always been women's work, and they have always had to learn it somewhere.

During the medieval period the noble lady bound up the wounds of her warring men, set their bones, and nursed them back to health. She was responsible not only for the physical care of her own family, but also for the nursing of everyone in the manor who was sick, noble or ignoble. The medieval herb garden was her pharmacopoeia, from which she concocted medicines whose recipes were passed down from mother to daughter, along with practical medical knowledge.

Nuns in convents were also expected to care for the sick. Famous saints, such as Scholastica, sister of St. Benedict, taught and practiced medicine. These women acquired their learning mainly by experience. The convent was a source of training in practical medicine and provided a kind of clinic for wayfarers who fell sick.

It is not surprising then that the name of a woman is connected with the first university medical school, at Salerno in Sicily. Sicily, a cosmopolitan center in the Mediterranean world, had never lost contact with the East. Christians, Jews, and Moslems mingled there and were part of the university, which began to take shape in the eleventh century around a medical faculty. If we can believe the considerable body of lore about the Salernitan School dating from the twelfth century, women also were a part of university life there.

This topic has been the subject of much scholarly debate, because the later universities in the north excluded women. It is only because of the nature of Salerno University—secular in origin, and organized around a medical faculty—that the Salernitan School of women physicians is believable.

The main figure of this school is known as Trotula, said to be the wife of a physician, mother of a surgeon. As a doctor she treated both men and women, and performed Caesarean sections. As a teacher, along with others of both sexes, she taught medicine to men and women.

Two medical manuscripts attributed to Trotula were widely circulated in late medieval and early modern Europe. One is a manual of gynecology and obstetrics that is far in advance of her time. The other treats of such diseases as epilepsy, malaria, typhoid fever, syphilis, and skin cancer. But with all her knowledge, Trotula believed that women were weaker than men because they menstruated instead of perspiring.

Trotula's texts, or others used at Salerno, were probably read by Hildegard von Bingen, a German abbess who had no formal training but traveled widely throughout Europe in the twelfth century teaching medicine in convents and monasteries. Her own medical writings are the most important Latin scientific works of this period. Among the other abbesses learned in medicine was the scholarly Héloïse, who in addition taught and practiced this art for twenty years at her hermitage in Paraclete.

There are some stories of other women teaching medicine in Italian universities, but in the north, where universities grew up around theological faculties, teachers and students were all celibate male clerics. Both men and women, however, practiced medicine without the licenses acquired by formal training. Women appear as doctors, distinct from midwives, in the 1292 Paris tax rolls. There were repeated efforts to confine medical practice to those formally trained. A 1311 statute reads: No surgeon or apothecary, man or woman, shall undertake work for which he or she has not been licensed. But statutes such as these could not be enforced. Wives and daughters of doctors learned medicine from their husbands and fathers. Some, in turn, took apprentices, a practice in midwifery since time immemorial. The result was a transmission of practical medicine, removed from scholastic theory. This extralegal practice of medicine probably kept alive many patients whom traditional treatment, which was based on Aristotle's works, would have killed.

Women connected with the Salernitan School of medicine wrote medical texts in the thirteenth century on such diverse subjects as fevers, ointments, care of wounds, urine, and the nature of human sperm. In France the practice of medicine by qualified women was legalized in the mid-fourteenth century. The Surgeon's Guild was opened to women in England in 1372; and in 1436 one Dorothea Bocchi was appointed professor of practical medicine and moral philosophy at the University of Bologna, replacing her father. From the thirteenth to the seventeenth centuries a few women moved from assisting medical professors at Italian universities to teaching courses in such subjects as anatomy, practical medicine, and even moral philosophy.

But outside Italy, and for the most part within it, women learned medicine from other women who had practical experience and had perhaps read a medical text. Some were related to male physicians and confined themselves to obstetrics and charity medicine. Although the Church issued an edict in 1421 completely forbidding women to engage in medicine or surgery, like laws prescribing celibacy for doctors, it was more honored in the breach. Whole families throughout Europe practiced medicine together.

Aristocratic women often studied the medical arts, and even founded hospitals for the poor in which they nursed. Queen Isabella and Margaret of the Netherlands founded hospitals. Elizabeth of England prescribed for herself; Sir Thomas More's daughters and Francis Bacon's mother were known for their medical skills. Most of the renowned ladies of the Renaissance practiced medicine. Hardly any women had formal training in medicine, since universities were closed to them and private tutors were both few and expensive.

The exception was Italy, where a few women continued to receive medical degrees until the sixteenth century from such universities as Bologna and Naples (which had absorbed Salerno). Costanza Calenda, in the fifteenth century, is considered the last of the Salernitan School stemming from Trotula.

By the sixteenth century the learned abbess who taught medicine in convents had all but disappeared, a victim of the Reformation. Women in medicine were secular rather than religious figures. Margarita Fuss, known as Mother Greta, practiced medicine throughout Germany, Holland, and Denmark. She traveled in a red and black striped skirt, a soldier's jacket, and a large cape trimmed with yellow fox fur; she carried a gold-headed cane and a bag decorated with the snake of Esculapius. German women continued to practice medicine in large numbers during the Thirty Years' War in the seventeenth century.

Women remained the only midwives in Germany for many centuries, practicing in large numbers. One, Dorothea Christina Leporin Erxleben, matriculated at the Halle medical faculty with the permission of Frederick the Great, who handed her the doctoral degree himself in 1754. At this time there was only one school of midwifery in Germany—at Strassburg—but Maria Theresa, an enlightened despot, established excellent schools for midwives in Austria in order to reduce female mortality. Similar schools were founded in Holland and the Scandinavian countries. Catherine the Great, also moved by Enlightenment ideals, founded them in Russia.

Midwifery was the most common employment of women doctors, of course, and some become famous through serving noblewomen. Many learned from other midwives, from books, and from male physicians. But in France men began to replace women in obstetrics for the upper classes in the seventeenth century. They had already pushed women out of other medical practice at the end of the religious war. In 1635 some midwives petitioned the University of Paris for public courses; the plea was ignored until 1669, when an examination was established for them and a course given to prepare for it.

Marguerite du Tertre de la Marche, a student of the Queen's midwife, Louyse Bourgeois, organized the three-month course and wrote a text for it. This was the origin of the modern obstetrical school called *La Maternité*. An alternative preparation for the examination was a three-year apprenticeship with a reputable midwife. Meanwhile Angélique Marguerite le Boursier de Coudray received a royal grant in 1759 to travel France teaching midwifery, which she had learned in Paris. She is said to have trained over 4,000 midwives. It was not until 1768 that midwives obtained permission to attend certain lectures at the Medical Faculty in Paris, and be present at autopsies and dissections (of female bodies only).

English midwives, such as Jane Sharp, also pleaded for better education. During the Puritan period in England midwives were licensed after three examinations. One Elizabeth Cellier collected statistics on female mortality in childbirth and presented them to James II with a petition for a royal hospital; she tried to get midwives incorporated under a royal charter. None of these plans materialized, and after 1662 to become a midwife a woman had only to pay money for a license. Although midwifery licenses were available to women, licenses for surgery and other medical arts were now difficult for women to acquire. Male doctors did not object to women if they confined themselves to charity medicine; for this one did not need a license.

In the eighteenth century men invaded the field of obstetrics in England. By midcentury male obstetricians were attending upperclass women in both England and the United States. When medical schools were opened in the United States, women were excluded from them. By 1810 there was hardly a female midwife left in New England, which followed the English fashion. Individual women, taught by husbands and fathers, continued to practice general medicine and obstetrics in England in the early nineteenth century, and a German midwife, Charlotte von Siebold, attended the birth of Queen Victoria in 1819.

In Russia, as in Germany, the midwife remained the rule. Four-year courses were provided in three schools for them in the early nineteenth century. Nicholas I reduced the courses to two years in the 1830s, and a gynecological clinic was attached to the midwives' schools in Moscow.

By the nineteenth century women had almost totally lost their once important role in medicine. In countries not yet industrialized they still served as midwives and unofficial ministers to the sick, but in countries where medicine, surgery, and pharmacy had been professionalized, women were excluded. In England and the United States they were even excluded from obstetrics, by being prevented from learning the most advanced techniques. It was unthinkable to men, and to most women, that students of both sexes should study anatomy, dissect bodies, and treat physical diseases together, and in most countries men were unwilling even to teach women in segregated classes. A woman who studied medical subjects lost her standing as a lady. A correspondent of the *English Woman's Journal* in 1862 wrote that "the extreme repugnance, amounting to disgust, felt for this kind of knowledge, including physiology, would frequently prove an obstacle, which could not be surmounted without the sacrifice of much which is very valuable in a young girl's mind." This statement is all the more ridiculous when it is considered that women had served for centuries as both informal and hospital nurses, and that a revolution in nursing education was even then taking place in London.

The late seventeenth century to the early nineteenth is known as the dark period in nursing history, because there was little formal medical training for nurses. In Catholic countries religious orders devoted themselves to tending the sick. The most notable of these was the Sisters of Charity, founded in the early seventeenth century by Saint Vincent de Paul, which eventually spread all over the world. (Elizabeth Bayley Seton, recently awarded sainthood, founded the United States branch of this order.) The training received by nursing nuns was on a strictly practical level, that is, they learned what other nuns could teach them about how to tend the sick. A hospital was not a place where formal medicine was practiced, but a place where ill people, usually of the lower classes, received care and feeding. They were endowed by churches and wealthy patrons, and staffed by the nursing orders, for whom the hospital was their convent.

When the Reformation came, secular boards in Protestant countries took control of existing hospitals, as a form of charity. But the convent form was retained for nurses. A head matron, corresponding to the traditional mother superior, supervised the nurses, who, though not nuns, were called sisters, and lived in the hospital. They in turn supervised poor women from the community who were paid to do menial tasks. The motherhouse system of Protestant countries, in which nurses trained at one hospital went out in groups, or sisterhoods, to found other hospitals, was also copied from the organization of Catholic religious orders. It began in Germany.

In the early nineteenth century one Pastor Theodor Fliedner and his wife Friedericke Munster established a Deaconess Institute to treat the sick and poor at Kaiserwerth. (Deaconess was then the highest church position a woman could hold; the duties of the office could be nursing, religion, or charitable work in the parish.) By 1843 Fliedner's second wife, Caroline Bertheau, who had worked in the Hamburg Hospital, was providing training in nursing for the deaconesses. Groups from Kaiserwerth went out to found hospitals in London, in the eastern Mediterranean countries, and even in Pittsburgh, Pennsylvania. By 1936 there were 35,000 of them. Elizabeth Gurney Fry, an English Quaker, visited Kaiserwerth in 1840 and returned to found a sisterhood of "Fry Nurses" in London.

Nursing sisterhoods were also established by the Church of England, but the sisters received little real training until St. John's House was established in 1848 as a nurses' training school. It provided a two-year course, followed by five years' training in a hospital, living in, to acquire a nursing certificate. Anglican sisterhoods were also established in the United States. The common feature of all these Protestant efforts was the motherhouse model.

Valerie Boissier, Countess Agenor de Gasparin, was the first to oppose this system. She pointed out that it restricted the freedom of women who undertook nursing, Instead of living in a controlled situation, under discipline, nurses should receive a salary, like other workers, and receive systematic training for their job from doctors. In 1859 she established a school of nursing in Lausanne, Switzerland, named *La Source*, which embodied these principles. Her example, however, did not produce any imitators on the Continent.

Florence Nightingale of England was to be the founder of modern nurses' training. Highly educated in the classics by her father, speaking a number of European languages, she desired to train for a career. Her parents refused to allow her to learn nursing in a London hospital, which was considered no place for a lady. In 1847 she visited Rome and became familiar with the Catholic nursing orders. She also visited Kaiserwerth in 1851, and took up a three-month residence at the school, but considered it inferior to some of the Catholic orders. Her subsequent stay with the Sisters of Charity in Paris was cut short by an attack of measles.

When the Crimean War broke out in 1854, Nightingale was in charge of the Establishment for Gentlewomen During Illness in London. As tales of neglect, disease, and death filtered back from the battlefield, the cry went up: Why have we no Sisters of Charity? Nightingale offered her services and was, miraculously, accepted. She left England with thirty-eight nurses of all religious denominations and found her career in the Barracks Hospital at Scutari—an unbelievable thing for an English woman.

What she found there were appalling sanitary conditions, obstruction from army doctors, even religious antagonism among the nurses she had brought, some of whom were not equal to the task. Those women who stayed, along with more who arrived later, served four miles of beds (straw pallets sewn by the nurses) set eighteen inches apart. By the end of the war Nightingale was supervising 125 nurses. But what she had seen of army health care determined her to fight for reform. She wrote later, "I stand at the altar of the murdered men, and while I live I fight their cause."[1] In traditional fashion, she fought through working informally with the all-male Commission on Health of the Army, appointed in 1857.

She was a heroine to the men who lived to tell what she had done. Immediately after the war the Florence Nightingale Fund was inaugurated to provide for a nurses' training school. It was established at St. Thomas' Hospital in London in 1860. By this time medicine had been professionalized by male doctors. They sat on the hospital boards and determined the tasks performed by nurses, through direction of the Matron. The novelty of the Nightingale Training School was that it aimed to enable nurses to master their profession just as men did theirs, in opposition to the traditional belief that every woman was by instinct a nurse. Another goal was to take the discipline and training of hospital nursing out of the hands of male doctors and administrators.

The Nightingale system, followed today in Britain, Holland, and Scandinavia, puts a matron in charge of all nursing, kitchen, laundry, and domestic personnel in a hospital, as well as the nursing school. The nurses live in and are provided theoretical training, based on the biological sciences. At first this education consisted of occasional lectures and demonstrations over a one-year period; later it was expanded to include a solid training in anatomy, physiology, pharmacology, and nutrition.

The American system, a variation of this, has a Superintendent of Nurses in charge only of nursing and nurses' training. The first school was established in 1872 at the New England Hospital for Women and Children, in Roxbury, Massachusetts. New York, New Haven, and Boston city hospitals started nurses' training schools the following year. The first bachelor's degree program was inaugurated at the University of Minnesota in 1910. But until 1925 training in hospitals accounted for the overwhelming majority of nursing programs in the United States. Not only were there few degree programs; there were also few courses in practical nursing for bedside care in the home. By that year all states had set standards for licensing nurses, beginning with North Carolina in 1903.

During World War II, two-year colleges seeking students began to offer associate's degrees in nursing, and standards for practical nursing licenses became general. The degree programs grew in the postwar era to regular four-year college courses, including liberal arts, basic sciences, and practical training in hospitals. In 1965, however, the majority of nurses was still being trained in the old hospital diploma programs. That year the American Nurses' Association published a Position Paper recommending that all nursing education take place in colleges and universities, and that diploma programs be phased out.

Since then there has been a proliferation of nursing colleges on university campuses. In 1975, 27,000 students were graduated from these with associate's degrees, 20,000 with bachelor's degrees, 2,000 with master's degrees, and 30 with doctorates. All programs include experience with patients, but the postgraduate degrees are mainly intended to provide teachers for nursing colleges. In the same year 37,000 persons received licenses in practical nursing.

The American system differs from the Nightingale in that more scientific and liberal arts education is included, and that nurses are no longer required to live in at the hospital.

Another variation, the Continental system, leaves male doctors in charge of the nurses in each division, while the school, which may or may not be attached to the hospital, is run by a Head Nurse. Theoretical training similar to that in England is provided in the school, and the nurses live either there or at the hospital. This is the higher level of education for nurses in Continental Europe. The motherhouse system also survives as a modern adaptation of the old convents, and is widespread in both Catholic and Protestant countries. Here also the ultimate control is in male hands—either of a religious chaplain or of a committee. There is a minimum of scientific training; practical training is directed by the Ward Sister.

The level of education for nurses thus varies widely. In some countries a girl needs merely an elementary education before being admitted to professional training. Only in the United States are schools of nursing integrated into universities. In all countries practical nurses, hospital attendants, and paramedical personnel receive separate training at a lower level.

Like teaching, nursing began as something women did informally in the home, developed into a religious vocation, and finally became a paid career. The last stage in both cases was accepted by society (in England, the United States, and some parts of the Continent) only in the late nineteenth century. But this acceptance did not extend to female physicians.

Since the seventeenth century men had been progressively barring women from the practice of medicine. By the time American medical schools were founded in the nineteenth century, it was not even considered necessary to exclude women explicitly in their charters. Thus when Elizabeth Blackwell, English born but living in the United States, applied to twenty-nine American medical schools in the 1840s, the decision was left to the faculties, all but one of which denied her entrance. In 1844 the Geneva College of Medicine in New York state dodged the issue by putting it to the students, ruling only that a single negative vote would represent a blackball. But the male students thought it would be great fun to have a woman, and voted her in.

Certainly they had guessed correctly that Blackwell would encounter endless difficulties. After fighting for her right to take anatomy classes, she had to steel herself not to show weakness during dissections. She was treated like a pariah in the small-town boarding house where she lived. Graduated at the head of her class in 1849, she decided it would not be ladylike to march in the commencement procession.

Seeking further training, Blackwell studied at *La Maternité*, the midwives' hospital in Paris, where she lost an eye, and the possibility of becoming a surgeon, to opthalmia. In England she met Florence Nightingale and through her became interested in sanitation and hygiene. Upon her return to New York she was faced with complete ostracism by the profession; even charity wards denied her access. She began to offer lectures on bodily hygiene and physical education for girls, which attracted her first supporters—a group of Quakers who helped her establish a dispensary on the lower east side.

In 1857 she raised the money to open the New York Infirmary, a forty-bed hospital staffed entirely by women. Her sister Emily, who had just completed her own medical training, and Marie Zakrzewska, a Polish midwife who wanted to be a doctor, formed the staff with her. Eight months later she opened a nurses' training school. During the Civil War army nurses were recruited and trained there.

By this time a small group of male doctors supported the hospital and sat on the board. At the war's end, they were persuaded to apply to the state for a medical school charter, since existing reputable schools still barred women. (At this time there were no state standards for medical schools, and their quality varied greatly.) The Woman's Infirmary Medical School opened in 1868. The following year Blackwell returned to her native England, where she took part in English women's struggle for access to medical schools. In the United States, medical schools began to open to women slowly through the 1870s. Schools restricted to women opened in New York, Philadelphia, Boston, and Chicago, which awarded 630 doctorates between 1880 and 1890. By 1929, there were 7,219 women doctors and surgeons in the United States.

Elizabeth Garrett-Anderson was the pioneer in England. She attended lectures at Apothecaries Hall, London, paying tutors to report to her on courses from which she was barred. Permitted to take her medical examinations in 1860, she passed, but was refused the degree. Later the University of Paris granted her an M.D. "with distinction." A single case was not unacceptable in England. But in 1869 Sophia Jex-Blake, an alumna of Queens College, applied to the medical faculty of Edinburgh University in Scotland. She was told that a single woman in a class of men would be improper, whereupon she advertised in newspapers for other women to join her. Eventually Jex-Blake and six other women applied and were accepted. This caused an uproar among teachers and students. Registration of women immediately ended. The seven already enrolled attended some lectures but were refused entrance to others. The male students petitioned to keep women out of the Royal Infirmary. When the women were refused degrees, friends tried to introduce an Enabling Bill into the House of Commons; it failed in 1875. Jex-Blake then returned to London and founded the School of Medicine for Women with Garrett-Anderson.

But their troubles were not over. Medicine can be neither taught nor practiced without clinical experience, and all hospitals were closed to women from the school. Finally, after three years, the Royal Free Hospital admitted them to its clinic. The University of London voted to admit them to their medical examinations and degrees, but only in 1877, after the Irish College of Physicians and Surgeons in Dublin had done so. The School of Medicine for Women was now legitimized, as its students could acquire medical degrees. Garrett-Anderson served as dean, and Blackwell took the Chair of Gynecology.

Jex-Blake obtained justice in Edinburgh by helping to found a women's medical school there. Edinburgh University finally opened its medical faculty to women in 1894. In the first mixed graduating class, a woman was placed third. But in general, women were held back in Britain by being segregated from men in medical schools well into the twentieth century.

Across the Channel, France's first recipient of the bachelor's degree, Mlle. Daubié, demanded in 1866 the right of women to be doctors on the grounds of their right to subsistence, of their ability to save lives, and of "morality, decency, and social economy properly understood." The first French woman to apply to the Faculty of Medicine at Paris was Madeleine Brès, a young widow with children, who first had to pass her baccalaureate, at age twenty-eight. When she entered the medical faculty in 1868 she found there Elizabeth Garrett from England and Emily Putnam from the United States, as well as a woman from Russia. They had entered by special dispensation from the Council of Ministers, urged on by Empress Eugénie; the Empress made women's medical education her own concern and planned to found a medical school for women. Unfortunately, the Franco-Prussian War ended her political power along with her husband's.

Male students whistled and hooted at the four women during lectures. Warned by the dean to be strict in their deportment, they sat in the front of the amphitheater near the professor. Sometimes male relatives accompanied French women to their medical classes in the early years, but gradually they came to sit on the benches with the men and were accepted. Garrett and Putnam finished their studies first, in 1870 and 1871; Brès received her degree with a dissertation on breast feeding in 1875. But women were denied the right to become interns, and thus complete their education.

In 1881 a deterimined woman named Blanche Edwards mounted a veritable campaign to be allowed to take the internship examinations. When she and another woman were finally given the tests and passed them, they were still barred from the hospitals. Their opponents claimed, among other things, that women were not strong enough to set hip bones and that male patients would be upset by female doctors. Doctors and interns signed petitions against allowing women to practice in hospitals. When the Municipal Council of Paris ordered that internship be opened to women in 1885, men demonstrated before City Hall, shouting "Down with Blanche"; when she passed the internship examination, she was burned in effigy at the interns' hall.

The medical profession in France was now open to women. Edwards married a doctor and at his death replaced him in the Chair of Physiology at Loriboisière Medical School. But women tended to confine themselves to women and children patients. It continued to be difficult for them to do their internship in hospitals. In 1928 women medical students were less than 20 percent of the total. In all France there were only 519 woman doctors in 1929, over half in Paris.

In Spain it was much worse. The first woman medical student, Pilar Tauregui, had stones thrown at her in class in 1881. Medical practice by women in Spain remained confined to women and children, and to some extent, opthalmology. In Italy, women were never completely barred from medicine, but few practiced it. After the Reformation there is no reference to women doctors until the mid-eighteenth century, when a handful of women, including a mother and daughter, Florence and Zaffira Petraccini, received medical degrees at Bologna. In the early nineteenth century one Maria della Donna still held the Chair of Obstetrics there. But reaction against educated women set in and continued through the century. In 1929 there were only 350 women doctors in Italy.

The attitude toward women's careers in Germany slowed the entrance of women into the medical profession. Some went to Switzerland to study, but were not allowed full freedom to practice medicine in Germany until 1899. After World War I, the new Weimar Republic declared equal rights for women, giving them access to the professions. By 1929 there were 2,231 women doctors, most of them with German degrees. There were even four women teaching medical subjects, although not as regular professors. By contrast, Zurich, which had given the first medical degrees to foreign women as early as 1867, treated native women in medicine as most other European countries. In 1928 there were practically no women doctors in Switzerland.

It was Russian women who opened the doors at Zurich; they were to take the lead in Europe in opening the profession to women, and to attain the greatest success in their field.

In Russia women's position in midwifery had never declined as it had in Western Europe. Women were also allowed to study and practice dentistry in the early nineteenth century. In 1861, with women as auditors in all faculties of Russian universities (See Chapter VII), the Medical Council agreed agreed to accept women as full students. In the reaction following university rioting, the women were barred from medical faculties in 1864. At this time there were over sixty female students in the St. Petersburg Medico-Surgical Academy alone.

Most of the women went abroad to complete their training. N. P. Souslova was the first woman to receive the doctorate of medicine, at Zurich in 1868. From this point on Russian women predominated in the medical schools of Europe. They were serious students, and more acceptable in the universities of France, Germany, and Switzerland than women native to those countries.

Meanwhile, the Russian government was worried that their students might acquire radical ideas in foreign universities. A number of plans for women's medical training were suggested and turned down in the late 1860s, but it was decided to add courses to the midwives' school in St. Petersburg. Finally in 1872 the higher medical degree was opened to women. They could become doctors, with the understanding that they would only practice on women and children. Women with a secondary school education would take the four-year program at the Medico-Surgical Academy, but completely separate from male students. They were forbidden to talk to the men and use the library. Ninety women out of the 106 who applied passed the entrance examination.

As in other areas of Russian higher education, it was the professors who championed the women's cause. They taught women complete courses and donated books, along with other interested citizens, to make up for lack of library facilities. The four-year course was extended to five; in the fifth year the women, like the men, received clinical and hospital experience.

In 1877, fifth-year medical students volunteered to serve in the Turkish War, over two dozen of them women. Both sexes worked in the front lines, performing the same duties. Those who survived received medals and returned to pass their medical examinations successfully. But instead of a diploma, the women received a certificate allowing them to treat only women and children.

But the need for doctors was so great in Russia that the district councils pressed the government for full certification for women. In 1880 the government relented, giving them the title of Women Doctors. As such, they were able to employ their skills in the outlying area of the Russian Empire, leaving the lucrative cities to men.

Three years later women doctors were finally placed on the official list of physicians entitled to treat all patients everywhere.

Medical education for women came to an abrupt halt in 1882, after the assassination of Alexander II. Medical training was under the control of the Ministry of War, from which women were now banned. All attempts failed to transfer the women's program to the Department of Education or the Interior. Women's medical education was confined to the midwives' school, and the female doctors already trained, almost a thousand, were restricted to posts in girls' schools and convents.

Yet the desire and need for doctors was a constant spur to the government. A committee established to lay out a program for midwifery training came up with a broad, five-year medical course, which received government approval in 1891, on the condition that it be privately supported. Even after money was collected there was a last-minute effort in the Council of State to require Greek as well as Latin for entrance. Since this was not required for male medical school candidates, it was voted down. The Medical Institute for Women was founded in St. Petersburg in 1897. The following year it admitted 118 out of 390 applicants. Each year fewer than half of those who applied were admitted. By 1903, there were 1,392 students, 226 of them on scholarship from district councils, public organizations, and the Institute itself. The government took over the school in 1904, lowering the fees and awarding women the title of Doctor after they passed a state examination.

After this, medical schools for women proliferated in Russia, either as additions to regular higher education or as separate schools. Moscow, St. Petersburg, and Kharkov had two each, Odessa and Yuriev (Estonia) one each. In Tomsk (Siberia), women were allowed into the medical school for men. In 1930, women made up 57.3 percent of the medical students in the U.S.S.R. Nor did Russian women find any difficulty in practicing medicine, the need for trained people was so great. Civil service medical posts were opened to them in 1898.

The story of medical education for women in Russia is one of conflict between the desire of a traditional society to keep women in their place and the need of a backward nation to bring its people's health care to a respectable standard. Trained women were willing to work in the villages, where the need was great. This solution was recognized first by the progressives, and then unwillingly by the government, which finally gave in and made Russia the country with more trained women doctors than any other. By the 1960s there were more women doctors in Russia than in all the rest of the world.

In other countries, even the need produced by two World Wars did not further opportunities for women in medicine. During the First World War, the English War Office refused the help of women doctors, some of whom went to France independently and formed the Women's Hospital Corps. In 1939 the Medical Women's Federation again contacted the War Office; the answer was much the same as twenty years before. As male doctors went to war, women were used on the home front, but were never fully recognized. In 1944 the Goodenough Report at last recommended that British women doctors be educated along with men, so as to obtain equal training and clinical experience.

At midcentury, England, the United States, and Italy had about the same number of women doctors (2,434 to 2,480), but while these women were about 10 percent of Italian doctors and about 19 percent of English doctors, they were only 8 percent of American doctors. Except for Spain's 3 percent, America's is the worst record of any sizeable country in the world. In 1950 in France and Germany women made up over 21 percent and over 25 percent of the profession, respectively. The Soviet Union continues to lead the great nations in the number and percentage of women doctors—72 percent in 1973. In the 1960s, however, women made up only 56 percent of the medical students, which indicates a move toward a more ideal equality of the sexes in the field.

In the West in general, women are still expected to become nurses and take orders from male physicians. The doctor is an authority figure and professional of great prestige, and most women as well as men prefer a male doctor. Modern women have a long way to go before they recover for themselves an area of life once considered natural to their sex.

CHAPTER IX

Limited Victory: the Twentieth Century

Although the year 1900 was hailed throughout the world with
great enthusiasm, it slipped by, like the thirteen years after it, without bringing great changes to the nineteenth-century view of life. By
that time women had gained entrance to almost all levels of education in the West. Primary education had almost eliminated illiteracy
in the United States, Britain, and Germany; in France and Italy better enforcement was to bring the same results during the new century. Russia was still predominantly illiterate. The United States had
been most effective in offering a high school education to girls, and a
similar type of education was available to them in British, French,
and German higher primary schools.

But European secondary education that prepared students for the
university was still largely confined to the upper classes who could
pay for it, and the curriculum often had to be supplemented by private lessons for university entrance. Only a small proportion of Russian and Italian girls received secondary education, even smaller
than the proportion of boys. As a result, few European women were
enrolled in universities as compared to the United States, where
high school opened the way to higher education.

The unfinished business in women's education was, then, primary and secondary education for all in Russia; equal access to good secondary education for girls in England, France, Germany, and Italy; and equal access to higher education for women in all Western countries.

Since 1900 the rate and variety of change has been so great that our world appears wholly different from the world at that time. For women, particularly in the West, there have been great advances. Almost every profession and vocation is now practiced by some women in the Western world. Yet the process of change has been less complete for women than it has been for men. Their participation in the wider world has been limited by the traditional view—often retained by men and women alike—of women as homemakers and mothers only, and also by the lack, until very recently, of a sure method of birth control. Thus women have tended to be slow to take advantage of the possibilities open to them.

As we have seen, women's roles are subject to the social pressures, economic needs, and ideology of the society in which they live. The great events of the twentieth century—World War I, the rise of fascism and communism, the Second World War, mass production—have all affected women's opportunities in education. This chapter will indicate some of the results for women's education, and point out the distance women have yet to go.

WORLD WAR I AND AFTERMATH

It is now generally agreed that the twentieth century, as we know it, did not begin before the Great War of 1914 to 1918. (Of course, its effects were felt more in Euope than in the United States, where one might say the twentieth century began with Henry Ford and mass production, but this did not affect women's lives until much later.) One of the by-products of this war, as of every war, was that women took the jobs of men who served at the front. In Britain, where women comprised 24 percent of all employees in July, 1914, they were 37 percent in July, 1918, with the percentage in local government and commerce going as high as 52 and 53 percent respectively. In France women workers increased most in the metal industries, administration, and transport. Even the number of female construction workers and miners tripled. This happened to a greater or smaller extent in all the countries involved in the war.

However, by 1920 the number of working women had dropped almost to prewar levels in most countries. Women's visibility in time of crisis had probably made some contribution to their campaign for the vote; by 1923 the United States, England, and Germany had granted women suffrage. But perhaps more important for the development of women's education, the war had killed a large part of a whole generation of men. One of the nineteenth-century arguments for careers for women—that unmarried women needed a means of support—was yet more cogent in the aftermath of the carnage.

This imbalance was particularly severe in France and Russia, which suffered the greatest loss of manpower. France lost fewer men than Germany during the war; but because her birth rate declined throughout the nineteenth century she faced Germany's 7.7 million men of military age with only 4.5 million, of which she lost 1½ million. Russia lost three million during the war, and more in the civil war that followed.

In France, where women had pushed for reform of girls' secondary education before the war, a commission of thirty-eight members, six of them women, began discussions on the matter in 1917. At first the traditional distinctive feminine education won out; the commission did not propose a public education for girls leading to the baccalaureate required for all professions. But in the midtwenties the door was finally opened by ministerial decree: over a six-year period, secondary schools for girls would introduce a program leading to a degree equivalent to that of boys' schools. By 1930 the full program was available and most girls chose it over the old, feminine program. During the 30s the class distinction between primary and secondary education was blurred, at least, by making secondary schools free and accessible to bright primary school students. As a result, exceptional women of all classes had a chance at the baccalaureate, the liberal professions, and administrative posts.

Careers for women, however, were thought likely to lower the birth rate. The economist Charles Gide saw a conflict between feminism and the birth rate, constituting a grave national danger. The only consolation was that "all the other nations will also undergo it more or less."[1] But this was small comfort for France, whose population growth had been the lowest in Europe for many decades. As it turned out, marriage and children remained the prime consideration for French women until after midcentury. A career was a last resort, a substitute for the desired traditional role in a society where men were in short supply.

Nevertheless, women accounted for just under half the students at the Faculty of Letters in Paris in 1929, and two-thirds of these were French. Although that year women took only 20 percent of the secondary education degrees, they were taking advantage of the new programs. Most were enrolled in the Faculty of Letters, fewer in Sciences, and very few in Law—less than one-eighth of all Paris law students.

The first higher education degree in France is the *licence*. By 1929, 1,506 women had obtained the French *licence* in letters, 1,026 in sciences, 991 in law. There are also two doctoral degrees, one a state and the other a university degree. The state degree corresponds to an American Ph.D. By 1929, only sixty-five women had received the degree in science, ninety in law. These two doctorates had been opened to women in 1888 and 1890, respectively. The last bastion was the doctorate of letters. Not until 1914 was it opened to women; from then until 1929, only twenty-three were awarded in Paris and a few in the provinces.

For the French, equality in letters represented intellectual parity between women and men—and it was only in 1927 that women were allowed to enroll as day students at the elite Ecole Normale supérieure, which had produced a century of France's intellectual and political leaders. It was ironic but inevitable that, soon after women managed to storm the heights of the Ecole Normale supérieure, it lost its position as the source of France's leadership to other, more modern schools. But in 1930 it did not seem inevitable. Gustave Cohen, professor at the Sorbonne, called the invasion of the Faculty of Letters the great revolution of his time: "At first they were a third, then half, then two-thirds [of the students], to the point where one asked oneself nervously if, having once been our mistresses, they were not about to become our masters."[2]

Certainly Professor Cohen was unnecessarily concerned. In that year there were only two women professors of letters in all France, neither of them in Paris, plus one in law, one in medicine, and two in science, including Curie. Women were allowed into the Ecole libre des Sciences politiques, which trains the administrative elite, after World War I, but they did not thereby get to fill top government positions, as male graduates did. In 1926, the number of women studying at universities in France was 12,000, as opposed to 291,000 in United States colleges and universities. Many of these women had no chance of leading the accepted housewifely existence in a country decimated by war. No "revolution" was occurring in France; the traditional female goals, modified by circumstance, still applied.

In Russia, on the other hand, tradition was overthrown by revolution in 1917; by 1920 there was also a 4 million surplus of women. The communist government decreed equality of the sexes. Because of the disastrous economic situation, the Soviet Union was unable to carry out changes immediately, in education or in any other area; but its aims in education were similar to those of Germany in the nineteenth century: education for citizenship in a new national society (the New Soviet Man) and education for technological and industrial growth. The first step was stamping out illiteracy, which was almost completed by 1934. Then the government inaugurated a system of universal primary education for both sexes. Such a system is always advantageous to girls. Plans for universal secondary education were announced in 1936; these did not mature, however, until after World War II.

Russia's serious economic condition was such that all were required to work, and in urban centers at least, this tended to buttress equality between the sexes. In rural areas traditional attitudes toward women persisted; and since the New Soviet Woman failed to provide the birth rate Stalin considered necessary, traditional attitudes toward marriage and motherhood returned. Soviet women were not to come into their own until after World War II. But, following communist ideology, the Soviet Union was the first nation to aim for complete equality of the sexes at all levels of education.

In Germany also the war brought down the old autocracy. Not communism, but Germany's first democratic government, led by socialists, replaced the old empire. Article 128 of the new Weimar constitution declared that women were equal under the law. By 1925 one-third of the white-collar workers were women, mostly unmarried. Through the 20s women made progress in schooling and employment, except when the Centre (Catholic) Party was in control. There was still prejudice against women in universities and as senior civil servants. By 1928 women constituted 10.4 percent of German university students. But there were only two regular woman professors and eighteen acting professors in the country.

The Depression brought a real effort to return women to the home. As male unemployment mounted, the first moves were made against working married women. Employment agencies discriminated against them by government order; women were dismissed from civil service posts. They were discouraged from seeking higher or professional education. It was not the Nazi takeover, but the Depression that preceded it, that initiated reaction in German women's education.

Nazi ideology stressed breeding—of the approved racial strain, of course—as the basis of world conquest. It called the family "the germ cell of the nation." After war and Depression, the German birth rate had fallen; the Nazis assigned high priority to raising it. So they adopted the traditional view that women were essentially different from men—subjective, emotional, and sentimental, as opposed to objective, creative, and rational. They believed that if women worked at all, they should perform only characteristically feminine roles in the society—"helping, healing, and teaching."

Although the worst of the Depression was over when the Nazis took control, they immediately instituted a program of marriage loans, child subsidies, and family allowances to encourage women to motherhood. In November 1933, 122 women, induced by government marriage loans and company bonuses to give up their jobs, were married at the Reemtsma cigarette factory in a combined wedding ceremony. Each child resulting from a marriage of this kind reduced by one quarter the loan that had to be repaid. Four children or more entitled a family to family allowances based on the number of children. On each August 12 (Hitler's mother's birthday) the Honor Cross of German Motherhood was awarded to particularly fertile women—bronze, silver, and gold, for over four, over six, and over eight children.

This program naturally affected women's schooling. Hitler announced: "Future motherhood is to be the definite aim of female education."[3] Women were to be freed from the unsuitable "masculine" elements of education—by which he meant the intellectual. Nazi pedagogues attacked coeducation under the Weimar Republic, and announced sharp reductions in the academic content of girls' school curricula. German history and culture were to be emphasized, and practical subjects benefiting health, physical education, and family life. (To be fair, one must admit that Nazi anti-intellectualism and belief in the practical affected boys' schooling also, in a somewhat different way. Secondary schooling for both sexes was shortened by a year—first for boys, because of conscription, and then for girls.) Girls' schools devoted to domestic science were expanded; proficiency in needlework was required in all secondary schools. Mathematics and foreign language courses were reduced. The only science that survived and flourished was biology, otherwise known as racial science. A campaign against private schools, which might not be ideologically pure, affected girls' education more than boys'.

On the university level, the Nazis took advantage of traditional prejudice against professional women. Encouragement of higher education for women was labeled "Jewish intellectual" and "liberal-democratic Marxist." During the Depression an academic proletariat had emerged: university graduates unable to find jobs. Male students blamed women, who constituted less than 19 percent of the total student body, arguing that they lowered academic standards and destroyed student fraternity. Women, they insisted, should not be allowed to matriculate; they should confine themselves to their "characteristic occupations."

Women fought back. But by 1933 their arguments were modified by party-line affirmations that motherhood was of course a woman's natural calling. The first limitations on university entrance, in 1933, were aimed only at non-Aryans, but eventually a women's quota of 10 percent was imposed. Thus the early 30s continued the Depression policy of returning women to the home. As Germany became more aggressive, however, economic needs conflicted with ideology; women were encouraged to educate themselves to take men's place on the home front.

The result was confusion in policy toward women's education. Because of the changing needs of the nation, the quota on women in universities was not rigorously enforced. The small generation born during the First War came of age in the midthirties, conscription began, and the proportion of women in the universities rose to 17 percent. Ironically, a surplus of teachers, resulting from the lowered school population, caused the Prussian government to bar all women from teachers' colleges in the 1936 fall semester.

The balance was reversed in 1939, when virtually all male teachers were inducted. New teacher training colleges for women were opened. In one year the percentage of women in these colleges jumped from 12 percent to 88 percent. For lack of male students, the government encouraged women to pursue regular university studies—particularly in mathematics and science, which had previously been considered improper for them. In medicine women constituted 20 percent of the students; in pharmacy, 52 percent. Whereas women were about 7 percent of all other science students in 1937, in 1940 they were 14 percent in chemistry, 17 percent in mathematics and physics. Although there was an acute shortage of law students, Hitler's refusal to allow women into the courts kept the number of women in that field low.

On the secondary level a similar relaxation of ideology took place. The Nazis failed to eliminate coeducation. Although they established a national educational system with different curricula for the two sexes in 1938, girls could in effect acquire a superior secondary education by attending coeducational schools, if they wished. The need for educated people was so great that, with the men away at war, the government pursued its ideological goals for women only halfheartedly. One might even say that the Nazi ideology of expansion by war vitiated their ideology of the domestication of women and expanded women's educational opportunities.

In Italy, the other fascist state, women were less fortunate. Unlike Germany, Italy did not undergo a period of liberalism after the war. In 1922 Mussolini and his followers took over the government. Mussolini believed that "women are inferior to men, but they are courageous."[4] Women's sole creativity was procreation. They were to have no part in public life, except to serve as an amusement for great men like himself.

For different reasons, the Church agreed that woman's place was in the home, and so when Mussolini settled the old Church-State problem through a Concordat with Pope Pius XI in 1929, the traditional view of women was doubly enforced in Italy. As in other European nations, unmarried Italian women worked until the Depression, when they were forced out of jobs in favor of men. But Italian women were declared totally unfit even for teaching positions, since they had peaceful natures which might impede fascist consciousness in their students; eventually they were dismissed from all government jobs. Mussolini too aimed to increase the birth rate by subsidizing large families, even though Italy could not support an increase in population.

While making sure that boys were educated in good fascist schools, Mussolini was content to leave women in the hands of the Church, which followed its traditional education of girls for piety. Thus it was more difficult for Italian women than for German to seize the opportunity afforded by the loss of manpower in wartime. In the 30s Portugal and Spain established fascist governments supported by the Church. (The survival of these regimes until the 70s put the women of these countries far behind the rest of Europe.) In 1931, 23 percent of Italians over fifteen years of age could not read; in 1940, 24 percent of Spaniards over fifteen could not read and write. It is reasonable to believe that most of these illiterates were women. In 1939, on the other hand, the Soviet Union reported only 19 percent illiteracy in the population over nine years of age.

England continued to lag behind France and Germany in women's education—mainly because the class system continued to bar most children from secondary schools. During the First War an act had been passed providing for more public high schools and raising the age limit for compulsory schooling, but postwar Depression cut the funds available for education, and the law was not enforced. Secondary school fees were raised, and teachers' salaries reduced. In 1936 compulsory schooling until age fifteen was enacted by Parliament; but this was not implemented until after World War II.

Scholarships for poor children in secondary schools preparing for university entrance were multiplied until there was only a minority paying fees in 1939, but places in these schools were limited and there were fewer places for girls than for boys. In the private schools subsidized by the government, only 25 percent of the places were reserved for girls under the Education Act of 1921. In 1931, despite a higher school-age population of girls than of boys, there were 249,303 boys and only 226,628 girls in all English secondary schools.

The assumption that few of the lower-class children, and even fewer girls than boys, would go on to the university was built into the system. The locally supported secondary schools, comparable to United States high schools, emphasized practical subjects for both sexes, particularly domestic science for girls. One hundred fifty boys' schools offered advanced programs in science, mathematics, and classics, as opposed to only twenty-seven girls' schools. Only in modern languages did girls' schools have more advanced courses than boys' (ninety-seven versus sixty).

The assumption thus became a self-fulfilling prophecy. Although more girls passed the first school examination taken at age sixteen, fewer girls than boys passed the second school examination taken at age eighteen. (The first school examination ends an English secondary education equivalent to our high school. The two years from sixteen to eighteen end with the second school examination, roughly equivalent to the baccalaureate of the French *lycée* or the associate's degree of an American college.) There were far fewer English women in higher education than men. University women were viewed as bluestockings. If they had male friends, it was assumed they were not serious about their studies; if they did not, they were considered unmarriageable.

In the United States, unlike most European countries, class education was confined to a small number of private schools. Secondary education in the extensive network of public high schools was designed to be free and universal, supported by local taxation. Movement from primary to secondary education was automatic; from the turn of the century, there were more girls in secondary education than boys, even though some southern states did not have compulsory primary education laws and few states had laws forbidding school-age children to work. (In 1976, the state of Mississippi still had no compulsory education law at all. Florida and California were considering revision of their laws to allow children to leave school before the ages of sixteen and eighteen.) The predominance of women teachers in secondary schools was also unique to the United States—138,761 in 1930 to 74,530 men teachers.

The early twentieth century was a time of growth for American women's higher education also. Although some of the state universities in the South delayed admitting women, the number and percentage of women in colleges and universities increased through the century until World War II. In 1900, they received 17 percent of all advanced degrees; in 1910, 23 percent; in 1920, 34 percent; in 1930, 40 percent; in 1940, 41 percent. Growth was partly due to equal secondary education for both sexes and partly to the impetus toward equal opportunity provided by the woman's suffrage amendment. The 1920s was the decade of greatest increase for American women in higher education; it has not been equalled since. The previous decade saw the greatest increase in women college and university teachers. From 1910 to 1920 women faculty members increased from 20 percent to 26 percent. By the outbreak of World War II they had increased to only 27 percent, a percentage they have never attained since.

The growth of American women's educational opportunities was partly owing to the society's relative freedom from postwar trauma. French women were encouraged to tend the family hearth and arrest the decline in population resulting from European war since 1870; German and Italian women were exhorted to produce cannon-fodder for new wars of expansion; even the Soviet Union, where sexual equality was part of communist ideology, began to encourage motherhood as the population fell off and war seemed imminent in the 30s. For the United States, the loss of manpower in World War I was not serious, and the country was determined never to be involved in another European war. It was after the Second World War that the ideology of the family was to affect American women's opportunities for education and professional status.

MIDCENTURY AND AFTER

World War II had catastrophic effects on the nations of Europe. All the results of previous wars were intensified in magnitude and severity. As men marched off to war, women took their place in unprecedented numbers, in farming, factory work, and administration, and in the declining colleges and universities. War brought destruction on a large scale to virtually every European country, and tremendous depopulation and social dislocation to most of them. It left behind a sense of horror and an urge to return to traditional values exemplified by family life—a desire shared by the United States.

The immediate postwar period and most of the 50s were devoted to the ideology of the family—"togetherness," as it was called in the United States, where young couples all wanted large families. All the forces in society supported this trend. In France, family allowances were raised and political leaders exhorted citizens to repopulate the nation. In the United States, communities erected elaborate schools for a child-centered society. Motherhood was exalted. Women might have taken men's roles during the war, but now the men were back to take care of them and provide for the families they would raise.

There were cogent social reasons behind the move to put women back in the home. The desire to repopulate decimated countries was only secondary. The main purpose was to make room for men, not only in the job market, but also in the universities. The *New York Times* reported in 1946 that returning veterans, who had priority in college admissions, were making it difficult for women to enter college at all. During the war, large numbers of women had taken the places left by men; fraternity houses had been converted to women's dormitories. This was all over. Now that the men were back, there were no dormitories for women. Using this excuse, colleges were turning away female applicants. Marshall College took six men to every woman; Marietta took 16 women and 263 men; Colby took no women at all.

There were some countertrends in Europe to compensate for the family ideology. First of all, the very real decrease in population made careers for women important, just to keep society operating. In France and Germany, women were given the vote and elected to office after the war. Second, in most European countries education at all levels became open to all classes without fee. Women of all classes did not immediately take advantage of these opportunities. At midcentury, for instance, there were still over twice as many boys as there were girls in secondary schools in all the countries of western Europe. In 1964, however, girls constituted over 40 percent of secondary school pupils in all western European countries except Austria (39 percent). In eastern Europe they were over 50 percent, 65 percent in Poland. Ironically, there was at the same time a residue of illiteracy in Europe, mostly female. In the midsixties there was still a rate of 30 percent female, versus 8.3 percent male illiteracy in Greece; in Spain, 17.7 percent versus 8.4 percent; in Yugoslavia, 33.6 percent versus 12.4 percent. The female illiteracy in Portugal was 44.6 percent.

In the twentieth century a good indicator of the progress of women's education is a country-by-country comparison of the percentage of women students in higher education. UNESCO's *World Survey of Education*, published just after midcentury, gives the most complete comparative figures available for this time. Unfortunately the survey does not give statistics for the Iron Curtain countries; the situation in the West was as follows:

Country		Total Students	Female	Students
France	university	137,332	47,911	(34.89%)
(1952)	higher teacher ed.	1,259	359	
	lower teacher ed.	16,167	8,714	
Italy	university	145,710	38,208	(26.32%)
(1951)	art & music acad.	5,687	2,660	
	teacher ed.	70,463	59,580	
England & Wales				
(1952)	university	68,447	15,626	(22.83%)
	teacher ed.	26,400	19,541	
West Germany				
(1951)	university	113,294	19,805	(17.48%)
	teacher ed.	11,386	5,184	
Spain	university	50,303	7,314	(14.54%)
(1949)	teacher ed.	19,942	14,329	
United States				
(1950)	all higher ed.	2,659,021	805,953	

The most notable aspect of these statistics is the much higher proportion of women in the teachers' colleges than in regular universities. The United States figures in the survey include those for teachers' colleges as well as for business, nursing, and fine arts colleges. If the figures for each country are added together, the comparative percentages of women in higher education at midcentury were:

Italy–45.39%
England & Wales–37.08%
France–36.82%
Spain–30.81%
United States–30.31%
West Germany–20.04%

Since the European countries, except Spain, were still in the process of rebuilding their educational systems, the United States position on the scale is striking. Because the first two years of college in this country would be considered secondary education in Europe, and as fewer women than men go beyond this level, true comparative percentages would be even worse.

These figures reflect fairly accurately the decline of American women's higher education at midcentury. In 1940, women received 41 percent of all higher degrees; in 1950, they received 24 percent. Although the figures have risen since then they had not, even in the burgeoning of higher education, returned to their prewar percentage by 1970, when women received 40 percent of the degrees.

The latest comparative statistics on higher education were gathered by UNESCO in the years 1972 to 1974. They are not broken down into university and teachers' college students, but they do include European communist countries, all of which show roughly the same proportion of women as East Germany.

Country	Total Students	Female	Students
U.S.S.R. (1973)	4,671,000	2,339,000	(50%)
East Germany (1974)	325,113	156,913	(48.26%)
West Germany (1973)	729,207	not available*	
France (1973)	737,207	344,585	(46.7%)
U.S.A. (1973)	9,602,123	4,231,071	(44.06%)
Italy (1973)	846,897	331,742	(39.17%)
England & Wales (1972)	538,469	182,737	(33.93%)

*In 1965, excluding teachers' colleges, West German women made up 24 percent of the university student body.

The figures bear out the theory that neither industrialization nor democratization is the determining factor for women's education. Population trends and ideology are more important. On both these counts France and the communist countries of Europe provide good examples. In both areas the need for womanpower at all levels of an underpopulated society has dictated that government equalize educational opportunities for women. Communist ideology has prescribed sexual equality from the beginning. But France, of the Western nations, proves that an egalitarian ideology in education need not be communist. French women, as we have seen, have a tradition of interest in education, and in this area at least, the egalitarian ideals of the Enlightenment, as expressed by Condorcet, are winning out. Few French women go into careers other than teaching. They make up 75 percent of the teachers in primary schools, 66 percent in the ordinary secondary schools, 54 percent in the prestigious lycées, and 24 percent in the universities. But until recently French women held more administrative posts in government than American women.

Of course, French woman professors tend to be concentrated in the lower academic ranks. But they are better off than their counterparts in the United States. Although American women received 41.5 percent of all bachelor's degrees and 39.7 percent of all master's degrees in 1970, they obtained only 13.3 percent of the Ph.Ds. Not only that, but they have also lost out in college and university faculties. From a high of 27 percent in 1940, they fell to 24 percent in 1950 and reached a low of 22 percent in 1960 and 1970. Not since the 1920s has the proportion of American women in academe been so low.

In the Soviet Union, where a much smaller percentage of women obtain the Ph.D. degree, women hold 52 percent of the faculty posts in higher education. On the undergraduate level, fewer Russian women drop out than American. Of the population under the age of thirty, women make up 60 percent of the college graduates.

What can one conclude from the experience of the twentieth century about the conditions under which women have the greatest educational opportunities? It seems that women do well in an ideologically egalitarian society, where access to all levels of education is automatic for all classes and both sexes. The Soviet Union, other communist nations, and France fit this category best, with the United States, still ideologically weak on sexual equality, trailing behind. Of the Western nations, England is weakest in equal access to education for all classes; this has affected sexual equality in education.

Another factor that has promoted women's opportunities is a national educational system, which serves to counteract inequalities in the society. As the governments of Continental Europe have expanded their educational systems to include all classes, they have provided education at all levels to increasing numbers of women, wherever sexual equality is a stated objective (France, Germany, Italy, Russia). University education is free and available to all who qualify for it. The professional schools—law, medicine, pharmacy, and administration—are included within the national systems. (Standing in Party circles influences university entrance behind the Iron Curtain, but this affects men and women equally.)

It may be argued, and has been argued in other connections, that governments have no business legislating an equality that the society itself does not desire. There are two answers to this: First, one of the objectives of every society should be justice, and governments should lead, not follow, in matters of justice. Second, a national education system can only prescribe equality of opportunity. Statistics from Italy show that where social custom is strongly against it, the opportunity will not be fully utilized.

In the United States, state universities have performed a role in equalizing higher education of the sexes similar to that of national universities in Europe, although they are not without cost to families. Since World War II the expansion of truly coeducational universities in England has done likewise. But in both countries women have long been discriminated against in the elite private universities. In England, the women's colleges in Oxford and Cambridge are far fewer than the men's colleges. In the United States, until the recent equal rights laws, women were discriminated against at all levels of private higher education, by an unwritten "gentleman's agreement." This was particularly true of the graduate faculties. Harvard Law School denied entrance to women until 1950. In 1968 to 1969 men received 96 percent of all medical, law, and theology degrees. As recently as 1972, although female undergraduates averaged higher grades than male, the average scholarship or loan for them was $518, as against $760 for men, and only a minority gained admittance to graduate schools.

Government action, including the threat to withdraw subsidies for special programs, has improved the situation somewhat. But enforcement has often been less than enthusiastic. It is clear that, in the absence of a system of education controlled by the government, some other type of national commitment to equality in higher education for women is important.

A libertarian tradition has interfered with women's opportunities in the United States and England, where governments are reluctant to interfere with the admissions policies of older, private educational institutions. There has been no attempt by the British government to equalize the number of places for women at Oxford and Cambridge, nor by the United States government at Princeton and Yale. Admission to these institutions directly influences careers and status. In the United States, education has become a big business since World War II. When the male clientele dwindles, as in war or depression, women are welcome; the recent attempt of Columbia University to swallow its sister college, Barnard, is an example. When men are flocking to universities, informal quotas are set on female students. Moreover, the cost of college education for families tends to eliminate some women to begin with, by family decision. Free, public education at all levels, in a context of sexual equality, seems to provide the ideal situation for women.

Now that women are obtaining higher education in large numbers throughout the industrialized world, it may be pertinent to ask: does equal education mean equal status for women, as nineteenth-century reformers believed? It is not clear that it does. In the Soviet Union, where 72 percent of the physicians are women, the prestige of the medical profession ranks below engineering. In the United States only 9 percent of the physicians are women (less than any country except Spain, Madagascar, and Viet Nam), and medical practice still carries high prestige. This situation follows the pattern set by the teaching profession, and has prompted much debate. Does the entry of women into a field in large numbers cause that field to lose prestige, or is it rather that, as a profession loses prestige women are allowed into it in large numbers? At present the answer can be only a matter of opinion. All we know is that, at all occupational levels, "women's work" has lower status than jobs filled mostly by men.

It is often argued that in the United States status is primarily related to salary. The same pattern noted concerning status emerges with regard to salary. A spokesman for Columbia Teachers' College said in 1931: "The presence of such a large proportion of women in the teaching profession has a decided tendency to lower salaries."[5] A survey of faculty salaries in 1972 showed 62 percent of the women and 27.9 percent of the men receiving less than $10,000, while 1.7 percent of the women and 9.4 percent of the men received more than $20,000. Recent statistics show that women's salaries in all fields in the United States have declined in relation to men's. This is despite the fact that female high school graduates outnumber male high school graduates; in 1974, 40.76 percent of white women over twenty-five had completed high school, and 37.35 percent of white men.

The traditional excuse for differentials has been that men support families and women's salaries are only supplemental. This ignores the large number of households headed by females and the large number of single males. It also ignores simple justice. But the strongest barrier to either high salaries or high status for women is the view that women belong at home, not in the public arena, and that they are naturally, if not inferior, at least different from men and destined to do different things. This view, internalized by women in childhood, has to some extent prevented them from taking even the opportunities available to them. When they take the opportunities, it has hampered them, causing them to try filling the traditional role as well as the new one.

A recent UNESCO publication on women's education stresses the importance of the "climate of opinion." The main fear in under-developed nations where UNESCO worked to improve women's status was that "sending girls to school would disrupt the pattern of traditional life."[6] In some societies even literacy is feared, as it was in the Western world in the Middle Ages; in others, a general education is acceptable but employment is not, as for upper-class European women until very recently; where advanced education is deemed proper, girls are limited to suitable fields and low-status positions.

UNESCO tried to make education of women "relevant to the requirements of development as well as to the requirements of women in a specific context."[7] As such, their projects are reminiscent of Madame de Maintenon's attempt to renew the French aristocracy

and provide for poor noble girls at Saint-Cyr in the seventeenth century. They are a reminder that women's education, like all education, corresponds to the needs of society—as viewed by the people
(usually the men) who live in it. Women's education will come into
full flower when it is realized that a society benefits by developing
the capabilities of all its members. Women's status will be equal
with men's when society is so structured as to make use of all those
capabilities.

Notes

All translations, except where otherwise indicated, are by Phyllis Stock.

PREFACE

1. Jean La Bruyère, *Les Caractères*, 2 vols. (Paris, 1749), I,115.

INTRODUCTION

1. Plato, "Republic," *The Dialogues of Plato*, trans. by Benjamin Jowett (New York and London, 1892), III, 148.
2. Aristotle, *Generation of Animals*, trans. by A.L. Peck (Cambridge, 1943), IV,vi,459.
3. *Oeuvres de Galen*, ed. and trans. by Charles Daremberg (Paris, 1854), II, 101.
4. Aristotle, "Politics," *Introduction to Aristotle*, ed. by Richard McKeon (New York, 1947), p. 576.
5. Xenophon, *The Economist*, trans. by A. D. O. Wedderburn and W. Collingwood (London, 1876), I, 42ff.
6. Galatians 3:28.

CHAPTER I

1. Leon Battista Alberti, *The Family in Renaissance Florence*, trans. by Renee Neu Watkins (Columbia, 1969), pp. 207ff.

2. William Harrison Woodward, *Vittorino da Feltre and Other Humanist Educators* (New York, 1970), pp. 126ff.

3. Baldesar Castiglione, *The Book of the Courtier*, trans. by Charles Singleton (Garden City, 1959), p. 207.

4. *Ibid.*, pp. 210, 211.

5. Giovanni Michele Bruto, *The Necessarie, Fit and Convenient Education of a Young Gentlewoman* (London & Amsterdam, 1598), unpaged.

6. Mathilde Laigle, *Le Livre des Trois Vertus de Christine de Pisan et son milieu historique et littéraire* (Paris, 1912), p. 120.

7. Fernand Zamaron, *Louise Labé, dame de franchise* (Paris, 1968), pp. 199-201.

8. Foster Watson, *Vives and the Renascence Education of Women* (New York, 1912), p. 179.

9. William Harrison Woodward, *Desiderius Erasmus Concerning the Aims and Methods of Education* (New York, 1964), pp. 149ff.

10. Watson, *op. cit.*, pp. 54-56.

11. *Ibid.*, pp. 64-66.

12. *Ibid.*, p. 69.

13. *Ibid.*, p. 86.

14. *Ibid.*, p. 84.

15. *Ibid.*, pp. 205-06.

16. Roger Ascham, *Works* (London, 1865), p. 191.

17. Allison Heisch, "Queen Elizabeth I: Parliamentary Rhetoric and the Exercise of Power," *Signs* I (Autumn, 1975), p. 34.

CHAPTER II

1. Martin Luther, *An den Christlichen Adel deutscher Nation* (Stuttgart, 1960), p. 106.

2. Erich Dauzenroth, *Kleine Geschichte der Mädchenbildung* (Dusseldorf, 1971), p. 33.

3. Friedrich Eby, *Early Protestant Educators* (New York, 1931), p. 42.

4. *Ibid.*, pp. 204-205.

5. *Ibid.*, pp. 209, 224.

6. Dauzenroth, *op. cit.*, p. 37.

7. Charles Leonidas Robbins, *Teachers in Germany in the Sixteenth Century* (New York, 1912), pp. 50-51.

8. Helene Lange and Gertrud Bäumer, *Handbuch der Frauenbewegung* (Berlin, 1902), III, 36.

9. Foster Watson, *The Old Grammar Schools* (New York, 1967), pp. 166-67; *English Writers on Education, 1480-1603* (Gainesville, 1967), p. 503.

10. *Ibid.*, pp. 665-66.

11. Joan Simon, *Education and Society in Tudor England* (Cambridge, 1966), p. 161.

12. Dorothy Gardiner, *English Girlhood at School* (London, 1929), p. 302.

13. Gustave Fagniez, *La Femme et la société française dans la première moitié du XVIIe siècle* (Paris, 1929), p. 11.

CHAPTER III

1. Anne Marie de Schurman, *Question célèbre, s'il est nécessaire, ou non, que les filles soient scavantes* (Paris, 1646), pp. 7-8, 14-16, 32-34, 71.

2. Gardiner, *op. cit.*, pp. 242-45.

3. Nicholas de Malebranche, *La Recherche de la vérité, Oeuvres complètes* (Paris, 1874), III, 222-23.

4. Gustave Reynier, *La Femme au XVIIe siècle, ses ennemis et ses défenseurs* (Paris, 1929), pp. 253-54.

5. Michel de Pure, *La Prétieuse*, 2 vols. (Paris, 1938), II, 17-18.

6. Reynier, *op. cit.*, pp. 115-16.

7. Paul Rousselot, *Histoire de l'éducation des femmes en France*, 2 vols. (Paris, 1883), II, 218.

8. François Fénelon, *De l'Education des filles* (Paris, 1844), pp. 60-62, 64.

9. Emile Faguet, ed., *Madame de Maintenon institutrice* (Paris, 1885), p. xviii.

10. Rousselot, *op. cit.*, p. 45.

11. Madame de Maintenon, *Lettres et entretiens sur l'éducation des filles* (Paris, 1861), p.40.

12. *Ibid.*, pp. 401-12.

13. Rousselot, *op. cit.*, pp. 87-89.

14. Ada Radford Wallas, *Before the Bluestockings* (London, 1929), pp. 21-24.

15. *Ibid.*, pp. 29, 40, 44-45, 50.

16. Josephine Kamm, *Hope Deferred* (London, 1965), pp. 74-75.

17. Wallas, *op. cit.*, p. 129.

18. Kamm, *op. cit.*, pp. 102-03.

19. Walter S. Scott, *The Bluestocking Ladies* (London, 1947), pp. 15-16.

20. Gardiner, *op. cit.*, p. 440.

NOTES

21. Scott, *op. cit.*, p. 198.
22. *Ibid.*

CHAPTER IV

1. Jean-Jacques Rousseau, *Emile* (Paris, no date), p. 435.
2. *Ibid.*, p. 440.
3. *Ibid.*, p. 471.
4. Kamm, *op. cit.*, p. 123.
5. P. J. G. Cabanis, *Travail sur l'éducation publique* (Paris, 1791), pp. 35-39.
6. Octave Gréard, *L'Education des femmes par les femmes* (Paris, 1897), p. 42.
7. Comtesse de Miremont, *Traité de l'éducation des femmes et cours complet d'instruction*, 7 vols. (Paris, 1779-89), I, 45.
8. Madame de Puisieux, *Conseils à une amie* (Paris, 1755), p. 16.
9. Madame de Genlis, *Adèle et Théodore*, 3 vols. (Paris, 1782), I, 39.
10. Nicholas de Condorcet, "Sur l'instruction publique," *Oeuvres* (Paris, 1847-49), VII, 224.
11. Mary Wollstonecraft, *A Vindication of the Rights of Woman*, ed. Carol H. Poston (New York, 1975), p. 200.
12. Mary Wollstonecraft, *A Vindication of the Rights of Woman* (New York, 1792), p. 38.
13. *Ibid.*, p. 102.
14. *Ibid.*, p. 76.
15. *Ibid.*, pp. 47-48.
16. *Ibid.*, p. 49.
17. *Ibid.*, pp. 97, 149.
18. *Ibid.*, p. 156.
19. *Ibid.*, p. 159.
20. *Ibid.*, p. 183.
21. *Ibid.*, p. 157.
22. Eleanor Flexner, *Mary Wollstonecraft* (New York, 1973), p. 165.
23. *Pétition des femmes du tiers état au roi, ler janvier, 1789* in Bibliothèque historique de la ville de Paris I, no. 17.
24. Edmée Charrier, *L'Evolution intellectuelle féminine* (Paris, 1931), p. 68.
25. Madame de Campan, *De l'Education*, 2 vols. (Paris, 1824), I, 151.
26. Eleanor Flexner, *Century of Struggle* (New York, 1974), p. 16.
27. Mary P. Ryan, *Womanhood in America* (New York, 1975), p. 127.

CHAPTER V

1. René Samuel, "L'Ecole Charlotte à Berlin," *Enseignement secondaire des jeunes filles* Oct. 1882 p. 236.
2. Dauzenroth, *op. cit.*, p. 158.
3. Cynthia Whittaker, "The Education of Women in Tsarist Russia," unpubished paper p. 10. Translation by Whittaker. See also Nikolai Gogol, *Dead Souls*, trans. Stephen Graham (New York, 1915), p. 26.
4. Cynthia Whittaker, "The Women's Movement during the Reign of Alexander II," p. 11. Abstracted *Journal of Modern History*, June, 1976.
5. Sophie Satina, *Education of Women in Pre-Revolutionary Russia*, trans. Alexandra Poustchine (New York, 1966), p. 114.
6. Cynthia Whittaker, unpublished paper, *op. cit.*, p. 12.

CHAPTER VI

1. Madame J. Bachellery, *Lettre au citoyen Carnot sur l'éducation nationale des filles* (Paris, 1848), p. 2.
2. Louis Bauzon, ed., *La Loi Camille Sée, documents, rapports et discours* (Paris, 1881), p. 148.
3. Madame de Rémusat, *Essai sur l'éducation des filles* (Paris, 1903), pp. 3, 92.
4. Félix Dupanloup, *La Femme studieuse* (Paris, 1867), pp. 7, 185.
5. Bauzon, *op. cit.*, p. 148.
6. Mona Ozouf, *L'Ecole, L'Eglise et la République* (Paris, 1963), p. 99
7. *Ibid.*, p. 107.
8. Bauzon, *op. cit.*, p. 190.
9. "Les lycées des jeunes filles en Italie," *Enseignement secondaire des jeunes filles* I (July, 1882), p. 47.

CHAPTER VII

1. Yoshi Kasuya, *A Complete Study of the Secondary Education of Girls in England, Germany and the United States* (New York, 1933), p. 44.
2. Kamm, *op. cit.*, p. 211.
3. Lee Holcombe, *Victorian Ladies at Work* (Devon, 1973), p. 27.
4. Kamm, *op. cit.*, p. 250.
5. Flexner, *op. cit.*, pp. 24-25.

6. Thomas Woody, *A History of Women's Education in the United States*, 2 vols. (New York, 1925), I, 527.

7. *Ibid.*, 516.

8. *Ibid.*, II, 2.

9. *Ibid.*, 153.

CHAPTER VIII

1. Lucy Ridgely Seymer, *A General History of Nursing.* (London, 1954), p. 89.

CHAPTER IX

1. Charrier, *op. cit.*, p. 525.

2. *Ibid.*, p. 149.

3. Jill Stephenson, *Women in Nazi Society* (New York, 1975), p. 116.

4. *New York Times*, March 6, 1927.

5. *Ibid.*, August 23, 1931.

6. UNESCO, *Women, Education and Equality* (Paris, 1975), p. 74.

7. *Ibid.*, p. 84.

Bibliography

BOOKS

Abel, James F. and Norman J. Bond. *Illiteracy in the Several Countries of the World*. Washington, 1929.

Abensour, Léon. *Le Féminisme sous le règne de Louis-Philippe*. Paris, 1913.

————. *La Femme et le féminisme avant la Révolution*. Paris, 1923.

Alberti, Leon Battista. *The Family in Renaissance Florence*. Translated by Renée Neu Watkins. Columbia, S.C., 1969.

Andrews, Marion. *The Most Illustrious Ladies of the Italian Renaissance*. London, 1911.

Aratò, Amélie. *L'Enseignement secondaire des jeunes filles en Europe*. Brussels, 1934.

Arouet, François Marie. *Oeuvres complètes*. Paris, 1885.

Ascham, Roger. *Works*. London, 1865.

Bachellery, Madame de. *Lettre au citoyen Carnot sur l'éducation nationale des filles*. Paris, 1848.

Barnard, H.C. *The French Tradition in Education*. Cambridge, 1922.

Barnard, Henry. *National Education in Europe*. New York, 1854.

Bauzon, Louis, ed. *Le Loi Camille Sée, documents, rapports et discours*. Paris, 1881.

Brantôme, Pierre de Bourdeille. *Vie des Dames illustres*. Paris, 1920.

Bibliothèque historique de la ville de Paris. *Recueil sur des Femmes*. 2 vols. #12807.

————. *Règlement de la Société patriotique et de bienfaisance des Amis de la*

Vérité pour l'établissement de quatre maisons déstinées à l'éducation des jeunes filles.

Bruto, Giovanni Michele Bruto. *The Necessarie, Fit and Convenient Education of a Young Gentlewoman.* London, 1598.

Board of Education, Great Britian. *Education in Germany.* London, 1902.

Bremner, C.S. *Education of Girls and Women in Great Britain.* London, 1897.

Buisson, Ferdinand. *Dictionnaire pédagogique.* Paris, 1911.

Bullough, Vern. *The Subordinate Sex.* New York, 1974.

Cabanis, P.J.G. *Travail sur l'éducation publique.* Paris, 1791.

Castiglione, Baldesar. *The Book of the Courtier.* Translated by Charles Singleton. New York, 1959.

Chamberlin, Frederick Carleton. *The Private Character of Queen Elizabeth.* London, 1921.

Charrier, Edmée. *L'Evolution intellectuelle féminine.* Paris, 1931.

Comenius, John Amos. *The Great Didactic.* Translated by M.W. Keatinge. New York, 1967.

Compayré, Gabriel. *Histoire critique des doctrines de l'éducation en France.* Paris, 1879.

Condorcet, Marquis de. *Oeuvres.* Paris, 1847-49.

Damagnez, Albert. *Influence de Calvin sur l'instruction.* Montauban, 1885.

Dauzenroth, Erich. *Kleine Geschichte der Mädchenbildung.* Düsseldorf, 1971.

Dennistoun, James. *Memoirs of the Dukes of Urbino.* 3 vols. London, 1851.

Dupanloup, Félix. *La Femme studieuse.* Paris, 1867.

Eby, Frederick. *Early Protestant Educators.* New York, 1931.

Fagniez, Gustave. *La Femme et la société française dans la première moitié du XVIIᵉ siècle.* Paris, 1929.

Faguet, Emile, ed. *Madame de Maintenon, institutrice.* Paris, 1885.

Fénelon, François. *De l'Education des filles.* Paris, 1844.

Ferriss, Abbott L. *Indicators of Trends in the Status of American Women.* New York, 1971.

Flexner, Eleanor. *Mary Wollstonecraft.* Baltimore, 1973.

———. *Century of Struggle.* New York, 1974.

Encyclopédie. Paris, 1751-65.

Fracard, M.-L. *L'Education des filles à Niort au XVIIIᵉ siècle.* Niort, 1952.

Franz, Nelly Alden. *English Women Enter the Professions.* New York, 1965.

Fraser, Antonia. *Mary Queen of Scots.* London, 1969.

Gardiner, Dorothy. *English Girlhood at School.* London, 1929.

Genlis, Madame de. *Adèle et Théodore.* Paris, 1782.

Goncourt, Edmond and Jules de. *The Woman of the Eighteenth Century.* Translated by Jacques le Clerq and Ralph Roeder. New York, 1927.

Gournay, Marie de. *Egalité des hommes et des femmes.* Paris, 1622.

Gréard, Octave. *L'Enseignement secondaire des filles.* Paris, 1883.

————. *L'Education des femmes par des femmes.* Paris, 1897.

Greene, Nathanael. *Fascism, an Anthology.* New York, 1968.

Grosclaude, Pierre. *La Vie intellectuelle à Lyon dans la deuxième moitié du XVIIIe siècle.* Paris, 1973.

Grunberger, Richard. *The Twelve Year Reich.* New York, 1971.

Herlihy, David. *The Family in the Renaissance in Italy.* St. Charles, Mo., 1974.

Hippeau, C. *L'Instruction publique en Russie.* Paris, 1878.

Holcombe, Lee. *Victorian Ladies at Work.* Devon, 1973.

Huizinga, Johan. *Erasmus and the Age of Reformation.* New York, 1957.

Hurd-Mead, Kate Campbell. *A History of Women in Medicine.* Haddam, 1938.

Jourda, Pierre. *Marguerite d'Angoulême.* 2 vols. Paris, 1930.

Kamm, Josephine. *Hope Deferred.* London, 1929.

Kasuya, Yoshi. *A Comparative Study of the Secondary Education of Girls in England, Germany and the United States.* New York, 1933.

Kelso, Ruth. *Doctrine for the Lady of the Renaissance.* Urbana, 1956.

Kilian, M. *De l'Instruction des filles à ses divers degrès.* Paris, 1842.

Laigle, Mathilde. *Le Livre des Trois Vertus de Christine de Pisan et son milieu historique et littéraire.* Paris, 1912.

Lambert, Madame de. *Avis d'une mère à sa fille.* Paris, 1811.

Lange, Helene. *Higher Education of Women in Europe.* Translated by L.R. Klemm, New York, 1890.

Lange, Helene and Gertrud Bäumer. *Handbuch der Frauenbewegung.* 4 vols. Berlin, 1902.

Lipinska, Melina. *Les Femmes et le progrès des sciences médicales.* Paris, 1930.

Lloyd, Trevor. *Suffragettes International.* New York and London, 1971.

Lorain, P. *Tableau de l'instruction primaire en France.* Paris, 1837.

Lougee, Caroline. *Le Paradis des femmes.* Princeton, 1976.

Luppé, Albert de. *Les Jeunes filles à la fin du XVIIIe siècle.* Paris, 1925.

Maintenon, Marquise de. *Lettres et entretiens sur l'éducation des filles.* Paris, 1861.

Mandel, William. *Soviet Women.* New York, 1975.

Maulde la Clavière, R. *Les Femmes de la Renaissance.* Paris, 1848.

Mazzetti, Serafino. *Memorie Storiche sopre l'università e l'instituto delle scienze di Bologna.* Bologna, 1840.

Miremont, Comtesse de. *Traité de l'éducation des femmes et cours complet d'instruction.* 7 vols. Paris, 1779-89.

Monica, Sister M. *Angela Merici and Her Teaching Idea.* New York, 1927.

Monroe, Paul. *A Cyclopedia of Education.* 5 vols. New York, 1906-13.

New York Times. Women, Their Changing Roles. New York, 1973.

O'Faolain, Julia and Lauro Martines, eds. *Not in God's Image.* New York, 1973.

Ozouf, Mona. *L'Ecole L'Eglise et la République, 1871-1914.* Paris, 1963.

Panckoucke, André-Joseph. *Les Etudes convenables aux demoiselles.* 2 vols. Paris, 1762.

Piéderrière, Abbé. *Les Petites écoles avant la Révolution dans la province de Bretagne.* Paris, 1877.

Pinet, Marie-Joseph. *Christine de Pisan.* Paris, 1927.

Power, Eileen. *Medieval Women.* Cambridge, 1975.

Puisieux, Madame de. *Conseils à une amie.* Paris, 1755.

Putnam, Emily James. *The Lady.* New York, 1910.

Rashdall, Hastings. *The Universities of the Middle Ages.* 3 vols. London, 1958.

Rémusat, Madame de. *Essai sur l'éducation des femmes.* Paris, 1903.

Reynier, Gustave. *La Femme au XVIIᵉ siècle, ses ennemies et ses défenseurs.* Paris, 1929.

Ribailler, Abbé. *De l'Education physique et morale des enfans des deux sexes.* Paris, 1785.

Richardson, Lula McDowell. *The Forerunners of Feminism in French Literature of the Renaissance.* Baltimore, 1929.

Robbins, Charles Leonidas. *Teachers in Germany in the Sixteenth Century.* New York, 1912.

Rollin, Charles. *Traité des études.* 3 vols. Paris, 1845.

Rousseau, Jean Jacques. *Emile.* Paris, no date.

Rousselot, Paul. *La Pédagogie féminine.* Paris, 1881.

———. *Histoire de l'éducation des femmes en France.* 2 vols. Paris, 1883.

Ryan, Mary P. *Womanhood in America from Colonial Times to the Present.* New York, 1975.

Satina, Sophie. *Education of Women in Pre-Revolutionary Russia.* Translated by Alexandra Poustchine. New York, 1966.

Schurmann, Anne-Marie von. *Question célèbre, s'il est nécessaire ou non, que les filles soient scavantes.* Paris, 1846.

Scott, Walter S. *The Bluestocking Ladies.* London, 1947.

Sichel, Edith. *Women and Men of the French Renaissance.* London, 1970.

Simon, Joan. *Education and Society in Tudor England.* Cambridge, 1966.

Snyders, George. *La Pédagogie en France au XVIᵉ et XVIIᵉ siècles.* Paris, 1965.

Stanton, Theodore. *The Woman Question in Europe.* New York, 1884.

Stephenson, Jill. *Women in Nazi Society.* New York, 1975.

Stone, Lawrence. *The Crisis of the Aristocracy, 1558-1641.* Oxford, 1965.

Sullerot, Evelyne. *Woman, Society and Change.* Translated by Margaret Scotford Archer. New York, 1971.

Telle, Emile V. *L'Oeuvre de Marguerite d'Angoulême, reine de Navarre.* Toulouse, 1937.

Transenster, L. *L'Enseignement supérieur pour les femmes.* Liège, 1882.

UNESCO. *Progress of Literacy in Various Countries.* Paris, 1953.

——. *World Survey of Education: Handbook of Educational Organization and Statistics.* Paris, 1955.

——. *World Literacy at Mid-Century.* Paris, 1957.

——. *Women, Education, Equality: A Decade of Experiment.* Paris, 1975.

——. *Statistical Yearbook.* Paris, 1976.

United States Department of Education. *Digest of Educational Statistics.* Washington, 1973.

United States Education Bureau. *Report of the Commissioner of Education for the Year 1894-95.* Washington, 1896.

Urseau, Charles. *L'Instruction primaire avant 1789 dans les paroisses du diocèse actuel d'Angers.* Paris, 1890.

Vetter, Betty M. and Eleanor L. Babco. *Professional Women and Minorities: A Manpower Resource Service.* Washington, 1975.

Wallas, Ada Radford. *Before the Bluestockings.* London, 1929.

Watson, Foster. *Vives and the Renascence Education of Women.* New York, 1912.

——. *English Writers on Education, 1408-1603.* Gainesville, 1967.

——. *The Old Grammar Schools.* New York, 1969.

Wollstonecraft, Mary. *A Vindication of the Rights of Woman.* New York, 1792.

——. *A Vindication of the Rights of Woman.* Critical edition by Carol H. Poston. New York, 1975.

Woodward, William Harrison. *Desiderius Erasmus Concerning the Aim and Method of Education.* New York, 1964.

——. *Vittorino da Feltre and Other Humanist Educators.* New York, 1970.

Woody, Thomas. *A History of Women's Education in the United States.* 2 vols. New York, 1929.

Zamaron, Fernand. *Louise Labé, dame de franchise.* Paris, 1968.

PERIODICALS

Enseignement secondaire des jeunes filles, 1882-84.
Revue internationale de l'enseignement, 1881-1900.

BIBLIOGRAPHY

PUBLISHED ARTICLES

Bell, Susan Groag. "Christine de Pizan [sic] (1364-1430): Humanism and the Problem of a Studious Woman." *Feminist Studies* III, 3/4 (Spring-Summer, 1976).

Bodek, Evelyn Gordon. "Salonières and Bluestockings: Educated Obsolescence and Germinating Feminism." *Feminist Studies* III, 3/4 (Spring-Summer, 1976).

Horvath, Sandra Ann. "Victor Duruy and the Controversy over Secondary Education for Girls." *French Historical Studies* IX (Spring, 1975).

Kelly-Gadol, Joan. "Did Women Have a Renaissance?" Renata Bridenthal and Claudia Koontz, *Becoming Visible: Women in European History.* (Boston, 1975).

Lyster, Mary A. "Higher Schools for Girls in Germany." Board of Education, Great Britain. *Special Reports on Educational Subjects #9.* London, 1902.

Silver, Catherine Bodard. "Salon, Foyer, Bureau: Women and the Professions in France." Mary Hartman and Louis W. Banner, *Clio's Consciousness Raised.* New York, 1974.

Stuart, Susan Mosher. "Dame Trot." *Signs I* (Winter, 1975).

Whittaker, Cynthia H. "The Women's Movement During the Reign of Alexander II." *Journal of Modern History*, XLVII (June, 1976).

UNPUBLISHED PAPERS

Bernstein, George. "The Curriculum for German Girls' Schools, 1871-1914." Berkshire Conference on the History of Women, Bryn Mawr, 1976.

Gold, Carol. "Education and Class in Pre-Industrial Society: A Case Study from Denmark." Berkshire Conference on the History of Women, Bryn Mawr, 1976.

Offen, Karen. "A Feminist Challenge to the Third Republic's Public Education for Girls." American Historical Association Convention, San Francisco, 1973. To be published in *Troisième République.*

Petschauer, Peter. "Changing Opportunities for Girls in Eighteenth Century Germany." Duquesne Forum, Pittsburgh, 1975.

———. "The Education of Women in Southern Germany in the Eighteenth Century." To be published in *Societas.*

Rosenberg, Rosalind. "The Academic Prism." Berkshire Conference on the History of Women, Bryn Mawr, 1976.

Struminger, Laura. "The Feminist Press of Lyon: *Le Conseiller des Femmes.*" Berkshire Conference on the History of Women, Radcliffe, 1974.

Whittaker, Cynthia H. "The Education of Women in Tsarist Russia." 1964.

INDEX

Schools, 124; Benjamin Rush,
125; Louisa School, 133; German
Association for Secondary
Education of Girls, 135; adult
education, Germany, 136;
gymnasia, Russia, 143–44;
Women's courses, Russia, 147;
institutes, France, 158; See Law,
France, 165; dame schools, 172;
Queen's College, 175–76; high
schools, England, 178; Mount
Holyoke, 185–86; high schools,
U. S., 186–87

Dall, Caroline H., 189
Dame schools, 69, 73, 172
Darwin, Erasmus, 100
Daubié, Julie Victoire, 166, 167, 206
Davies, Emily, 176–77, 180, 181, 182
Day, Elizabeth, 175
Dewey, John, 193–94
Dolce, Ludovico, 36
Donna, Maria della, 208
Douglas Commission on Industrial
and Technical Education,
Massachusetts, 189
Dupanloup, Félix, Archbishop of
Orléans, 161, 162, 163
Duruy, Victor, 156, 162–63

École libre des Science politiques,
France, 217
Ecole Normale supérieure, France,
216
Edinburgh University, 206
Education Acts, England: 1870, 173;
1902, 178, 183; 1921, 221
Edwards, Blanche, 207
Eleanor of Aquitaine, 27
Elizabeth I, Queen of England, 44,
55–56, 197
Ellis, Mrs. William, 175
Elstob, Elizabeth, 102
Elyot, Sir Thomas, 55
Emma Willard School (formerly
Troy Female Seminary), 184, 186

Encyclopedia, 109–10
Endowed Schools Act, England,
1869, 177, 178
Epinay, Louise, Madame de, 86
Erasmus, Desiderius, 50, 52, 54
Este, Beatrice d', 39
Este, Isabella d', 39

Falloux Law, France, 156
Fénelon, Francois, 91–93, 97
Ferry Law, France, 157
Filosofova, A.P., 145
Fliedner, Theodor, 201
Fontenelle, Bernard Le Bovier de,
86
Fourier, Charles, 158–59
Frances de Bremond, 76
Frances of Suffolk, 50
Francis I, King of France, 45–46
Francke, August Hermann, 67, 96,
97
Frederick the Great of Prussia, 68
Frederick William I, King of
Prussia, 68
Fröbel, Friedrich, 108
Fry, Elizabeth Gurney, 201
Fuss, Margarita, 198

Galen, 20–21
Galinda, Beatriz, 51
Garrett-Anderson, Elizabeth,
205–6, 207
Garrick, David, 100
Geneva (N.Y.) College of Medicine,
204
Genlis, Stéphanie Félicité,
Comtesse de, 111–12, 123
Geoffrin, Marie-Thérèse, Madame
de, 86
German Association for the
Secondary Education of Girls,
135, 138
German Women's Movement
(Frauenbewegung), 134, 136
Girls' Public Day School Company,
178